Unexpected Places

UNEXPECTED PLACES

Relocating Nineteenth-Century African American Literature

ERIC GARDNER

UNIVERSITY PRESS OF MISSISSIPPI

JACKSON

www.upress.state.ms.us

Margaret Walker Alexander Series in African American Studies

The University Press of Mississippi is a member of the
Association of American University Presses.

First printing 2009

∞

Library of Congress Cataloging-in-Publication Data

Gardner, Eric.
Unexpected places : relocating nineteenth-century African American
literature / Eric Gardner.
p. cm. — (Margaret Walker Alexander series in African American studies)
Includes bibliographical references and index.
ISBN 978-1-60473-283-2 (cloth : alk. paper) 1. American literature—African American
authors—History and criticism. 2. American literature—19th century—History and criticism.
3. African Americans in literature. 4. Place (Philosophy) in literature.
5. West (U.S.)—In literature. 6. Regionalism in literature. I. Title.
PS153.N5G25 2009
810.9'896073—dc22   2009009672

British Library Cataloging-in-Publication Data available

as always, for my family

Contents

ACKNOWLEDGMENTS

The completion of this book owes a great deal to my friends at Saginaw Valley State University. A Ruth and Ted Braun Research Fellowship, administered by the Saginaw Community Foundation and SVSU, provided both much-needed time and key resources. Vice President Donald Bachand and Dean Mary Hedberg have been consistently supportive of my work. Colleagues and students have listened to some of the arguments here, shared some of the joys of discovery, and always commented thoughtfully; I am especially thankful to Ken Jolly, Paul Teed, and Melissa Teed. Several colleagues in the English department have made my time as chair not only livable but sometimes even enjoyable. Pat Latty and Sharon Opheim have consistently been of great help in daily tasks.

Part of the research for chapter 1 was funded by a Summer Stipend from the National Endowment for the Humanities; any views, findings, conclusions, or recommendations expressed in this volume do not necessarily reflect those of the National Endowment for the Humanities. Although centering on another project, my time at the Library Company of Philadelphia on a Mellon Fellowship allowed valuable discussion that contributed to some of chapter 4.

Librarians and archivists across the nation aided me thoughtfully and consistently; they are the unsung heroes of nineteenth-century African American studies. Michael Everman at the Missouri State Archives at St. Louis, especially, provided a great deal of help and good conversation. Library staff members at the Allen County Public Library (Fort Wayne, Indiana), Ball State University, the California Historical Society, the California State Library, the Doris Foley Historical Library (Nevada City, California), the Indiana Historical Society, the Indiana State Library, the Library Company of Philadelphia, the Library of Michigan, the Missouri Historical Society, the Missouri State Archives, the New Jersey State Archives, the

New-York Historical Society, the Pennsylvania Historical Society, the San Francisco Public Library, the St. Louis Public Library, the Searls Historical Library (Nevada City, California), Tulane University (including the Amistad Research Center and American Missionary Association collections), the University of Colorado, the University of Michigan, and the University of Pennsylvania were uniformly helpful. The Warren County (Ohio) Genealogical Society kindly answered queries on the Hart family. The library staff at Saginaw Valley has not only been adept at securing materials through interlibrary loan but has also been supportive in obtaining key reference sources.

The reader for the University Press of Mississippi provided astute commentary that helped shaped the book's argument. Mississippi's staff members—starting with Director Emerita Seetha Srinivasan, whose contributions to African American studies will long be celebrated—have aided the project almost from its inception. I am deeply thankful for the chance to work with Walter Biggins, Anne Stascavage, and Shane Gong. Debbie Self copyedited the book with great care.

Colleagues at panels at the African American Literature and Culture Society, the American Literature Association, the American Studies Association, the Modern Language Association, the Society for the Study of American Women Writers, and the Western Literature Association provided useful feedback on pieces of various chapters. Editors and readers at *Legacy, PMLA,* and especially *African American Review* provided both similarly useful comments and forums for earlier versions of some of the ideas included here; they and the editorial staff at the *African American National Biography* have deeply shaped my thinking about the field. Particularly useful feedback on this earlier work came from John Ernest, P. Gabrielle Foreman, Michael K. Johnson, Joycelyn Moody, and Hollis Robbins. Nina Baym has consistently remained a model for what it means to be a student, teacher, and scholar.

Of course, my greatest debts are to my family—teachers, students, readers all. My parents raised me in a house full of texts, and it has been my joy to make such a home with my wife, Jodie, who read almost every page of every draft of this book and supported me in more ways that I can describe. It has also been my joy to share with Jodie the introduction of our wondrous daughters, Elisabeth and Abigail, to reading. While there is much that separates me from the writers studied in this volume, I unite with them in recognizing the value of literacy and the literary, of remembering the richness and the complexities of a diverse history, and of teaching our children with great care and deep hope.

Unexpected Places

INTRODUCTION
Duty and Daily Bread

On 11 December 1856, David Lewis rose to address sixty fellow African Americans: "I am a friend to this [news]paper, and go for supporting it; the changes we are seeking . . . for the sake of the common security of life and property must be effected through it, and as a result of an altered public sentiment; to produce this latter, we greatly need a paper; it seems, then, my duty to support the paper, as to labor for my daily bread" (Foner 155).

Lewis's sense that a textual outlet like a newspaper might be as important to some antebellum black Americans as their "daily bread" could have been offered by any number of nineteenth-century black writers now familiar to scholars and students. Frederick Douglass, Martin Delany, Sojourner Truth, William Wells Brown, and Frances Ellen Watkins Harper all called for—indeed, fought for—a black presence in American print culture. Lewis's sense that black texts spoke to a broad "public sentiment"—not just to a "white sentiment" or to ideologies operating solely within African American communities—could have been voiced by any number of these figures, too. Like a host of other nineteenth-century African American activists, Lewis recognized that, because black presences in the textual world were essential "for the sake . . . of life and property," outlets for black stories were also, as Jonas Holland Townsend (who spoke just before Lewis) asserted, "imperatively necessary" (154).

Today's readers may, however, find the physical location of Lewis's speech disconcerting. His remarks might well have been made at meetings in New York (perhaps in support of the Rochester-based *Frederick Douglass's Paper* or as part of the initial rumblings that led to the later *Anglo-African Magazine*), or in Philadelphia (in African Methodist Episcopal [A.M.E.] Church meetings about the financially troubled church organ, the *Christian Record-er*), or even in Boston (where the white-run *Liberator* continued to provide an outlet for black voices, albeit generally those in line with William Lloyd Garrison). Instead, the body he addressed was the Second Annual Convention of the Colored Citizens of the State of California, and he spoke in the midst of four intense days of meetings in a Sacramento church that stood thousands of miles away from the expected urban northeastern locations for such activity. The paper he was supporting was the San Francisco–based *Mirror of the Times,* the first black newspaper in the West. Largely an outgrowth of a convention of California African Americans held a year earlier, the *Mirror* shared black western stories in modes ranging from biographical sketches to accounts of struggles for the right to testify—or, put another way, to gain legal validation of black stories in public settings with public consequences.

Convention attendees represented an impressive collection of black literary activists: Lewis addressed, among others, *Mirror* cofounders Townsend and William H. Newby (the "Nubia" of *Frederick Douglass's Paper*), *Pacific Appeal* founder Peter Anderson, Mifflin Wistar Gibbs (whose 1901 autobiography was not recovered until 1995), and Thomas Detter (author of the first book of fiction published by a black westerner, the 1871 *Nellie Brown,* which was not recovered until 1996).[1] However, in the twentieth century, these figures and others like them across the nation essentially fell off most maps of African American literary history. How these figures were pushed to the margins of black cultural studies and how some were almost completely forgotten are central subjects of this introduction. The ways in which we might bring them—as well as their fellows from a set of "unexpected places"—back into our sense of nineteenth-century African American literature and culture is the subject of this volume.

Certainly some of the specific phenomena leading to the attendees' modern absences are tied to the lack of consideration of the black West generally. Though no less than Langston Hughes cautioned historians with "Don't leave out the cowboys!" until the landmark work of historians like Quintard Taylor, William Loren Katz, Rudolph Lapp, and Shirley Ann Wilson Moore over the last two decades, early California was largely absent from maps of early African American history (qtd. in Katz xi).[2] Until recently, other areas outside of the South and the urban Northeast (especially the centers of activism noted above) have similarly suffered from historical neglect.[3]

However, while these absences in historical scholarship certainly shaped similar gaps in literary criticism, so, too, have the ways in which key literary scholars located black stories. Houston Baker, for example, near the beginning of his landmark *Long Black Song,* asserts that "tales of pioneers enduring the hardships of the West for the promise of immense wealth are not the tales of black America" (2). Baker's narrowing is in some ways understandable; he had a much more limited number of texts than are becoming available today. Further, like the generation of pioneers he immediately followed—Darwin Turner and Robert Stepto, for example—he was attempting the radical, indeed revolutionary, task of fashioning a literary history where much of the academy still largely saw no *literature* and so need for any such history. But he and others largely wrote out whole bodies of texts—including those produced in the black West.[4] Broadly speaking, while there were notable exceptions, most critics of African American literature during the first three-quarters of the twentieth century concentrated heavily on rescuing texts within a set of specific areas and on creating the trajectories—the slave narrative to the novels and poetry of the Harlem Renaissance to the protest novel to Toni Morrison's work, for example—that have formed the backbone of many black literature surveys.

The end of the twentieth century brought a flowering of projects that richly complicated these basic frameworks—most notably, the forty-volume Schomburg Library of Nineteenth-Century Black Women Writers, edited by Henry Louis Gates Jr., but also key (re)visionary texts like Gates's critical studies, Frances Smith Foster's 1993 *Written by Herself,* William Andrews's 1986 *To Tell a Free Story,* Hazel Carby's 1987 *Reconstructing Womanhood,* Carla Peterson's 1995 *Doers of the Word,* Joan Sherman's continuing work on early black poetry, among others. While each of these studies—and a handful of others like them—were innovative in theory and exemplary in close, contextual reading, what remains striking about them is simply how many *more* texts they considered than their predecessors. They named names and read texts that were often simply left out of earlier critics' work, and they often asserted that generalizations about genre, content, approach, and even sometimes publication, distribution, and audience could not be made without fuller bibliographic and historical pictures.

Much of the best recent literary history and criticism in the field has built from these texts and has complicated, corrected, and broadened their assertions. Joycelyn Moody's 2001 *Sentimental Confessions,* John Ernest's 2004 *Liberation Historiography,* and Daphne Brooks's 2006 *Bodies of*

Dissent all challenge boundaries of subject and genre, as do the attempts at larger-scale literary history like those in Dickson D. Bruce's 2001 *Origins of African American Literature* (and his earlier 1989 *Black American Writing from the Nadir*). Frances Smith Foster's ouevre—including her germinal "A Narrative of the Interesting Origins and (Somewhat) Surprising Development of African American Print Culture"—has challenged us to (re)consider the place of black periodicals in literary study, and this call has been taken up in different ways in texts ranging from Todd Vogl's 2001 collection *The Black Press* to Noliwe Rooks's 2004 *Ladies' Pages*. The parameters of literary biography have been challenged (and enriched) by texts ranging from Robert Levine's 1997 *Martin Delany, Frederick Douglass, and the Politics of Representative Identity* (a text that goes far beyond traditional "biographies") to Lois Brown's mammoth 2008 study *Pauline Hopkins*. Barbara McCaskill and Caroline Gebhard's recent edited collection *Post-Bellum, Pre-Harlem* challenges the temporal gap in some of the trajectories noted above. And while we do not have the kinds of close studies of nineteenth-century black authors' interactions with publishers (and questions of reception generally) that can be found for nineteenth-century white writers in books like Susan Coultrap-McQuin's 1990 *Doing Literary Business* and for modern black writers in texts like John K. Young's 2006 *Black Writers, White Publishers* (or even Abby Johnson and Ronald Johnson's much earlier 1979 *Propaganda and Aesthetics*), the available archive to support such work is growing, and Elizabeth McHenry's 2002 *Forgotten Readers* offers a powerful template for considering black readers vis-à-vis black texts. [5]

That said, for many students—and even for some strong scholars—nineteenth-century African American literature still consists of a tiny handful of texts. Consider the words of one representative critic in prefacing what is actually an important example of localized recovery: "The newness of representing an ex-slave's life in freedom helps to explain why African American literary works published in the 1840s and 1850s, an era of slavery's expansion, greatly exceed all works published between 1867 and 1876, a period of legal freedom. While hundreds of slave narratives were published before the Civil War, only 67 were published after freedom came." The slippage between the first sentence's "African American literary works" and the second sentence's "slave narratives" illustrates the common reduction of antebellum (and even postbellum) black literature to a single genre—albeit a rich one. [6]

But there are other assumptions here, too. The quote offers an implicit sense that slavery and the move from slavery must be the subject of "African American literary works"—and so asserts that "ex-slaves" must be the central authors of nineteenth-century black literature. The quote also emphasizes the bound book as the measure of literature—as the "67" above counts only narratives published in book form. In turn, this means that, given the locations of most of the publishers willing to handle slave narratives, the quote places the locations for composition and publication of most black texts firmly in the urban Northeast. All of these assumptions define the landscape of nineteenth-century black literature as much, much narrower than it really was.

For all of this, however, the quote above is *much* more nuanced than the sense of the field suggested by searching the Modern Language Association's *International Bibliography* of publications in language and literature.[7] The quote above recognizes that nineteenth-century black literature encompasses "hundreds" of texts worthy of study, and that those "hundreds" include not just antebellum slave narratives but also postbellum texts. Running a series of searches on the MLA Index suggests that African American literary study is skewed heavily in favor of twentieth century texts—that is, toward often ignoring the texts noted in the quote above—and that it is specifically conversant with only a very small number of nineteenth-century texts. In searches carried out in August 2008, Toni Morrison came up as a subject of 1,106 entries; Richard Wright, of 530 entries; Langston Hughes, of 418 entries; Zora Neale Hurston, of 398 entries; and Ralph Ellison, of 375 entries.[8] Leading pre-twentieth-century black authors, Frederick Douglass was listed as a subject of 311 entries—164 of which specify his 1845 *Narrative* as a key text. After Douglass, though, the drop is stunning: Harriet Jacobs's 1861 *Incidents in the Life of a Slave Girl* was the subject of 165 entries, and two eighteenth-century authors, Olaudah Equiano and Phillis Wheatley, also passed a hundred entries each, with 116 and 110, respectively. Texts and authors recognized as deeply important—if not canonical—within nineteenth-century African American studies received far fewer hits. William Wells Brown, for example, was listed as a subject of only 35 entries (13 citing his 1853 novel *Clotel* and only four, his *Narrative*—the same number of hits on Solomon Northup's important 1853 narrative). The postbellum slave narratives suggested in the quote above fared worse: Elizabeth Keckley's 1868 *Behind the Scenes* was the subject of 21 entries, for example, and Lucy Delaney's circa 1891 *From the Darkness Cometh the Light,* only five. Early black fiction also returned strikingly low numbers: Harper's 1892 *Iola Leroy* was listed as a subject of 41 entries; Martin Delany's 1859/1861–1862 serialized novel *Blake,* of 22 entries; Frank Webb's 1857 *The Garies,* of 15 entries; Brown's *Clotel,* as noted above, of only 13 entries. Julia C. Collins's serialized 1865 *The Curse of Caste* promises to pass several of these, in part because of a special issue of *African American Review* devoted to its 2006 recovery; still, it seems unlikely that Collins will approach the attention focused on Douglass and Jacobs, much less Morrison. A handful of other texts received similar results: Harriet Wilson's 1859 novelized autobiography (or autobiographical novel) *Our Nig* was the subject of 46 entries, and Hannah Crafts's (re)discovered pseudonymous novel *The Bondwoman's Narrative,* of 31 entries since its publication in 2002. Pauline Hopkins—generally thought of as a turn-of-the-century writer, was the subject of 45 entries (the vast majority on her 1900 novel *Contending Forces*). In many ways, then, the MLA Index suggests not only that, for many scholars, slave narratives (and/or perhaps a novel or two that look like slave narratives) *are* nineteenth-century African American literature, but that this complex genre is embodied solely in a tiny number of texts—perhaps, in the worst cases, just two (albeit fascinating) texts, Douglass's *Narrative* and Jacobs's *Incidents.*

In the last decade or so, Douglass and Jacobs have, in some ways, entered the "mainstream" of American literature, and this is, of course, in some ways, a very exciting development. Further, consideration of nineteenth-century black authors has generally increased. But even these facts carry complications, given the structures described above. Often, Douglass and Jacobs have been cast as "representative" black authors. Jacobs's work has especially fallen prey to being lumped into considerations of white authors (especially in dissertations and surveys) without much attention to the complex racial and movement-based contexts that shaped the composition, publication, and distribution of her *Incidents.* In observing this, I certainly don't mean to imply that we shouldn't consider Douglass and Jacobs alongside figures like Hawthorne, Poe, or Margaret Fuller in studies of temporality, or property, or physicality vis-à-vis nineteenth-century American literature. I am, however, deeply troubled when tokenism leads to ahistorical misreadings of texts (and authors); to the reduction of a large, rich, and wondrously complex and conflicted body of literature to single supposedly representative texts, and to generalizations by scholars who have not taken the time to understand what we know—and what we don't know—of the black literary nineteenth century.[9]

One of the readers for the drafts of this volume conveyed a hope that it would be "both a call and a response." If it is, its first call simply asks that we broaden even further the list of authors and texts that we study—because nineteenth-century black literature was simply much richer than our scholarship and our teaching often suggest. In this way, the selection of authors and texts in *Unexpected Places* can be seen as offering a small sampling of what could be added to that list. This naturally leads this study to also call for an expanded sense of genre and the literary. While there is no doubt of the slave narrative's importance and while early black novels are clearly crucial to thinking about both black literature and American literature generally, our near-obsession with specific kinds of narratives has drawn sharp and narrow boundaries around "what counts" as and in black literature.

Those boundaries are often defined in decidedly modern and ahistorical terms. In an 1858 essay in the African Methodist Episcopal Church's *Repository of Religion and Literature* titled "On General Literature," for example, Bishop Daniel Payne—himself both a poet and a literary activist—outlined five key types of literature: historical, scientific, religious, "light," and philosophical. His definition of literature drew on the senses common in the eighteenth century—and still very present in the nineteenth century—that literature and the textual writ broadly were synonymous, that "the object of literature is to collect, preserve and transmit to posterity the fruits of intelligence, the knowledge and the learning of the men of all nations and all ages," that writers of literature should "exhibit in their own native forms, things past, things present and things to come," and that literature "is the great medium of instruction to mankind" (110). Given this didactic approach to literature, it is no surprise that Payne placed novels, grudgingly, under "light literature"—though he then quickly marked "newspaper tales" and "novels and romances" as "those gilded baits by which Satan leads so many young men and women to *shame,* to *infamy,* to *misery,* and to *hell!*" (110) Payne asserted that other types of literature allowed "the most brilliant thoughts of genius, the most judicious maxims of sages, the most valuable discoveries of empiric philosophy, the predictions of prophets; still more, the very teaching of the incarnate Deity" to touch readers (111).[10]

I quote from Payne not because his definition of literature governs this study—or because I think it should govern our larger endeavors. Rather, I introduce Payne to remind readers of one important set of conditions of textual production, consumption, and reception among African Americans in the nineteenth century. While some of the writers in this study—and some in nineteenth-century African American literature broadly—would have disagreed with Payne, almost all knew of him and many *knew* him.[11] Further, recognizing that the nascent black periodical press (in which Payne was a major player) was *the* central publication outlet for many black writers—and especially for texts that were *not* slave narratives—we need to consider how the demands of the short or serialized forms of periodicals (and especially newspapers) within editorial processes shaped by figures like Payne might (re)define African American literature of the period. Zeroing in on the bound book and even more specifically on the genre of the slave narrative (especially if such is shorthand for just Douglass's *Narrative* and Jacobs's *Incidents*) radically circumscribes the senses of genre and literature held by many nineteenth-century African Americans.[12]

If we understand that most nineteenth-century black writers were working in dialogue with definitions like Payne's and thinking about periodical publication as often (or more often) than book publication, our sense of the literary—and of genre—must shift to include essays, letters to editors, and a wide range of other types of texts.[13] As Elizabeth McHenry persuasively argues, "one reason scholars have posited the African American literary tradition as a monolithic entity that begins with the slave narrative is that they have not valued . . . other literary forms. . . . [But] letters, essays, poems and narratives—all considered 'literature' according to contemporary definitions—appeared regularly" and "survive as both a remarkable record of the wide variety of writing done by early black Americans and evidence of what they were reading as well" (12).

Thus, while figures like Douglass, Harper, and Brown do tread through the pages of this volume, they walk with a host of writers who have few if any entries in the MLA Index, in many black literature surveys, and in most critical and bibliographic works on nineteenth century African Americans. While the slave narrative and the early novel are backdrops to discussions in most chapters in this study—and sometimes even step to the fore—they are figured in dialogue with travel narratives, essays, letters to editors, poems, newspaper columns, and a host of other forms.

In this and in my other calls to broaden our sense of nineteenth-century black literature, I echo challenges made by several recent scholars—including John Ernest, who asserts that "reenvisioning the literary history might well begin by bringing more of it into view, and what is radical about this work might be little more than the insistence that we attend to an African

American calendar of literary scholarship" to establish basic information on authors and texts and to piece "together some sense of the complex cultural processes that shaped the writers' various approaches" ("Race" 49). Our field needs the kind of sweeping and exhaustive works that combine bibliography, history, and criticism that scholars like Nina Baym—in *Woman's Fiction, American Women Writers and the Work of History,* and *American Women of Letters and the Nineteenth Century Sciences,* for example—have built for nineteenth-century American women writers. It also needs a much richer set of basic and readily available reference sources.[14]

But in addition to the temporal—perhaps even genealogical—qualities of Ernest's calendar reference, I also call for attention to geography. Consider, for example, the online "Map of Early London," which, in the words of general editor Janella Jenstad, attempts to offer a "cultural geography"— tracing literature in not just time, but space, and so giving a much richer sense of not just authors and texts, but networks and affinities between such. Alternately, consider Matthew Jockers's work on "georeferencing" Irish American literature, which, through marking texts' geographical ties and references, has allowed him to challenge generalizations about how— and, importantly, where—this body of texts evolved.[15] Thus, I argue that the reader of Lucy Delaney's fascinating postbellum St. Louis slave narrative, *From the Darkness Cometh the Light,* should know that Delaney's mother (who filed the freedom suit that freed Delaney and that is the centerpiece of her narrative) may well have interacted not only with Dred and Harriet Scott but also William Wells Brown—and that Delaney herself may well have engaged with Susan Paul Vashon, widow of poet George Boyer Vashon, descendant of the powerful Paul family of black ministers and writers, and cousin of Pauline Hopkins. Delaney's narrative draws from and works in dialogue not just with the antebellum slave narrative, but also with the court records of enslaved men and women, various traditions in northeastern black literature, all sorts of specifically St. Louis stories, black masonic texts, and a range of other works. Affinities of place may well tell us much about questions of influence, composition, content, publication, and reception in this text and others—and may begin, for example, to thicken our sense of the homonymic character Lucille Delaney in Frances Harper's much better known *Iola Leroy.*[16] But that same reader should also know that one of Delaney's St. Louis residences is now a parking lot across the street from the *Globe* building—the building that houses the archive that cares for the rescued (partial) documents pertaining to Delaney's and her mother's freedom suits—and thus that, even when paved over, sites in downtown St. Louis hold a complex mass of early black stories that appear on few—if any—maps of the African American literary landscape.

Because of limits on authors, genres, subjects, and locations drawn by previous scholars (and by the larger academy), nineteenth-century African American literature has often been reduced to southern stories told in bound books that were written by blacks in the urban Northeast and published in one of the handful of urban Northeast centers of activism like New York, Philadelphia, and Boston.

In broadening our sense of the places of nineteenth-century blackness and the black literary, *Unexpected Places* certainly functions in conversation with moves to recognize and study larger diasporic communities; it shares with critics interested in the "Black Atlantic" and trans-Atlantic conceptions of African American literature and culture a desire to, in the words of Ifeoma Kiddoe Nwankwo, read "the identificatory and idealogical border crossings of people of African descent" to produce "a reconceptualization of these literatures as arising of intra-Diasporic dialogues" (17). It also recognizes, though, that even many of the best works on the black Atlantic fall prey to the oversimplifications discussed above.[17] Thus, while I see scholarship—especially strong work like Nwankwo's—that thoughtfully reaches outward from national boundaries as essential, this volume focuses on complicating the sense of place, power, and nation embodied in Nwankwo's sense of "national affinity." If we are to do good comparative work, we need a much better idea of just what we're comparing—and why; we have not yet fully built that base.

In this, *Unexpected Places* is perhaps closer in scope to a group of projects I would loosely label as the "new regionalism" in nineteenth-century African American studies—a sense that, in the title words of Elizabeth McHenry's 1999 *American Quarterly* review essay, black Americans were "undeniably there," undeniably present in locations across the early nation. This impulse began to flower in historical studies at the tail-end of the twentieth century in texts like Stephen Vincent's 1999 *Southern Seed, Northern Soil*, which begins as a story of black Americans in the South, but shifts to offer a deep sense of early black Indiana. William Pierson's 1988 *Black Yankees* (which carefully reads a rich, if somewhat expected, region) and Valerie Cunningham and Mark J. Sammons's *Black Portsmouth* (which discusses three centuries of black history in the individual location of Portsmouth, New Hampshire) are certainly inflected by this new regionalist awareness. It is also deeply evident in collections like B. Eugene McCarthy and Thomas L. Doughton's 2007 *From Bondage to Belonging: The Worcester Slave Narratives* and especially William Andrews's recent work on North Carolina, including both his 2003 *North Carolina Slave Narratives* and his 2006 *North Carolina Roots of African American Literature*. Each of these projects—and a small score of others—emphasizes placing African American culture and literature more complexly, with more awareness of the ways in which specific locations shaped enactions of African American-ness. The ways in which a new regionalist approach to early African American literature can work to transform communities (and the fact that the field should have a larger public presence) are perhaps best embodied in the efforts of the Harriet Wilson Project, which has, through considering the deep ties of Harriet Wilson to Milford, New Hampshire, led to community reading projects, a walking tour of the area, a scholarly collection of new approaches to Wilson's *Our Nig,* and a statue of Wilson in Milford's Bicentennial Park. The Harriet Wilson Project—like the new regionalism in nineteenth-century African American studies more broadly—has dared to echo David Lewis's sense that attending to black texts and authors might be a duty and might be as valuable as daily bread. While this volume's approach to nineteenth-century black literature certainly recognizes the value of broader diasporic studies, then, and while it is based upon a recognition of the difficulties and desires nineteenth-century African Americans had in defining themselves as residents, citizens, and members of the United States, it also asserts that black struggles for identity formation were carried out in specific locations—locations that have often fallen off of our maps of early black culture.

In the broadest sense, then, *Unexpected Places* hopes to push nineteenth-century black studies toward considering and practicing what W. Lawrence Hogue (in his germinal work on modern black literature) calls "a polycentric approach"—one that presents "a vision of African American life, literature, criticism, and history that displays their hybridity, heterogeneity, and variety" (xi). Hogue defines polycentrism as "the principle of advocating the existence of independent centers of power within a singular political, cultural, or economic system," and he is especially interested in the ways "in which differences cannot be accommodated adequately in a hierarchical system that priviliges a center with a subordinated periphery" and so challenges "the construction of a canon of African American literature that privileges select African American texts and ignores others" (3, 4).[18] Especially important for this study—and for the new regionalism in nineteenth-century black studies—Hogue asserts that he hopes to "eschew historical narratives and an African American literary canon whose focus/center is on racial oppression exclusively" and wants to "challenge the African American sociopolitical mission of racial uplift" as simply signifying "the journey of the African American from the colonized subaltern to the values and definitions of mainstream society" (9). This means that his readings "do not position the once marginal communities and traditions as" in the words of Ella Shohat and Robert Stam, "'interest groups' to be added on to a 'preexisting nucleus'" (9). In this vein, Hogue might also echo the words of Michael Berube in *Marginal Forces / Cultural Centers*: "my work is not simply a comparative exposé; I am not dealing with two artists in the same medium, one who made it and one who didn't, and seeking thereby to disclose hidden and explicit biases" (5). Rather, Hogue wants to examine a full range of texts, without falling into the preset senses of canon-forming critics and without falling into easy comparisons and value judgments.

When I went to my shelves hoping to find the range of texts Hogue considers in *The African American Male, Writing, and Difference*, however, I was initially deflated: one of the great virtues of Hogue's work is that it demonstrates an amazing sense of a massive number of texts and authors, of all sorts of "places" that are certainly unexpected (even if they aren't essentially absent from our conversations). Even if my figurative shelves weren't as bare as the MLA Index might suggest, I was nonetheless reminded of how much basic "calendar" and "geospace" work to recover and republish texts, to create basic reference sources, to understand authors' biographies and contexts, and so to fill our shelves remains yet to be done.

Where I took great hope, though, is that, had I made that journey three decades ago, I would have found much, much less. Even though this study involved a great deal of traveling to archival sites and work with texts that have not yet been collected and/or republished in modern editions, it was also aided greatly by database products like the Accessible Archives digitization of the *Christian Recorder* and a small set of other black newspapers, by improvements in microforming and interlibrary loan processes, by genealogical products like those offered by ancestry.com, and by the growing set of powerful and free online projects like the wondrous *Documenting the American South* project (which includes, among other texts, electronic editions of many of the major histories of the A.M.E. Church written in the late nineteenth and early twentieth century).

Two pioneering projects led by Gates have the potential to cause even more sweeping change. The *African American National Biography*—published in eight volumes in 2008—offers the kind of basic reference tool (biographical entries on over six thousand African Americans written by scholars and rigorously fact-checked and edited) that has been wanting for so long; the project's promises to continue adding entries and to make them available through a fee-based online service (the Oxford African American Studies Center) will likely only broaden its impact.[19] The Black Periodical Literature Project offers a mammoth and unprecedented collection of early black literature, even if access to that collection is still limited: combing through dozens of black periodicals, microforming literary works and reviews, and indexing what's been found, the project has compiled a treasure trove of the black texts; unfortunately, the resulting collection of thousands of fiche is so large and so expensive that only a handful of the largest research libraries have purchased it (causing another split between "expected" and "unexpected" places, centers and margins, in the field). Hopefully digitization will increase access to this valuable resource.[20] And this is to say nothing of the wealth of new editions and scholarly volumes published in the past two decades, some of which are mentioned above.

We are getting closer to the kinds of collections, calendars, and maps that would allow a fuller application of Hogue's conception of a polycentric approach to nineteenth-century African American literature. Part of the goal of *Unexpected Places* is to make the locations studied herein more available to scholars and students—and so *less* unexpected—by documenting some of the events within the lively and complex literate and literary black cultures that grew in such unexpected places. Throughout this study, I thus use "locations" not simply to designate physical places—although this is certainly a key component of the term—but also to invoke the complex and shifting collections of people who populated those locations and who helped build and define them, as well as the generic "places" in which their texts were created and functioned.

In chapter 1 I look at antebellum St. Louis not simply as a location of the kinds of cruelty central to slave narratives, but also as a complex nexus of American conceptions of the frontier and civilization. Against this backdrop, I consider antebellum texts by John Berry Meachum, a St. Louis black minister who was born a slave, and Cyprian Clamorgan, a gadabout mixed-race barber descended from one of St. Louis's founders; I also begin to assess how we might weigh the stories told in places like court records—and specifically in the freedom suit case file of Polly Wash, Lucy Delaney's mother—in dialogue with more traditional genres. Chapter 2 moves East—but is set in what, in the 1850s, was still very much thought of as the West. It reads a group of texts surrounding the African Methodist Episcopal Church's *Repository of Religion and Literature,* an Indianapolis-based quarterly magazine that began in 1858. Central to the story of the *Repository* is the story of Elisha Weaver, who would eventually leave his Indiana home to resurrect the Philadelphia-based *Christian Recorder* and publish, among other texts, Julia C. Collins's 1865 *Curse of Caste.* However, while much of this chapter follows Weaver's complex growth, it also offers the first close reading of a newly discovered book of plays—perhaps the first published by an African American—William Jay Greenly's 1858 *The Three Drunkards,* as well as the first consideration of the *Repository*'s later shift away from its western roots, a shift embodied in a pair of recently recovered *Repository* texts by activist Maria W. Stewart.

Chapters 3 and 4 shift to postbellum "unexpected places." Chapter 3 introduces the rich black literary community that grew from early activism in San Francisco (like that lauded in David Lewis's remarks) and that, during the Reconstruction, found its center in the weekly San Francisco *Elevator.* Through reading the *Elevator* letters of Peter Cole, a black expatriate living in Japan, alongside texts by the *Elevator*'s columnist "Semper Fidelis"—recently revealed as Jennie Carter—and by Thomas Detter (including *Nellie Brown*), this chapter begins to map a larger black literary West that used San Francisco—and specifically Philip Bell's *Elevator*—as a conduit for a radical rethinking of the places possible for blackness. In chapter 4 I pick up several of these questions through studying what may initially seem to be a much more expected "place" for black writing. However, in examining the Philadelphia-based *Christian Recorder* in the 1860s and 1870s, I focus on the ways in which *Recorder* writers from a much wider swath of locations made Philadelphia—as the writers studied in chapter 3 did with San Francisco—into a venue for sharing the ways in which their own unexpected places might shape the nation. In addition to surveying the larger landscape of the *Recorder*—a landscape that included, among other texts, Frances Ellen Watkins Harper's first novels—chapter 4 introduces readers to Sallie Daffin, who left her Philadelphia home to teach the newly freed; Lizzie Hart, who, from her home in the tiny Ohio town of

Morrow, advocated not only specific modes of pursuing the Civil War, but also a plan for the Reconstruction; and New Jersey–based William Steward, whose serialized novel *John Blye*—published under the pseudonym "Will"—has never been analyzed by literary critics or historians.

While each chapter introduces a fascinating group of black writers and texts worthy of study in and of itself, I also hope that each functions as a kind of case study for how we might respond to the much larger calls I have articulated here. Each chapter thus offers information on a range of social, political, economic, and racial factors that surrounded the various sites of textual production before sharing close readings of key texts produced within given locations. The close readings are, in turn, as much as possible, paired with discussion of circumstances of composition, genre, publication, audience, reception, and, above all, approaches to community based on geography, influence, and a host of other factors. Even as I attend deeply to questions of physicality—ranging from the location of a given printing press in Indianapolis to the residences of sales agents for the San Francisco *Elevator*—I want to also suggest the importance of ideological, even metaphysical "unexpected places."

In this, perhaps not surprisingly (given both the study's focus and the lives of the various authors it considers), two issues have become centerpieces of the close readings in each chapter: conceptions of place and of black mobility. My sense of place as simultaneously both physical and metaphysical is certainly influenced by the two generations of critics of nineteenth-century American women's writing (especially sentimentalism), who have described complex and interconnected relationships between the "domestic" of the home and the "domestic" of the nation.[21] However, the sense of that second "domestic," as scholars like Frances Smith Foster, John Ernest, and Elizabeth McHenry have thoughtfully asserted, was always more (and differently) conflicted for African Americans. Even as many nineteenth-century black activists and writers articulated deep connections to the United States (in the rhetorics of patriotism, nationalism, manifest destiny, and even, as chapter 3 considers, xenophobia), African Americans, per McHenry's words, found it "readily apparent that free blacks needed to develop their own internal strength, identify and articulate their own needs, and develop their own strategies and institutions to meet those needs if they were to survive in the United States" (42). This means that, again in McHenry's words, while "the quest for citizenship among African Americans has often been cast as another manifestation of the desire to assimilate into white society," African Americans "throughout the nineteenth and into the twentieth century believed that their future in the United States depended on creating *for themselves* the educational and cultural opportunities that would prepare them" (18; 19, italics mine).[22]

One of the "places" that runs throughout the locations considered in this study is thus the metaphorical black nation within a nation. While this "place" certainly functions, per Benedict Anderson's insightful discussion of nations and nationalism, as "an imagined political community— and imagined as both inherently limited and sovereign," its defining conditions also include the physical circumstances of specific locations (6). Thus, for example, the literature produced by the community surrounding the *Repository of Religion and Literature* was empowered—and sometimes limited—by the journal's dependence not simply on the A.M.E. Church but more specifically on the itinerant nature of that church's construction of a (mid)western ministry and the ways in which that itinerancy created or shut down opportunities to raise enough capital to print and distribute black writing. In this vein, each chapter of *Unexpected Places* attends to the need for biography, local history, and other forms of thick-contexting in "placing" the literary texts, and each chapter discusses how individual writers represented their physical *and* metaphysical places as part of not just the United States, not just the black nation within the nation, and not just, say, St. Louis or San Francisco, but all of these and other "locations."

Central to all of these conceptions of place—in the work of almost every writer included in this study—is the question of black mobility. Certainly some of this emphasis should be expected. The vast majority of the writers in this study exercised different forms of mobility to reach the places they wrote from and about: John Berry Meachum traveled from Virginia to North Carolina to Kentucky to St. Louis; Elisha Weaver, from his birthplace in North Carolina, to Indiana, to Philadelphia; Thomas Detter, from Washington, D.C., to the black West; Sallie Daffin, from Philadelphia to locations throughout the upper South; the list could go on. They knew—often all too well—that such mobility was specifically denied not only to many of their free brethren (through economic as well as legal barriers, including various states' and localities' formal and informal "Black laws") but also, of course, to enslaved African Americans.[23]

Further, as Mark Simpson persuasively argues, there was a "longstanding tendency, inscribed again and again in the American nineteenth century, to articulate entangled ideologies of national identity and progress, using mobility as their prime sign or symptom. Treating mobility as the key to national temperament became habitual, even hegemonic, serving to bind together two traits supposedly intrinsic to 'the American': the need to move (freedom as geographical expansiveness) and the need to rise (freedom as social uplift)" (xxv).

In my discussions of black mobility to, from, and within various "unexpected places," I agree with a set of recent scholars that "travel" and "mobility" have been deeply and wrongly conflated. The writers noted above were not simply "travelers." As Inderpal Grewal notes, "the deployment of the term *travel* as a universal form of mobility . . . erases or conflates those mobilities that are not part of this Eurocentric formation," and this means that "migration, immigration, deportation, indenture, and slavery are often erased" from discussions of "travel" (2); the "traveling ideal," as Simpson asserts, emphasizes "individuation, freedom, leisure, solitude, refinement, taste, reflection, discernment, sensibility, and disinterested detachment" and "treats as universal, as the common condition and capacity of all persons, what are in fact the dispositions, privileges, and values (the habitus, to use Pierre Bourdieu's term) of a particular social class under capitalism" (xxiii). Certainly, "travel" narratives are a subset of some of the texts embracing the larger issues of black mobility studied here, but they are *only* a small subset—and, even then, talk back in complex ways to readerly and critical assumptions about the literature of travel.[24] "Travel literature" has also often implicitly suggested that its writers have (or, rather, own) a permanent home, that their travels are temporary, and that they will return to their homes. Many African American writers in this study— even those engaging in more expected senses of travel writing—conceived of their journeys, rather, in the language of Cheryl Fish, "as a choice of vocation and . . . a geographical space" and so as a "mobile subjectivity" with an "agency, even if incomplete or compromised" that "reflects a desire for empowerment" (3, 6, 7). That sense emphasized forms of mobility less discussed in the criticism of travel literature—the mobility of the itinerant minister, for example, and the germinal mobility (and perhaps "manifest domesticity") of the settler, both of which were tied to creating new homes, albeit in different ways.

In short, like Simpson, I find that "'travel,' the concept most ubiquitous when naming modern human movement, will clearly fail to describe the full complexity of the dynamics" I find in these texts, and so, again in Simpson's words, "by directing the emphasis . . . toward . . . the politics of mobility, I mean to refuse travel's hegemony in favor of mobility's contest" (xvi). The African American writers I locate in unexpected places did not only "get there" by exercising mobility, but were continually concerned with the proper practices of mobility to ensure racial elevation, citizenship, and broader participation that would make their places seem more expected and more deeply tied to the rest of the black nation, as well as to the deeply contested broader multiracial nation.

I want to end this introduction with a brief text from the archive, a text that I found paging through California newspapers as I was building chapter 3, a text that has haunted me. Drawn from the 24 July 1865 *Stockton Daily Independent,* it reads:

> INSANE—James E. M. Gilliard, a colored man, formerly of this city, but more recently of Petaluma, arrived in charge of officer Myers, on the steamer Cornelia yesterday morning and was taken to the Insane Asylum. An exchange says that he imagines himself a fountain of intelligence, a living embodiment of greatness, and the grand central luminosity around which all the white shape and talent revolve. His insanity is of the lively and garrulous type. He says people call him a "crazy ni**er" because he talks like a sensible white man, and "quotes Latin from Homer's Iliad." No wonder.

Gilliard's is one of those stories we are only just beginning to recover. He *was*—the text's tone to the contrary—indeed a "fountain of intelligence," and undoubtedly *could* quote Homer with skill and understanding. Born circa 1835, he worked as a barber, a teacher, and sometime A.M.E. minister, and, in the later 1860s, began writing for the *Elevator* and lecturing more widely. I have uncovered no evidence of mental disease—or of his being committed to an asylum. I *have* documented the fact that A.M.E. bishop Thomas M. D. Ward said that "as an orator, he has no superior and few equals on this side of the American Continent" and that he won similar praise from (white) California governor Newton Booth. Gilliard moved to Texas—though he lectured as far east as Philadelphia—in the early 1870s, and was a leading force behind the A.M.E. secondary school in Austin (an ancestor of Paul Quinn College). His pride and willingness to fight for black rights, though, led to his assassination at the hands of a white mob on 6 June 1876 in Van Zandt County, Texas.[25]

Gilliard certainly represents a sense in nineteenth-century white California that a person who was both black and literary was not simply "unexpected" but was so fanciful—or, perhaps put more truthfully, so flat-out frightening to the existing power structures—as to be marked as Insane Other. It was arguably that same sense and that same racist fear that led the lecturer, writer, and teacher to be executed in rural Texas—precisely because, in some racist white minds, Gilliard was not only a "crazy ni**er" but because he hoped to aid more African Americans to become literate, literary, and, through such, more fully participatory citizens. "No wonder."

But what strikes me now is that, very much like Lewis's speech to the 1856 California Colored Convention,[26] while specific location matters deeply, there are tenets and principles of Gilliard's story that are more transportable. It is not surprising, given the interconnectedness of African American communities that comes up repeatedly in the following pages, that both the *Christian Recorder* and San Francisco black newspapers mourned Gilliard's death and decried the circumstances that allowed his killing. In some ways, within the dominant structures of the time, *any* black literary location—be it in the person of an individual or in the instance of a cluster of individuals—was *and had to be* "unexpected." Cornering the black literary into the "not" and the "un" of expectations powerfully marginalized generations of authors and texts; that such cornering marked not only the nineteenth century but also the twentieth century's efforts toward defining canons in American literature (and articulating an American literary history generally sans African Americans) should remind us of the multiple reasons why so many black literary locations are still thought of as "unexpected."

Critics and literary historians, especially those engaged specifically in nineteenth-century studies, have skillfully claimed the rhetorics of recovery and of discovery to combat these limitations (albeit sometimes with some complications, as I discuss in this study's epilogue). Here, I want to remind that recovery and discovery are goal-oriented rhetorics—that is, they have at least a theoretical end. The goal of *Unexpected Places* is thus to contribute to its own obsolescence. We may never discover, recover, or rescue *all* of the literary history that has been lost (and sometimes stolen), but we may be able to make the places of that history more and more expected—and then, perhaps, more and more understood.

Chapter 1

GATEWAYS AND BORDERS

Black St. Louis in the 1840s and 1850s

There was no shortage of discussion of St. Louis vis-à-vis slavery, race, and American values in the decades before the Civil War. In many ways, it was an "expected place" for a very specific kind of black story: "Though slavery is thought, by some, to be mild in Missouri when compared with the cotton, sugar and rice growing States," William Wells Brown wrote in his 1847 *Narrative,* "no part of our slave-holding country, is more noted for the barbarity of its inhabitants, than St. Louis. It was here that Col. Harney, a United States officer, whipped a slave woman to death. It was here that Francis McIntosh, a free colored man from Pittsburgh, was taken from the steamboat Flora, and burned at the stake. During a residence of eight years in this city, numerous cases of extreme cruelty came under my own observation;—to record them all, would occupy more space than could possibly be allowed in this little volume" (34).

In this "expected" story, St. Louis was a locus of the evils of the slave system; in this framework, St. Louis black stories had to be stories of the kind of violent oppression that spread like a virus, stories that could only be told by those who had left (in Brown's case, escaped). Indeed, the 1836 McIntosh case—a lynching that St. Louis authorities let go unpunished— led St. Louis journalist Elijah Lovejoy to protest in ways that caused his own exile from the city. That exile began the sequence of events that led to his 1837 martyrdom in nearby Alton, Illinois, which abolitionist activists used to engineer national outrage.[1]

However, while there were certainly deep truths in the St. Louis stories of McIntosh, Lovejoy, Brown, and post-Lovejoy abolitionism generally, they were not the only black St. Louis stories of the 1840s and 1850s. Both the known and several of the generally unknown St. Louis black stories were part and parcel of the city's amazing growth based on its central role in American mobility. The *St. Louis City Directory for 1840–1841* boasted that "the commercial relations of the city are extended over the entire west" and that St. Louis would soon be "the commercial emporium of the valley of the Mississippi" (vi). It noted that the city had hosted 1,721 steamboat arrivals in 1840; as James Neal Primm points out, it had become "a major collecting point for agricultural produce" within the region (vii, 135).[2] The *Directory* further bragged that the city was home to six daily newspapers and thirteen churches and had a population of 16,291; while the 1840 federal census actually put the number at 16,439, both sources agreed that the population had more than doubled within the space of a decade. By 1845, the population would double again—to over 35,000; given this amazing growth, it is no wonder that, as Primm notes, "after 1835 . . . housing construction fell far behind demand" (179). Still, the *Directory* authors were especially proud of "the public and private buildings" which had "been erected within the last few years," saying that they gave "evidence of much taste and munificence" (viii). Though the authors noted nationwide economic reversals, they were confident that "there is much in the steady, onward progress of St. Louis to gratify all" (viii).

One of the unnamed engines of this growth was St. Louis's African American population. Almost a tenth of the 1840 city population—a group of just over 1,500 souls—was enslaved; 531 more African Americans were nominally free.[3] By 1850, even though their percentage weight would go down in the face of rapid white immigration, the number of African Americans in St. Louis would rise to 2,636 enslaved and 1,398 free. They kept the households of St. Louis's prominent and wealthy running: Primm notes that, by 1850, the "affluent central section" of the city held over two-thirds of the city's slaves and more than half of its free blacks (147). But blacks were also key to the city's massive shipping industry, and served in almost all of the menial positions both on board steamers (Polly Wash, one of the central figures in this chapter, was hired out as a chambermaid) and on the docks.

Of course, these African Americans were not the only blacks in the city. As a regional hub, both slaves and free blacks regularly entered the city limits on brief business; Thomas C. Buchanan's 2004 *Black Life on the Mississippi* marks the St. Louis and "the Mississippi world" generally as a site of surprising black mobility. That said, however, the vast majority of

blacks passing through St. Louis were tied to the city's massive and growing place within the slave trade. As several historians have noted, St. Louis
functioned—along with other regional hubs in the upper South like Nashville and Richmond—as a key conduit for trading slaves not only within
the region but also to markets deeper South like those in New Orleans; as
Primm notes, "St. Louis became a busy slave market, serving as a collecting point for slaves from outstate areas. More than two dozen dealers had
agents in the city, and slave auctions at the courthouse were commonplace
spectacles" (187).[4] This was the St. Louis perhaps freshest in William Wells
Brown's mind as he composed his *Narrative*—a St. Louis where blacks were
viciously "moved" (often to Deep South deaths) amid the white westward
mobility that supposedly held the promise of the nation.

After briefly examining key components of Brown's more "expected"
story—including his sense of slavery's violence and attempts to destroy
black personhood and domesticity, his positioning of St. Louis as a gateway, and his representation of possible black locations and mobility—this
chapter considers three texts that expand our sense of the black stories
located in and even told from within antebellum St. Louis: John Berry
Meachum's 1846 *Address to All the Colored Citizens of the United States,*
Cyprian Clamorgan's 1858 *The Colored Aristocracy of St. Louis,* and the St.
Louis freedom suit case file of Polly Wash. As case studies of "other" African American texts in and of St. Louis, my discussions consider how African Americans negotiated the boundaries that both authorized and limited
their voices. I focus on how their texts begin to articulate stories of a black
St. Louis that is, at times, very different from the city in Lovejoy/Brown
abolitionism, even as these stories share—in different ways—Brown's attention to mobility, location, domestic ideals, and black personhood (in
and beyond the slave system). While I certainly don't suggest that these
texts represent a literary renaissance in antebellum St. Louis, their presence demonstrates the complexity, the black textual lives, and the black
stories possible in even the most surprising of places, Brown's locus and
location of brutality.

Brown's text and his specific depiction of St. Louis certainly depended
in part on the outrage generated by Lovejoy's murder.[5] That Brown had
actually been hired out to work in Lovejoy's St. Louis print shop, knew
Lovejoy as both "a very good man" and "a very humane man" (34, 35), and
could invoke his memory directly reminded readers that the slaveholder
violence Brown depicted in his own story was part and parcel of what (and

who) killed Elijah Lovejoy. Brown's very first reported experience of St. Louis—being hired out to a tavern keeper while still a child—illustrates the tri-part linkage of St. Louis, slavery, and evil. Near the opening of his "little volume," Brown tells of the drunken "cut and slash—knock down and drag out" temporary master from whom he eventually ran (31). Caught by dogs, Brown was taken to the St. Louis jail before being returned to the tavern keeper to be "tied up in the smoke-house," "very severely whipped," and then "smoked" through prolonged exposure to "a fire of tobacco stems," in what the taverner's son referred to as "the way his father used to do to his slaves in Virginia" (32).

Brown fared no better when he was next hired to the manager of St. Louis's Missouri Hotel, who not only abused his wife with sadist regularity but savagely beat the slaves under his control—including one named Aaron, who, for a minor offense, received "fifty lashes on the bare back with a cow-hide," after which Brown was ordered to "wash him down with rum," causing even "more agony than the whipping" (33). Very much in the spirit of earlier abolitionist movement-supported slave narratives like Frederick Douglass's famous 1845 volume and of white abolitionist depictions of McIntosh and Lovejoy, violence thus quickly becomes central to the book's sense of slavery. This violence, though, defines not only slavery, but also the physical location of St. Louis—a specifically Southern location where slaveholders might attach "a ball and chain" to a slave's leg as punishment for any small infraction (35).

Brown, however, adds a key component not found in the McIntosh-Lovejoy nexus: the conception of St. Louis as a "gateway" to the heart of slavery, a representation clearly designed to challenge the depictions of St. Louis as the gateway to the West (and thus to America's future) that dominated white texts from guidebooks and city directories to early St. Louis newspapers.[6] St. Louis's claim as a center of American mobility (and the independence that came with such) is frighteningly revised in Brown's account of being hired out to the notorious "soul driver," slave trader James Walker (41).[7] Describing a time that made him "heart-sick," Brown repeatedly shows how St. Louis served as a key entry point for the slave trader's "cargo of flesh" (42–43). Brown tells of Walker chaining "a gang of slaves" in St. Louis and carrying them down the Mississippi to New Orleans, where they were "placed in a negro-pen" and sold (42). Such sales, Brown quickly reminds readers, doubly damn domestic ideals: he tells, for example, of seeing a slave named Lewis "tied up to a beam, with his toes just touching the floor" for hours before receiving a hundred lashes for attempting to see his family, from whom he had been separated by sale (44).

All of Brown's hellish journeys down the Mississippi notably end where they began: "back to St. Louis" (45). Each return marks St. Louis's accretion of more of slavery's evil, including Walker's return "home" with an enslaved "mistress" named Cynthia, who "bewailed her sad fate with floods of tears" and who Walker sold after fathering four of her children (45). Brown thus constructs St. Louis as the beginning of a repeated process of "tearing the husband from the wife, the child from the mother, and the sister from the brother"—a sense that is only solidified by Brown's account of the St. Louis sale of his sister, who "expressed her determination to die, rather than to go to the far south" (55). As in much of the abolitionist movement's sponsored literature, such scenes reminded readers that slavery was the antithesis of domestic ideals. That such was a key feature of the "gateway" to the West thus augured horrifically for America's future domestic bliss.

Brown's representation of St. Louis as a perverted gateway, like much of the rest of his depiction of slavery and race, shares another crucial component with the earlier stories of McIntosh and Lovejoy: the sense that St. Louis *held* black stories, but could not be a location for the *telling* of those stories. Lovejoy certainly represented such: his sympathetic telling of the story of free African American Francis McIntosh forced him from the city and toward his death.[8]

Purchasers and readers of Brown's *Narrative* were barraged with reminders that, to tell his story, Brown could *not* be in St. Louis. Some purchasers would have bought the *Narrative* at one of the many antislavery lectures and fairs that sprang up across the North in the 1840s; some might even have seen Brown speak, shaken his hand, taken the book from the fugitive himself. The title page reminds readers that Brown was "a fugitive slave," the dedication to the first edition ("to Wells Brown, of Ohio") echoes this status, and New Yorker J. C. Hathaway's preface describes how Brown's antislavery "labors have been chiefly confined to Western New York, where he has secured many friends" (24). Hathaway's preface further argues that Brown's narrative "is a voice from the prison-house" and that Brown "has been behind the curtain. He has visited its secret chambers" (23). And, of course, the *Narrative* was published by William Lloyd Garrison's Boston "Anti-Slavery Office." In essence, all of the book's front matter demonstrates that Brown had crossed the border into freedom, into a place—the urban

American Northeast—where he could finally articulate the truth of black St. Louis because he was finally outside of it.

In the narrative proper, Brown repeatedly marks his first escape attempt from St. Louis as an exodus designed to save his soul—telling of how, "anxiously" looking "for our friend and leader—the NORTH STAR," he "left the city" and of how, "as we traveled towards a land of liberty, my heart would at times leap for joy" (58, 57, 59). When he finally succeeded in escaping, he writes, "I wanted to see my fellow-slaves in St. Louis, and let them know that the chains were no longer upon my limbs" (77). He thus reminds readers again that his story can only be told because he is *not* in St. Louis—because he is, as he says only two paragraphs later, "seated here in sight of the Bunker Hill Monument, writing this narrative"; he also tells readers that the full stories of his "fellow-slaves" may never be known because they are still in St. Louis (77–78). In thus rewriting the idealized and independent mobility promised by the gateway of St. Louis—first as the site of a slave trader's destruction of domestic ideals and then ultimately as the site of his own desperate escape—Brown firmly situated the *only* black stories of St. Louis as stories of the "prison house." This representation held sway in most abolitionist discussions of St. Louis—from Brown's later work to pieces in the *Liberator*—and it has deeply shaped literary critics' and historians' sense of black St. Louis to the present day. In many ways, then, Brown's *Narrative* contributed to making black St. Louis a deeply unexpected place for stories of and by African American residents—the stories this chapter begins to study.

JOHN BERRY MEACHUM'S "LITTLE BOOK"

John Berry Meachum came by his freedom far differently than did William Wells Brown, and that difference shaped both the story of his life and the stories in his major published text, *An Address to All the Colored Citizens of the United States.* Building from this recognition, after briefly examining Meachum's path to freedom, this section reads Meachum's *Address* as a story of a St. Louis that offered select free blacks (and perhaps, in some theoretical future, select enslaved blacks) opportunities deeply tied to black unity, religious-industrial education, and especially western expansionism and a domesticated, germinal sense of mobility.

Born into slavery in 1789 in Goochland County, Virginia, Meachum accompanied his owner, Paul Meachum, when he moved to North Carolina and then to Hardin County, Kentucky. In his *Address,* Meachum would remember his owner as "a good man" (3). By the time they settled in Kentucky, Paul Meachum was elderly. John Berry Meachum, a carpenter and cooper, "proposed to him to hire my time," and he was allowed to keep enough of his wages to eventually buy himself and later return briefly to Virginia to buy his father (3). However, the realities of slavery and white mobility continued to shape Meachum's life: he married Mary, a slave whose owner moved from Kentucky to St. Louis in 1815. Meachum followed. By all accounts, Meachum's initial years in St. Louis were, for an African American in a territory that permitted slavery, an amazing success story: he earned enough to buy and then free his wife and children, opened his own coopering business, began buying real estate, and began preaching to a small congregation of both free blacks and slaves. Meachum also began participating in the trade that made William Wells Brown "heartsick": he began buying slaves. His stated purpose, though, was to teach them a trade, allow them to work for him long enough to buy themselves, and emancipate them.

By 1846, he claimed that he had purchased "twenty colored friends," emancipated all, and seen all but one (a drunkard) find success and freedom in St. Louis (5).[9] Some readers outside of St. Louis may have known of this work, as well as of Meachum's "temperance boat" (a steamer he purchased in 1835 and equipped with a library and probably a school for African Americans), as both were discussed in "Capacity of Negroes to Take Care of Themselves," which appeared in the 10 December 1836 *Liberator* and was republished in the 11 March 1837 *Colored American.*

Regardless of Meachum's motives—which may well have been humanitarian and communitarian, but may also have figured in his economic status, relative personal power within St. Louis's black community, or a combination of these and/or other factors—Meachum did clearly and creatively consider the limitations and possibilities of "racial elevation" in St. Louis. The post-Lovejoy era, when abolitionism became more organized and more national, saw increasing restrictions on free and enslaved African Americans in St. Louis. At the end of 1838, St. Louis mayor William Carr issued an edict that, because of "the recent extensive distribution, in this city, of incendiary abolition newspapers, tracts and pictures, effected secretly in the night time, by casting packages into yards and other places, where

they would be found by servants," all "officers . . . concerned in maintaining the public peace" would have "to deny the colored people some of their
usual privileges, until those enemies of the human race, the abolitionists
. . . are discovered." Carr's notice, which was reprinted in the 15 February
1839 *Liberator,* continued, "the usual permits, from this office, to colored
people, for social parties and religious meetings, after night, will be with-
held, until information is given of the hiding places of the incendiaries,
which must be known to some of our colored people" and asserted that "it
is the special duty of the colored race, to give the police such information."
The city government's continuing concern led to periodic sweeps of black
neighborhoods that were reported in national venues like the *Liberator* and
the *Colored American.* The crackdown was a harbinger of the next decades'
increasing legal limits on free blacks—including toughened rules for free
black registration and bonding, more arrests for not carrying free papers,
and further restrictions on black gatherings—all tied to growing suspicion
of abolitionist activity among the city's free black and enslaved populations.[10]

Meachum demonstrated a fairly creative if sometimes accommodationist sense of working within these limits. If instruction of blacks took place
on his boat, for example, as it may well have, such would center at least
nominally on temperance and piety—values much of the white St. Louis
hierarchy said they desired in African Americans—and such would likely
take place closer to the Illinois side of the river. Meachum's preaching had
also long been deemed generally safe, and so, when laws against gatherings
of African Americans became stricter, most of white St. Louis seems to
have been willing to turn a blind eye.[11] (That the *Liberator* noted, "among
the fruits" of Meachum's "arduous, persevering labor," "a deep-toned missionary spirit, uncommon order and correctness among the slave population in the city, [and] strict and regular discipline in the church" speaks
volumes.) Even Meachum's emancipations were carefully regulated and
limited: not only did the newly emancipated have to register like all free
blacks in the city, they had to be bonded and carefully monitored.

Meachum's *Address* differed from this earlier community work not simply in that it was textual. It was clearly national in intent—even as many
of its components made it very much a St. Louis story. Virtually unknown
today even though it is easily accessible through the electronic *Documenting the American South* project, the sixty-two-page booklet was originally
published in Philadelphia. Its stated purpose was to call representatives

to a "National Convention of Colored Citizens of America" to be held in September 1847, and its title consciously addressed "all" of "the Colored Citizens of the United States." Its stated theme was "union," and so it focused much energy on how black Americans "must therefore be united in love and affection—our interests, aims, and hopes must be one" (9).[12]

In taking as his central text Psalm 68: 31—"Ethiopia shall soon stretch out her hands unto God"—Meachum argued not only for black potential but also for a unified black nation within a larger Christian nation. This kind of nascent black nationalism, though, cannot be read as simply radical or simply conservative: it was, simultaneously, deeply negative about Africa, but certainly not assimilationist; hopeful of a "union" between select free (and eventually, select formerly enslaved) blacks, but not abolitionist; at times proud of black accomplishments, but often quite critical of the "laziness" Meachum saw among free African Americans; assertive about the need for economic self-sufficiency within the black community, but generally uncritical of the white racism, system of slavery, and racially inflected capitalist structures that kept economic power from African Americans.

After a brief preface, the *Address* opens with a comparison of African Americans and their African ancestors, asserting that war and division into "separate kingdoms" in Africa led to slavery (8). Meachum worried that enslaved Africans "brought with them the same principles here,—envy, hatred, malice, jealous[ness] . . . principles which they possessed" and that "originated doubtless, from ignorance" (8). These dubious conclusions led Meachum to argue that, only when "union of sentiment, feeling and affection is formed and established among us" could African Americans "arrive to the same scale of being which those who are considered our superiors have attained" (12). Meachum's "those who are considered" language may both nod to the segregationist ethos that dominated the nineteenth century and subtly dig at whiteness.[13] Certainly it demonstrates Meachum's recognition that, however much whites shaped many details of his and his audience's existence, black unity must come from within the black community. (Thus, whites are mentioned only briefly in the *Address;* all of the first-person pronouns and group nouns that Meachum uses are clearly marked as African American.)

Like many black writers both before and after, Meachum constructed the African American nation as analogous to the "children of Israel," whose "rebellious" turn of heart caused God to make "them wander forty years before they reached Canaan" (6).[14] This rhetoric allowed Meachum to assert that "all will admit that we are capable of elevating ourselves," but it also led Meachum to consistently criticize his fellow free blacks (7). In short, to argue that "righteousness will exalt us," Meachum had to argue that "sin has degraded us" (7). Thus, Meachum regularly claimed that African Americans were "in darkness, ignorance, and superstition, in a state of moral and intellectual degradation"; that while it is common "to suppose that our oppression is occasioned by severe restrictions . . . laid upon us by others . . . the truth is that you keep yourselves down"; that "you do not respect yourselves sufficiently"; that "we have been asleep" or dominated by "strife and confusion"; that, "with few exceptions, you are too idle or too wasteful" (9, 11, 12, 16, 25).

While Meachum claimed that unity would help African Americans "shake off our lethargy," piety, education, economic consciousness, and domesticated mobility were just as important (12). In each of these areas, Meachum saw racial elevation as doubly domestic—"as in family relations, so in national affairs" (10). Meachum's construction of piety and education were not out of the ordinary: he argued that "we must live godly and soberly in Christ Jesus the Lord" and felt that African Americans should focus on "manual labor schools" that would fit young blacks for trades and farming, as such would allow some measure of economic security (41, 19). Bemoaning his sense that African Americans had generally been "too idle or too wasteful" to invest in the settled ideal of the church-centered community of well-tended farms and light industry driven by skilled craftsmen, Meachum called for such schools to teach piety as well as "industry" (25, 19).[15]

But Meachum's sense of what should happen beyond such religious-industrial education places a surprising emphasis on black mobility. While he notes that if a reader has given a son "a trade, he might set up a business in the same city," he also suggests that that son might "travel off to find a better place; and when he has worked long enough . . . writes to them to come on where he is" (30). Meachum found models for such among "foreigners who have emigrated to this country" who, "in a few years . . . have good homes" because of industry (28). Meachum also praised immigrants' willingness to invest in real estate—because "just as long as you are living in rented houses you are making yourself a slave for somebody else" (45).[16] In short, this was mobility with the end goal of settlement and domesticity, and this specific sense of mobility was further emphasized in Meachum's criticism of forms of mobility that lacked roots. Perhaps remembering white St. Louis's views of river worker Francis McIntosh,

Meachum asserted, for example, that "boatmen are very apt to be rude" because they lacked community ties (31).

Implicitly embracing an anticolonization ethos—perhaps surprising given his often accommodationist stance—Meachum ignored the possibility of germinal, settler-centered mobility that involved leaving the United States. While Meachum "would not recommend this people to settle on poor ground, like many of the free people in old Virginia and North Carolina," however, he advocated moving to "the state of Illinois, it is a fine country and a free state. And there is the state of Michigan, the finest country likely in America, and many others that I could mention, such as Iowa and Wisconsin" (26). "Stop dreaming over poor land," Meachum told his readers: "go and see, and please yourselves" (26). On the frontier, Meachum asserted, "farming is the most independent life that a man can live, most especially for the colored citizens of America, who cannot hold any office . . . but . . . can hold a farm . . . the greatest office in the United States of America" (26–27). In short, Meachum's sense of worthwhile mobility was doubly domestic—of and for the home and of and for the nation.

Meachum's placement of his intended audience—"All the Colored Citizens in the United States"—on the cusp between African-ness and American-ness, between factionalism and union, and between "wandering in the wilderness" and finding a Canaan in the American (Mid)West reemphasizes that many of his arguments come through the language of location and dislocation (6). It also bluntly asserts that not all African Americans were ready for his relocation plans: "if you will not come and join this honorable society, and endeavor to live an honorable life, we must leave you" and "if we cannot carry the whole race along, we will carry just as many as we can get to join" (52, 53). This meant that, for the time, the question of slavery would have to wait, because "it is more in the power of the free to promote" unity "than those who are differently situated" (11). Further, Meachum "verily believe[d] that only a portion of the free should be consulted in the outset—they should be men of worth, good, moral, religious, intelligent, influential men, whose only object would be to promote the glory of God and to do good to their fellow men" (11). For that select mobile and prepared few, Meachum offered a western black place, one that grounded black personhood in the domestic ideals of family/community and piety while at the same time directly addressing national domestic ideals of agrarian and trades-based economic self-sufficiency and (segregated) community.

What makes these very national calls into a St. Louis story—beyond Meachum's physical location and his byline tag ("Pastor of the African Baptist Church, St. Louis, Mo.")—is Meachum's autobiographical preface. That preface also complicates easy generic classification of his *Address* as a simple convention call. While the *Address* proper certainly fits into the black sermonic and pamphleteering traditions and has much in common with other convention calls, the preface begins, for example, with a personal narrative of slavery, albeit a very different kind of slavery than that in Brown's soon-to-come *Narrative*. While the preface's very first sentence gives the kind of "was born" line common in many slave narratives tied to the abolitionist movement, it also offers the kind of specific birth date—3 May 1789—whose absence is often mourned in abolitionist movement-supported slave narratives. In sharing information on his owner, Meachum again followed a pattern in such slave narratives, but he also, again, veered far from the typical slave narrative's cataloging of cruelty to say that his owner "was a good man and I loved him" (3). Again like many movement-supported slave narratives—albeit in much tamer terms—Meachum asserted that he "could not feel myself satisfied" while in slavery; however, Meachum's way to freedom—rather than the escape, the culminating exercise of "stolen" mobility in many slave narratives—is to gain permission and resources to purchase himself.

That his single paragraph of slave narrative goes so completely against post-Lovejoy abolitionist literature—indeed, that the *Address* never even mentions Lovejoy or McIntosh—emphasizes Meachum's very different definition of black St. Louis. From *his* black St. Louis, Meachum could both assert that "I have written this little book to show you the great desire I have for the welfare of this people" *and* elide the kinds of discussion of the slave system that dominate better-known black stories of St. Louis. Instead, the bulk of Meachum's preface shares repeated examples of black freedom and opportunity—how (after purchasing himself and his father) he had a conversion experience that led to his baptism and eventual preaching, how he exercised the same germinal westward mobility he argues for in the *Address,* how his skilled practice of his trade and his strong moral fiber brought first money and then property, and how he began "giving back" to his community through pastoring and through engaging in a small-scale gradualist emancipation scheme. He even details the life of one of the unnamed enslaved men he reputedly purchased and eventually freed as an echo to his own story: "One of the twenty colored friends that I bought is [especially] worthy to be taken notice of, to show what industry will do. I paid for him one thousand dollars. He worked and paid back the thousand dollars. He has also bought a lot of ground for which he paid a thousand dollars. He married a slave and purchased her, and paid seven hundred dollars for her. He has built a house that cost him six hundred dollars. He is a blacksmith, and has worked for one man ever since he has been in St. Louis" (5). Meachum's St. Louis, then, like the St. Louis of this nameless emancipated blacksmith, has the potential to be the kind of Canaan he notes in Michigan, Wisconsin, Iowa, and even nearby Illinois.

Meachum went even further in suggesting that there might be *other* stories from other black places—stories and places and names that needed to be textualized. He asked the "Colored men of America, wherever you are scattered in different directions upon American soil," to specifically "Send your name, and place of residence, with your desire and pledge, that the same may be recorded in the great Ledger that shall be handed down from generation to generation" (57). That "ledger," a collection of letters to the proposed national convention from "each state or county, or city or village, or town or any place below the sun," would collect the names of representatives from across the nation, thus letting all know "that a union is already formed as to your part" and so doing much to stop African Americans' "scattered condition" (57–58, 27).

Meachum's accommodationist and gradualist stance is certainly unpalatable to many contemporary readers—as it undoubtedly was to some of his contemporaries (like William Wells Brown). However, he was nonetheless able to use that stance in his *Address* to represent a domestic ideal of blackness centered on a germinal, settler-centered mobility that sometimes challenged racial stereotypes and began to counter the sense that the only black St. Louis stories could be stories of the tragedy of slavery.

CYPRIAN CLAMORGAN AND ARISTOCRACY

If Meachum's "little book" questioned the representations of black St. Louis found in post-Lovejoy abolitionist literature, then Cyprian Clamorgan's 1858 *Colored Aristocracy of St. Louis* (reissued in 1999 and edited by Julie Winch[17]) attempted a much larger rewriting of not only black St. Louis but also the general representation of blackness in literature. That revision almost completely ignores contemporary slavery, constructs a much narrower black elite than Meachum's *Address* (one based largely on wealth and lineage), describes and sometimes revels in that elite's excesses, and removes much of Meachum's sense of the domestic from the still-essential component of mobility.

Though Clamorgan never mentioned William Wells Brown's by-then famous *Narrative,* he seemed to accept the fact that "the romantic autobiographies of Solomon Northrup [*sic*], Box Brown, and other colored gentleman, have been read in every quarter of the globe" and that "respectable white men and women can sit and listen to the oratorical displays of Fred. Douglass and his able compatriots" (45). That said, the gossipy mixed-race barber found much to object to in the more popular abolitionist fiction with which he lumped these black voices: "Thousands have wept," Clamorgan tells readers at the opening of his short pamphlet, "over the fictitious sorrows of 'Uncle Tom,' as delineated by the facile pen of Mrs. Stowe; while the imaginary 'Dred,' a monstrous creation of the same morbid and diseased brain, has awakened the sympathies of all classes of readers" (45). Characterizing himself as "a faithful historian," Clamorgan claimed that even though "the history" of the families considered in *The Colored Aristocracy* would provide "material for a dozen such volumes as 'Uncle Tom's Cabin,'" he could "only aim at the simple truth" and would "leave all flights of fancy to such romancists [*sic*] as Mrs. Stowe and her colleagues" (54).

Clamorgan shared such "simple truth" through the form of a compendium of brief biographies of some of St. Louis's wealthiest black citizens.[18] He spiced those biographies, however, with a recognition that it was his "unpleasant duty to speak of the vile and unworthy" among this class "as well as the good and virtuous" (54). Clamorgan's text certainly hints that these factors—as well as the wealth and mobility key to his sense of aristocracy—were exotic enough to be interesting, even titillating, to white as well as black readers. Because of these shifts from a moral emphasis and from a primarily black intended audience, Clamorgan's St. Louis is, even more than Meachum's, a sea of seeming contradictions: a black St. Louis at once tied to ideas of economic uplift and flat-out greed, at once broad in terms of opportunity and narrow in who was allowed such opportunity, at once politically engaged and deeply self-interested, and at once deeply tied to the frontier but eminently civil and civilized.

Clamorgan seems almost obsessed with net worth. We learn, early and prominently in most of the entries, his estimate of each figure's wealth— Pelagie Rutgers, a "half a million dollars"; Pelagie Nash, "five thousand dollars" including "nearly the whole block in which she resides"; Sarah Hazlett, "a comfortable fortune of seventy thousand dollars," and so on (48–49). He also regularly mentions key possessions denoting wealth, like Rutgers's "piano which cost two thousand dollars" (49). If readers assumed Clamorgan was correct and tallied his figures, they would see an elite group of black St. Louisians who had combined real estate, cash, and other assets worth close to $1.7 million.[19]

Some of those funds were raised, as were the elder William Johnson's, through "clear foresight and shrewdness in business" or, as were those of nurse Mary Obuchon, through "patience, gentleness, and watchfulness," or even, as were those of Elenius Henley, through "upright deportment and business qualifications" (55, 50, 53). Much more of the wealth Clamorgan notes, however, came from, as did "inveterate gambler" Samuel Mordecai's, "the turn of the cards," or from, as Albert White's did, good luck in "the California fever," or from, as did that of Pelagie Rutgers's late husband, inheritance from white forbears (51, 52). Some even came from much more "questionable" activities like those of the "saucy" and "imprudent" social "outcast," Pelagie Foreman, who began "her career" as "the mistress of a white man" and "like Delilah of old," had "sheared the strength of more than one Samson" (60).

What emerges is an elite black St. Louis focused, like Meachum's, on gaining power through economics. However—deeply unlike Meachum's— this elite lives for material wealth. Some of Clamorgan's commentary is certainly critical of such; for example, he says that he writes about Pelagie Foreman "with extreme reluctance," as it means that he must "speak in terms of disrespect of a lady" (59). However, other wealth that Meachum would find horribly tainted (especially that tied to gambling) is joked about, tolerated, and even lauded. Robert Smith, for example, while "not received into society on account of his wife" is still recognized as "proud and dignified" and "of good moral habits"—even though "he sells intoxicating liquors" at his "coffee house" (61).[20]

Clamorgan is blunt in his prefatory remarks that "wealth is power," and he echoes this sentiment directly and indirectly throughout the volume— as in his reporting of Pelagie Nash's motto, a revision of Pope: "Wealth makes the man, the want of it the fellow" (47, 49). Thus, even though he occasionally objects to some excesses—calling, for example, the wife of Ludwell Lee "more ornamental than useful" because she "has all the vanity of a peacock" and attacking Pelagie Rutgers because "she worships the almighty dollar more than Almighty God"—he maintains that "every one knows that money, in whose hands soever it may be found, has an influence proportioned to its amount" (58, 49, 47). Even as he makes the token assertion that "there is not a colored man in our midst who would not cheerfully part with his last dollar to effect the elevation of his race," Clamorgan shows no such parting and no such community; indeed, he says nothing about political or social activism outside of his brief prefatory remarks (47).[21]

Still, wealth alone did not, in Clamorgan's mind, guarantee entrance into the privileged "first circles." As Winch succinctly explains, "if wealth was the prime qualification for membership of the 'aristocracy,' it was not the only prerequisite. . . . He believed one instinctively *knew* who 'belonged,' who 'counted'" (9). Clamorgan asserts that he could simply tell "who moved in a certain circle" regardless of wealth (46). Thus, Clamorgan could write of how Pelagie Foreman was "an outcast from society, into which all her infamous wealth cannot gain her admittance" and of how Virginia Berry's attendance at a ball given by "the colored people of the second class" removed her for a season from any "first class" events (60). Robert Smith and Henry Alexander McGee, both noted as "good businessmen," were excluded from the true aristocracy by their wives' deeds; McGee, "owing to certain reports in regard to the character of his wife before marriage" (57).[22] Ironically, as Winch notes, "Clamorgan did not count a single African American minister among his 'aristocrats'" (8).

Clamorgan's definition of the "colored aristocracy" was, in fact, even narrower than the above suggests; it focused largely on a sense of lineage and mobility that revised Meachum's ideals significantly. In his prefatory remarks, Clamorgan offers a brief history of how, "when Upper Louisiana was settled by the French and Spaniards, the emigrants were necessarily nearly all of the sterner sex" and, because they longed "for the endearments of a wife, and . . . the prattle of children," they "sought wives among the sylvan maids of the forest" (46). Into this Greco-Roman analogy— Clamorgan even references the rape of the Sabine women—he adds, to the "sylvan" Native American women, West Indians who had "the blood of Africa" (46). Clamorgan was arguably directly describing his own "voyageur" ancestor—who, Winch notes, was born in "the French West Indian colony of Guadeloupe," was "according to various accounts, of mixed Spanish, Portuguese, Scottish, Welsh, French, and perhaps West African extraction," and had sexual relationships with several black women (22). Clamorgan was also, however, defining the kind of wealth that had been gained through pioneering (specifically through westward expansion) that he saw as crucial to understanding St. Louis. The African / West Indian women who "many of the voyageurs up the Mississippi obtained [as] wives" went on, Clamorgan says, "to share their fortunes in the wilderness; and from this union have sprung up many of those whom we designate the 'colored aristocracy'" (46).[23]

Clamorgan creates an analogue to the original mobility of the voyageurs in his discussions of newer St. Louis blacks—immigrants to St. Louis from Kentucky, Cincinnati, Pennsylvania, Tennessee, Baltimore, the District of Columbia, Detroit, and especially "the prolific old State of Virginia, the mother of Presidents and mullatos [sic]" (58). These neo-elite share many of the attributes of the voyageurs' descendants, albeit with British, rather than French or Spanish, ancestors. Clamorgan prominently notes, for example, that many of those he lists were, like Byertere Hickman, descendants from "the first families of Virginia" (53). Central, too, was an entrepreneurial spirit—as in Albert White, who "came to St. Louis some sixteen years ago, and has amassed a fortune" since (52). Beyond this, of immediate interest is the fact that most of Clamorgan's neo-elite came from the South. Sidestepping the question of slavery's full impact on African Americans, Clamorgan reflects briefly on his sense that "the colored people who have come here . . . from the free States, bring with them more faults and vices than . . . those who have been reared upon the soil" of slave states like Missouri (57). However, he decides to "leave it to the abolition philosophers to solve the problem" (57).

Clamorgan is careful to note that St. Louis is *not* the true frontier for either group of the elite—even if it served and serves as a gateway to such. Much more dependent on a sense of civilization, modernity, and urbanity than Meachum's agrarian model, Clamorgan's St. Louis is a kind of "home base" to which pioneers return. He tells, for example, of several of the black elite going West—as in his description of Albert White and his wife, "when the California fever was raging some years ago," accumulating "a comfortable pile of dust," and then returning to live in St. Louis (52). A similar sense of St. Louis marks Clamorgan's depiction of those among his "aristocracy" who made their money through the river trade. Far from Meachum's ill-mannered roustabouts, Clamorgan depicts the wealthiest of these as men who have "seen the world" and are "genteel" (59, 63). In Clamorgan's black St. Louis, then, money and lineage—and perhaps physical features that allowed some (like Clamorgan himself) to occasionally pass—might be able to make the city's borders more permeable.[24]

Clamorgan's own incessant traveling may have shaped both his choice of rhetoric and his sense of the "first circles." Winch's landmark research traces Clamorgan's ancestors' complex cross-racial place in early St. Louis—especially the relationship of the voyageur Jacques Clamorgan and "his 'Negro wives,' as a contemporary described his mistresses" (23). One of several grandchildren of Jacques, Cyprian Clamorgan was born 27 April 1830 in St. Louis; after the early death of his unwed mother, he and his three siblings were cared for and educated by the white Charles Collins. Two of his brothers became successful barbers in the city, and Clamorgan also learned the trade. He, however, turned to the Mississippi, and—sometimes living as a white man, sometimes not—worked up and down the great river. As for his westward-looking colleagues, St. Louis remained his touchstone—though this was in part because he was, in Winch's words, a "perennial litigant" involved in the messiness (and massiveness) of the battles over his grandfather's estate.[25] By the time he wrote *Colored Aristocracy,* he had a black wife and two sons in St. Louis, a second (and white) wife and a daughter in New Orleans, varied experiences up and down the Mississippi, strained ties with his immediate family (partially because of arguments over his brothers' St. Louis barbershop), and a unique combination of the perspectives of both deep insider and perennial outsider vis-à-vis the "colored elite" he wrote about.[26]

But, unlike Meachum, Clamorgan chose not to place himself as a model; *Colored Aristocracy* does not do the kind of autobiographical work that Meachum's preface did. Instead, Clamorgan took the novel step of giving himself the power of mobility within his narrative voice. Specifically, much of Clamorgan's presentation of "history" and "simple truth" borrows from the language of the travel narrative—exemplified by his transition from general prefatory remarks to specific biographies: "If the reader will accompany me down Seventh street to the vicinity of Rutgers, I will show him a large mansion. . . . Entering the mansion, I will introduce him to its mistress" (48). After his two-paragraph discussion of Rutgers, he transitions with "Turning up the street, we come to Third street, between Lombard and Hazel, to the residence of Mrs. Pelagie Nash," and after a single paragraph on Nash, he brings us "next door to Mrs. Nash," where "resides Mrs. Sarah Hazlett" (49). This language of a tour guide, which is repeated throughout the volume, positions his black St. Louisian subjects as familiar and understandable Others, Clamorgan as an expert participant-narrator, and readers (both white and black) as simultaneously interested in "the colored aristocracy of St. Louis" and able to separate such from the "flights of fancy" of abolitionist agitators.

This approach vacillates between placing readers as welcomed visitors, voyeurs, and perhaps even voyageurs. Clamorgan emphasizes what readers "see," ranging from Rutgers's above-noted piano to her body—"a brown-skinned, straight-haired woman of about fifty years of age . . . fine-looking and healthy" who had "been quite handsome" (48–50). But we also learn that Rutgers is "illiterate," "not noted for her piety," "too penurious to give her [daughter] an education," and a woman who "exposes her ignorance when she attempts to converse"; similarly, Clamorgan tells us that "a mystery hangs over the gay" Hazlett, "which curious eyes have in vain endeavored to penetrate" because she "has thus far been shrewd enough to keep her own secret, and to effectually conceal all proofs of criminality" (48–50).

His tone was certainly calculated to attract readers—Winch rightly notes that Clamorgan was "always the opportunist" (3)—and his booklet was, much more than Meachum's text, also self-consciously literary. If Clamorgan's weaving of travel narrative with wit (in the sense of Pope and his circle, whom Clamorgan alludes to more than once) was successful, it would mark its author as a man of culture and taste—an urbane "colored aristocrat."[27] Still, this approach had its risks: at many moments, Clamorgan's elite become simple exotica, and his St. Louis, a kind of gallery of oddities. In this vein, while Clamorgan's text certainly joined Meachum's in offering a very different literary representation of black St. Louis from that in the Elijah Lovejoy–William Wells Brown nexus of abolitionist literature—another story *of* black St. Louis *from* black St. Louis—it ran the very real risk of losing its already-limited political efficacy through its tabloid approach and its complete sidestepping of the condition of most African Americans in the city and in the nation.

(RE)READING POLLY WASH

While Meachum and Clamorgan's texts both represent black St. Louis far differently than post-Lovejoy abolitionist texts, they nonetheless could not—or would not—share the stories of those still caught in the slave system. The vast majority of those men, women, and children would, as William Wells Brown suggested, never see their stories in print, and most of those stories have now been lost and forgotten. Still, if, in a more speculative mode, we begin to broaden our sense of what might constitute a black story, a black text, a black author, or even a "slave narrative," we can begin to tap into another unexpected location of black textual presences and black stories in antebellum St. Louis, the stories built into court records.

One of the largest single manuscript collections of such stories sits in the massive, warehouse-like building that once housed the *St. Louis Globe.* Amid centuries of civil case files heard by the St. Louis Circuit Court, there are over three hundred "freedom suits"—suits brought by enslaved African Americans seeking their freedom through openings in Missouri slave law. Few historians or literary critics have considered the collection, in part because, until recently, only a handful of city and state workers knew of the suits, even though both the infamous Dred Scott case as well as the case that became the basis for Lucy Delaney's *From the Darkness Cometh the Light* began as St. Louis freedom suits.[28]

Some of the continuing silence surrounding these cases can also be explained by the fact that, while the basic concepts behind the suits were fairly simple, their place(s) as slaves' stories were not. The remainder of this chapter offers an introductory discussion of the structures and implications of freedom suits before sharing a close reading of the case file of one freedom suit litigant, Polly Wash. Wash's case demonstrates yet again the centrality of mobility in "other" textual versions of black St. Louis, though the mobility that this case file illustrates is neither Meachum's westward pioneering nor Clamorgan's flexible exit and entry (though it has similarities with both—and even with Brown's dialectic between the river-based slave trade and the escape). Further, while economics are key to the mobility of Meachum and Clamorgan (and even Brown), for the Wash case file, comity and domesticity become central questions surrounding the exercise of mobility and, more largely, of representing a black St. Louis.

The St. Louis freedom suits had corollaries in several Southern states: if an enslaved plaintiff could prove that she or he met requirements specified by statute, that person could obtain freedom through the court system. Most of the basic requirements for such suits in Missouri were codified by the 1820s—with the Missouri Supreme Court's decision in *Winny v. Whitesides* (1824) marking out the most common grounds for freedom: extended residence in a free state or territory. Such residence made one free, and, "once free, always free."[29]

In essence, this logic of exceptions functioned as a kind of safety mechanism: freedom suit law implicitly argued that if a handful of slaves in exceptional situations should be freed, most "regular" slaves were properly and legally enslaved. Demonstrating that slavery was governed by law and thus based on a civil (and so civilized) system was essential to some whites in St. Louis, especially in the aftermath of the McIntosh and Lovejoy incidents.[30] That the most prominent reason for exceptional status—extended residence—addressed the key legal principle of comity was no mistake: white slaveholding Missourians granted the fact that the occasional (and probably foolish) slaveholder might bring a slave into free spaces for too long and thus be bound by the laws of such spaces. In return, they expected residents of free states to have similar respect for the laws supporting slavery, including the various fugitive slave laws, and, by extension, the sense that slavery had a legal basis. That sense of comity, of mutual respect for individual states' laws, was—pro-slavery legal theorists argued—essential to a national version of domestic bliss.[31]

Freedom suit law was also a reasonably cheap and safe way to demonstrate that Missouri was civilized, governed by law, and shaped by mutual domestic respect: few slaves met the needed qualifications. Fewer still were able to file suit because doing so took significant time, effort, and resources. Enslaved plaintiffs had to first establish that they could sue as "poor persons," in part so that the court would cover some of their costs. This process required a written statement to the circuit court, and so enslaved plaintiffs generally had to find an attorney who would prepare and submit such a petition—a problem not only of money, but of time and access to a limited number of willing attorneys.[32] (Thus, archivists speculate that urban slaves who had some mobility—generally through being hired out and so moving about more freely within city limits—were much more likely to file freedom suits.) Once counsel was found, enslaved plaintiffs had to worry about payment. Scholars initially thought that the state covered all of the costs associated with pursuing a freedom suit, but recently uncovered evidence shows that, while some court fees seem to have been covered or excused, slaves themselves were probably responsible for attorneys' fees.[33]

Slaveholders also used a variety of techniques to delay and sometimes quash suits. Legally, owners of enslaved plaintiffs had to allow access to counsel and court proceedings after freedom suits were filed—though not

before. Slaveholders were also nominally forbidden from punishing enslaved plaintiffs for bringing suit, but, beyond personal threats of physical
violence, they retained the power to, for example, sell or abuse any of the
plaintiff's family members who they owned. The fact that the court com-
monly, in essence, confiscated enslaved plaintiffs during the pendancy of
freedom suits suggests that legal protections were difficult to enforce.

This "confiscation" also meant that the court entered the business of
slaveholding: when the court "took" enslaved plaintiffs, they were generally
lodged in the same St. Louis jail William Wells Brown was once thrown
into, although the court and slaveowner defendants often agreed that it was
better for both parties for the jailed slave to be hired out—with the money
from the hiring (less lodging costs) to go to the suit's victor. If the plaintiff
was not hirable, or the owner feared escape, or the owner simply wished to
punish the slave through imprisonment (as David Mitchell did in revenge
for Lucy Delaney's suit),[34] enslaved plaintiffs could be held in jail throughout the pendancy of their suits—a foreboding prospect, as suits often took
a long time to resolve.[35] Still, in the face of these obstacles, some enslaved
St. Louisians could and did explore, file, pursue, and even occasionally win
freedom suits during the decades before the Civil War. In so doing, they
caused the creation of case files that tell stories of their lives and of the black
St. Louis they inhabited.

Those stories and their sources do not fit neatly within a conception of
African American literature dominated by the single-authored book published in the Northeast—or even within an expanded sense that includes
texts like Meachum's (which has ties to both the sermonic and pamphleteering traditions) and Clamorgan's (which has ties to both the biographical compendium and travel narrative traditions). While I stop short of suggesting that the black stories of slavery at the heart of these suits represent
the same kind of literary endeavors that texts classified as slave narratives
did, I do assert that the freedom suit case files clearly attempt, to para-
phrase William Andrews's formulation about the slave narrative genre, to
tell free stories, to publicly declare personhood, to articulate blackness.[36]
Thus, before turning to Polly Wash's specific case file, we need to consider
how freedom suit case files might be read both within and against an expanded sense of the slave narrative tradition.

First, the freedom suits were not, of course, the stories of slavery and
race that organized abolitionism—the driving force behind the publication of many major slave narratives like William Wells Brown's—wanted at

the fore. As Jeannine Marie DeLombard demonstrates in *Slavery on Trial,* while "abolitionist propagandists worked hard to ensure that the era's exciting court cases provided Americans with both entertaining spectacles and object lessons in the jurisprudence of slavery and freedom," abolitionism's depictions of such cases and its appropriations of judicial rhetoric were, more often than not, tied to larger, extralegal goals (10). Abolitionist publicists, DeLombard argues, consistently positioned slavery as a crime against the nation and against God—thus fixing slaves as victims and slave owners as perpetrators—and marked slavery as "more than a dispute over the right of individual slaveholders to hold human property versus the right of individual blacks to property in themselves" and so as "an offense against the entire society, and thus one that required adjudication by that society" (15).[37]

Thus, while freedom suits certainly included some of the abolitionist tropes seen in slave narratives like William Wells Brown's (e.g., the violence of the slave system, the system's destruction of families), freedom suit law rested on principles that directly contradicted abolitionism's sense of slavery on trial. Because freedom suit law centered on establishing a plaintiff's exceptional status, the suits assumed a local and civil basis for—rather than national criminal questions about—slavery: the freedom suit cases were heard in the circuit court and treated slavery as a property issue; successful plaintiffs even occasionally won monetary damages. Slaveholders as a class were never at issue in these suits; freedom suits were very much about, to use DeLombard's language, *individual* slaveholders and *individual* blacks. All of these differences meant that freedom suits constructed slaveholders not just as noncriminals, but as appropriate administrators of justice: most freedom suit juries *included* slaveholders who likely understood the argumentative value of the law of exceptions; Delaney's *From the Darkness* even features Edward Bates arguing, "I am a slave-holder myself, but, thanks to the Almighty God, I am above . . . holding anybody a slave that has as good a right to her freedom as this girl" (42).

Freedom suit law thus also asserted the primacy of the judicial process and especially the principle of comity. Comity allowed the careful slaveholder to bring slaves into free territory under the rules of time set by that territory; that is, it destroyed the idea of slaves as agents with mobility by making slaves objects *to be moved* by whites.[38] It further marked white mobility as a legally governed process—and as the only legal power for moving the enslaved.[39] Again, the existence of exceptions—slaves whose owners failed to govern their time in free territory—emphasized the validity of the law itself. Slave narratives like Brown's, to the contrary, decried the idea of interstate comity by their very existence: Brown, as a fugitive slave, was a walking violation of comity, as comity would demand that he be returned to his "rightful owner."

It thus comes as no surprise that the abolitionist press said very, very little about freedom suits; that absence has certainly shaped the continuing silence. Beyond these issues, literary scholars' consideration of freedom suits is also complicated by a set of factors. First, the stories in the freedom suits are deeply fragmented. Case files contain initial statements, depositions, subpoenas, and such, but there are no trial transcripts; even if there were transcripts, very few would contain direct remnants of black voices, as the enslaved plaintiffs were not allowed to testify. Second, the case files are multivocal—and not simply via novelistic heteroglossia. Petitions were written by lawyers, depositions were recorded by local officials and contained questions by attorneys and answers by deponents, sheriffs regularly wrote on warrants, and some documents were even partially pre-printed with standard language—the voice of the state. All this—as well as the fact that many enslaved plaintiffs may have been illiterate or semiliterate—means that, third, the voices of the enslaved were, at best, mediated through white "writers." Even the sections of the case files that purport to share the actual words of enslaved persons were written and likely edited by attorneys or justices of the peace. Beyond complicating "authorship," these circumstances lead to questions about the faithfulness of attorneys to their clients' stories. Enslaved plaintiffs are never "I." At most, they are "the undersigned," and they are generally referred to in the third person. Thus, while the suits clearly contain autobiographical information, they often seem biographical—even though such biography was drawn from enslaved speech and likely shaped by and read back to the enslaved plaintiffs. Finally, the texts of these stories were not intended to function as literary objects.[40]

Still, these features also suggest some fascinating echoes of issues in slave narratives. Arguably, many slave narratives are rich collections of fragments unified only by the central structuring device of the quest— a device that also structures freedom suits. That device, in turn, further limited the stories authors of slave narratives could tell: for example, the revolution in Frederick Douglass's second autobiography—embodied in his title claim that the volume would talk about "my bondage" *and* "my freedom"—reminds us of just how fragmented a quest narrative is when considered as autobiography. Douglass's elision of the specific details of his escape (like Douglass's criticism of Henry "Box" Brown's specificity about his escape) marks another moment where external functions both shaped and disrupted narrative cohesiveness.[41] The multivocality of the case files similarly evokes issues in slave narratives. White authenticating statements like those attached to William Wells Brown's and many others offer an interesting initial analogue to the case file structure.[42] However, the boundaries between the main text and the appended documents in most slave narratives are often much clearer than in the case files, and there are simply *many* more voices in the case files. A better analogy might be the dictated narrative—running the spectrum from the 1838 *Narrative of James Williams* to the 1861 *Louisa Picquet, the Octoroon*—or even the antislavery compendium, a genre that has received little attention from literary scholars but includes key abolitionist texts full of black stories like Theodore Weld's 1839 *American Slavery As It Is* and Harriet Beecher Stowe's 1853 *Key to Uncle Tom's Cabin*. Such texts call on scholars to carefully consider the mediation of voices, the interplay of different subject positions and agendas, and a range of other rhetorical factors—and to recognize the ways in which African American subjects might shape black stories not *written* by them.

With these issues in mind, I want to begin to speculatively read Polly Wash's case file—and specifically to recognize two alternate stories within that case file, stories that are very much of black St. Louis and that complicate our sense of this unexpected place for black textual presences and especially of the representations of mobility and black ideals like those offered by Brown, Meachum, and Clamorgan.

Like many freedom suit case files, Polly Wash's focuses on events that happened long before she filed the suit in 1839—events that happened when she was, according to deponent and Illinois farmer Jubilee Posey, "a slip of a girl apparently between 14 & 16 years of age."[43] Though Wash's daughter Lucy Delaney later claimed that Wash was born free,[44] Naomi Wood, another deponent, claimed that she had known Polly Wash "almost ever since" Wash was born and said that, when Wash was "about seven or eight years of age or thereabouts," she was sold by her original owners, the Beatty family of Wayne County, Kentucky, to "Joseph Crockett, a one-armed man." Even those deponents favorable to Wash said that she "was treated as a slave, was talked as such by Crockett & generally considered as such."

While the case file talks briefly about a more recent period of slavery—when, as a slave of Robert Wash, she was hired out to steamers working the Mississippi[45]—Wash's case file focuses mainly on her time with the aged Crockett, who originally came from Fredericks County, Virginia, and was one of the uncles of frontiersman Davy Crockett.[46] Never successful, Crockett moved between Kentucky and Tennessee doing a range of jobs; in late 1817, he sold his property in Tennessee and moved to Illinois, seemingly with the intent of going on to Missouri when weather allowed. Crockett's decision to winter in Illinois—with his wife, belongings, and stock—became key to his slave Polly Wash, whom he hired out to neighbors before allowing his son to take her to Missouri several months later and sell her.[47] Polly Wash's freedom suit argued that Wash was held in Illinois long enough for that (free) state to govern her status. Put another way, Wash was made "exceptional" in the eyes of Missouri law because of the fact that, out of respect for comity, Missouri had to admit that Wash was "once free" and so must be "always free."

While one Missourian—Joseph Magehan, Polly Wash's owner when she filed the suit and the named defendant—would lose significantly from this reading of comity, the gains for Missouri and slaveholders generally were obvious: in addition to asserting that Wash would have properly remained a slave if Crockett had simply followed the law, this reading also recognized that *all* agency in the question of Wash's location was white and was specifically held by slaveholder Crockett. In other words, legal mobility was white, and slaves could only be legally and properly moved by their owners. (If Wash had "settled" as a fugitive like, say, William Wells Brown—that is, without legal white agency—comity would have demanded that she stay a slave.)[48]

Much of the suit centers on proving Wash's extended stay in Illinois: Wash's initial petition, her attorney's questions to deponents, and many answers by deponents focus on just how long Crockett stayed in Illinois, whether the weather and other factors would have allowed him to continue to Missouri if he had wanted to, whether he indeed meant to go there, how long Wash was with Crockett in Illinois, and so on. While we have no trial transcripts, it is clear that this story—which addressed standard freedom suit law and practice, accepted the principle of comity as it applied to slavery, and so removed all sense of black agency and mobility—would have been the basis for Wash's claims of freedom.

But this is *not* the only story of Wash in her freedom suit case file; a second story—the story I suggest is more "hers"—focuses on a different sense of exceptional status, of comity, and so of the conception of domestic propriety implicit in comity. That second story concentrates much more on a promise of one individual to another—made in a domestic setting—with the clear sense that honoring such a promise is key to any idea of comity, even one tied to national ("domestic") promises of mutual respect between states.

Before examining that second story, we need to be clear that Polly Wash wrote *none* of the texts included in her case file. The "X" in place of a signature on her post-trial release form and her free bond suggests that she was illiterate.[49] Even the statements made directly by Wash—in her petition to sue as a poor person and her initial pleading—were written down by white men (the first by a justice of the peace, perhaps with a lawyer's aid, and the second by Wash's attorney). Yet I want to suggest that the case file documents not only tell this second story *of* Wash but that it may well be a story *authorized* and shaped—perhaps even, if we stretch our sense of the term, authored—by Wash.

I base this claim on the fact that Polly Wash took actions that may initially seem simply stunning. The court ordered that she be hired out during the pendency of her suit, and this meant that, between roughly October 1839 and June 1843, she worked for Elijah Haydon, a St. Louis resident and sometime schoolteacher. When Naomi Wood gave her deposition in April 1840 at the Wood homestead in Madison County, Illinois, she told those present:

> I know the plaintiff well. I have not seen the plaintiff since she was here with Crockett until something like a fortnight ago when *she came to my house.* I knew then that I had seen her before [;] her face was familiar to me [;] after talking about old times & facts & person[s] I became fully convinced that she was the same person that was here with Crockett some twenty two years ago. She said *she had come to hunt us* and after talking some time about the Beattys and Crocketts & other neighbors & things she I asked Pol where she had been all this time & why she had come here. She said she had come to see if they could say how long she had stayed here & said she had an idea of endeavoring to get her freedom. I then stated to her that I recollected such facts as I have stated & I told her I was willing to testify to such facts as I know here as at St. Louis. [italics mine]

In short, whether Wash made a sanctioned trip into a free state or took it on herself to go as a fugitive, it is clear from Naomi Wood's deposition that Polly Wash left St. Louis, traveled to Illinois, and spoke to several potential deponents.[50] While she asked deponents to specifically address the key criteria of her suit (extended residence in a free state), Wash also—as the friendly "Pol"—seems to have interacted with the deponents in ways designed to create sympathy as she "endeavored to get her freedom."

Polly Wash did not stop her shaping of the depositions with these border-crossing pre-deposition conversations. She attended the depositions themselves at the Woods' Illinois farmhouse. Nothing she said there is recorded; as at her trial, nothing she said at the depositions would be admissible.[51] Even if she did not converse with the deponents—hard to believe given the small Wood home and the fact that the depositions were spread out over three days—she was literally at the table when the depositions were given. A nod or a smile from her might have influenced deponents even further.

While we cannot assume that the deponents willingly served as Polly Wash's mouthpieces—at best, her story would have been mediated by their white voices—the majority of the deponents clearly liked and favored Polly Wash. This seems especially true of Naomi Wood, who grew quite cross with the defendant's representative—answering a question about Crockett's final destination with "I heard him say that he was bound for Missouri & this is all that I know about it. I don't know what he said to other folks & don't care" and ending her deposition with, "I do not know of any persons who have made up a [story?] to aid plaintiff in her suit for freedom. Deponent never heard of such a thing in her life." Thus, all four of the depositions included in Wash's case file assert that Crockett held Wash as a slave in Illinois roughly between October 1817 and April 1818, but all also offer significant information designed to mark Polly Wash as both a sympathetic and exceptional slave, information that was not necessary to prove the "first" story of comity and information that was generally not even called for by the attorneys.

That additional information running through all four depositions included a rhetorical/remembered representation of Polly Wash as a youth who was taken advantage of. Naomi Wood, for example, spoke in some depth about how she had known the plaintiff Polly "almost ever since the plff was born," including "frequently" seeing "the mother of plff carry the

child (now plff) about." She further offered that Crockett hired "Pol" out
even though she was often "a little sick." Jubilee Posey, as noted above, referred to her as "a slip of a girl." Samuel Wood, Naomi Wood's husband, referred to her as the "young Negro girl," and Mary Wood Moore (the Woods'
daughter) even recalled Crockett saying that Polly "was kinder to him than
his own children."

Deponents were more mixed on Crockett's character. While Samuel
Wood, for example, remembered Crockett as having "the character of an
honest & good citizen," even though "he was a little addicted to drink,"
and noted that he treated Wash "in a favorable & indulgent way," Naomi
Wood was much less kind: "Crockett & the brother in law of deponent that
is James Wood were both drinking men," and, by the time he moved to Illinois, Crockett "was failing in constitution as any drinking man does."

More damning, though, were Naomi Wood and Mary Wood Moore's
assertions that Crockett understood that keeping Polly Wash in Illinois
would free her and initially favored making such happen, but that his resolve crumbled. Mary Wood Moore specifically remembered that Crockett "intended when he & his wife were dead that she should be free," and
Naomi Wood asserted that "old Mr. Crockett was in the habit of saying that
he intended to set the plaintiff free at the death of him & his wife—that she
should serve nobody but him & his wife." Both Wood and Moore argued,
in Naomi Wood's language, that "Mr. Crockett, could have taken Polly away
if he had chosen. There was nothing to hinder him from so doing and from
traveling." Moore, who had heard her mother's earlier deposition, even said
that she "heard my husband[,] Old Mr. Crockett & his son talking about the
consequences of keeping plaintiff in Illinois; the son said she would be free
according to the laws of Illinois if his father kept the plaintiff there until
spring."

Now a widow, Mary Moore went much further in describing a conversation between her husband, Crockett, and Crockett's son William that she
seemed to find quite distasteful:

> My husband advised old Mr. Crockett to have the plaintiff bound to
> him by indenture. The Old Man said he would [not] have her inden-
> tured & he would keep her there untill [sic] spring if she did get free
> he said he wanted plaintiff with him for she was kinder to him than
> his own children & he intended when he & his wife were dead she
> should be free. They spoke to the old man of another plan to prevent

her from becoming free. It was to send her to Missouri for a term of time & then fetch her back so that she should not be in Illinois for more than 60 days at a time. The old man refused to adopt this plan. I know of no reason or cause which prevented or could prevent Old Mr. Crockett from going on to Missouri or elsewhere. . . . Polly the plff was actually here in the last of April. Dep[onen]t knows this from the baptist meeting about that time. The plff was carried away by a son of Mr. Crockett & before Mr. Crockett left himself.

In essence, then, Moore's husband and Crockett's son William schemed to keep Polly Wash a slave. The frustrated son eventually took action—action that, given Moore's phrase "carried away," sounds almost like a kidnapping—to guarantee that she would remain a slave.

This story is much closer to what Polly Wash seems to have told her own family: Lucy Delaney's narrative, written over fifty years after Wash's freedom suit was filed, began thus: "In the year 18—, Mr. and Mrs. John Woods and Mr. and Mrs. Andrew Posey lived as one family in the State of Illinois. Living with Mrs. Posey was a little negro girl, named Polly Crockett, who had made her home there, in peace and happiness, for five years. On a dismal night in the month of September, Polly, with four other colored persons, were kidnapped, and, after being securely bound and gagged, were put into a skiff and carried across the Mississippi River to the city of St. Louis. Shortly after, these unfortunate negroes were taken up the Missouri River and sold into slavery" (9–10).[52]

While there are notable differences—ranging from Wash being born free to her living in Illinois for *five* years—the sense that Polly Wash's freedom was stolen from her, that the Woods and Posey families were a happy memory, and that Polly Wash's forced crossing into Missouri was a landmark in her life are all still here. That Delaney reported not only these items but also commented on her mother's agency and mobility—even suggesting that Wash later escaped from and returned to St. Louis to care for Delaney[53]—hint that the conception of Wash in the freedom suit's second story was the sense that she carried throughout her life.

More immediately, Moore's deposition—extending and expanding on ideas raised in her mother's earlier deposition—arguably moved the emphasis toward a very different reason to free Polly Wash: a promise of freedom offered by Crockett.[54] That shift suggested that comity should extend beyond laws to promises, and it suggested that, because promises could be made to African Americans, blacks like Polly Wash were full persons. Further, as problematic as Wash's rhetorical positioning as a child in the depositions might seem, it was as a child who was *better* than Crockett's own (white) children; that is, she more fully realized the domestic ideals of antebellum American culture and she was rewarded for such by a promise. Naomi Wood and Mary Moore clearly thought this an eminently proper reason to free "Pol."

This second story—a story marked by a contested sense of mobility (Polly Wash's kidnapping versus her border-crossing interactions with deponents) and by a much larger and more multiracial sense of domestic comity—thus emerges to counter both the standard narrative of freedom suit law and the stories later told by figures like Brown, Meachum, and Clamorgan.

But beyond being a set of stories about comity, domesticity, Missouri's permeable borders, and mobility, the stories in Wash's case file are very much St. Louis stories. Like thousands of other whites, Joseph Crockett at one point saw St. Louis as a gateway to the West, and so a land that held more promise for the final years of his life. Like thousands of other enslaved African Americans, St. Louis was, to Polly Wash, a site of yet another sale— a borderland not just between East and West, but also between North and South, and, very concretely, slavery and freedom. And it was a permeable border for some—as Whaley Moore and William Crockett's scheming to shuttle Polly Wash in and out of Missouri (to avoid allowing her more than sixty consecutive days in Illinois) illustrates. Finally, her case touched some of the city's most prominent citizens: as noted, former Supreme Court justice Robert Wash was a previous owner; further, Wash's initial petition to sue as a poor person went to the same Judge Luke Lawless who had let those who participated in the lynching of Francis McIntosh go free only three years before.

These facts, though, and the hints of the second story in Wash's case file were probably radically de-emphasized in the single formal oral telling of her story in the St. Louis Circuit Court—one where she was legally silenced and had to depend on her attorney Harris Sproat and the depositions for any "voice." There, on 6 June 1843, twelve white male residents of the city— including at least two slaveholders and at least two men who may have had business dealings with her owner[55]—heard her case. Most of them probably wanted to see St. Louis not simply as a boundary land but also as a center of the rational rule of (white) law; thus, they were probably more comfortable accepting the first story of the case file—the story of Polly Wash as an object moved about by white subjects. However, they might have heard bits of the second story; as her daughter's autobiography hints, Polly Wash distributed her story when and where and how she could—even if only in pieces.

The jury's verdict demonstrated both the potential of Polly Wash's various stories and their limitations. The jury found that she "was not nor is she now a slave in the manner and form the said defendant has in his Plea alleged"; that is, they granted her freedom. But her claim of damages (she sought five hundred dollars because of her false imprisonment and because Magehan had "with force and arms an assault made on the said plaintiff and then & there beat bruised and ill-treated her") was reduced to a single dollar. Beyond this insult—which arguably marked the jurors' evaluation of the worth of the suffering of a free black woman—what is more telling is that Lucy Delaney's pending freedom suit was not automatically resolved when Polly Wash was freed. The assertion of the basic matrilineal principle of slave status would wait eight months, and Lucy Delaney would, as her narrative and recent scholarship discuss, have to go through a trial of her own.

Black St. Louis and Neglect

The study of reception and neglect is always, in part, hypothetical: who might have read a text, who might have purchased it, what kept others from doing so. The neglect of Polly Wash's case file is perhaps easiest to guess about: it was not considered literature, was not even considered *important* for decades—and it might have been completely forgotten were it not for her daughter's better-known slave narrative and the rescue efforts of a handful of heroic archivists. Still, in her time, the stories in her case file did the job she needed. They allowed her to be freed, and then, because the child's condition followed that of the mother, eventually allowed her daughter to be freed. And it is not unlikely that her case—and the stories she told of it in St. Louis's relatively small black community—may have shaped other, better-known stories. Her daughter's initial attorney, Francis Murdoch, was also the initial attorney for Dred and Harriet Scott; Harriet Scott, like Polly Wash and Lucy Delaney, worked as a laundress. The possibility that they knew each other and talked about freedom, even about freedom suits, is tantalizing, if unproven and perhaps unprovable.[56]

The neglect of Meachum's *Address* is a bit more difficult to explain. Certainly, as the biographical comments in the *Liberator* and the *Colored American* demonstrate, he could be held up as an example of the "Capacity of Negroes to Take Care of Themselves." However, when his *Address* is compared with another roughly contemporary "Address" (given earlier but not published until 1848), Henry Highland Garnet's "Address to the Slaves of the United States of America," Meachum's gradualist and accommodationist work seems anachronistic. Garnet's famous speech, delivered at an 1843 national convention, rhetorically addressed the slaves so absent in Meachum's text and, of course, physically absent from Garnet's convention audience. He told them that, though "your brethren of the north, east, and west have been accustomed to meet together in National Conventions, to sympathize with each other, and to weep over your unhappy condition," slaves needed to decide "whether it is better to choose LIBERTY or DEATH!" and rise up in a revolution (90, 95). Though that 1843 convention—including a young Frederick Douglass—rejected Garnet's speech by a narrow margin, it remained in the black public consciousness. Garnet's move to publish it himself only reemphasized the growing sense that many free African Americans did not want to hear Meachum's story. The format emphasized such even more: Garnet bound his address with a brief account of early radical David Walker and a reprint of Walker's fiery *Appeal*, the text that arguably began the national abolitionist movement and laid the groundwork for Garrison's writing and the furor over Lovejoy's murder (less than a decade after Walker's own death).[57]

The neglect of Clamorgan's text seems even more curious—in part because its precursor, Joseph Willson's consideration of black Philadelphia, is still discussed today. Still, Winch notes only one extant copy of *Colored Aristocracy*, and I have been unable to find any others. The title term found its way into later nineteenth-century minstrelsy, but tracing its genealogy solely to Clamorgan is a doubtful venture. All that said, Clamorgan's text did circulate in some fashion; specifically, it reached the community studied in the next chapter—a group of free African Americans in Indiana who were instrumental in publishing the little-studied African Methodist Episcopal Church quarterly *The Repository of Religion and Literature and of Science and Art*. The copy of *Colored Aristocracy* they read may have been either damaged or badly printed: their review, newly rediscovered and possibly written by a young Elisha Weaver, was headed "Colored Aristocracy of Saint Louis. By Cyprian Ola Morgan." It noted that the "pamphlet of 22 pages . . . has considerable literary merit" (45). But, it concluded, "Its moral bearing is as disgraceful to its author, as it is libelous to some of the people whom he represents as the aristocracy of St. Louis. If his statements be true, the majority of those whom he styles the Colored Aristocracy of St. Louis, are a disgrace to their race, and no honorable man of color need desire their acquaintance" (45). The *Repository* singled out one instance: "We have little personal knowledge of any of the parties beside Mr. Frances Robinson"; Robinson, whom Clamorgan insulted,[58] was, the *Repository* asserted, a man "whose shoe latchet Cyprian is not worthy to unloose" (45).

Nonetheless, neglected or not—or, in Clamorgan's case (perhaps rightfully) attacked or not—these texts demonstrate that even in antebellum St. Louis, there was a complex black textual presence that went beyond the stories of slavery told by abolitionists like William Wells Brown. The existence of these other stories, of course, does not negate the deep truths Brown shared about St. Louis slavery; indeed, all were shaped by such—as well as by the restrictions placed on free African Americans. Antebellum St. Louis was never able to build the kind of literary communities studied in the next chapters—and certainly never able to create the kind of flowering discussed in chapters 3 and 4 of this study. Still, the three texts considered in this chapter remind us that nineteenth-century black stories (including stories of mobility, agency, and domestic values) as well as black authors happened in unexpected places, even places marked by the shadow of slavery.

Chapter 2

FRONTIERS AND DOMESTIC CENTERS
Black Indiana, 1857–1862

In a letter published in the *Christian Recorder* on 19 January 1861—as the United States moved closer and closer to civil war—the Reverend John Mifflin Brown celebrated the *Recorder*'s return after a hiatus of several years. Brown especially praised the recently appointed A.M.E. book steward and *Recorder* editor, Elisha Weaver: "I thank you for proving that we can do something," Brown wrote. "It takes our Western boys to lead off. I am proud of your paper. I wish most heartily for your success."

In many ways, Brown's wish would be fulfilled by the end of the Civil War. Weaver turned the *Recorder* into a paper with a nationwide reach, solicited and published extensive coverage of the Civil War (including letters from and about black troops),[1] facilitated diverse political and theological commentary, highlighted the struggles of newly freed African Americans in the South, and asserted an important place for literature in black political and cultural life through, for example, his serialization of Julia C. Collins's 1865 novel *The Curse of Caste*. His efforts set the groundwork for the flowering of the *Recorder* under later editor Benjamin Tucker Tanner, who made the weekly paper a key site for later-nineteenth-century black political and theological discussion and for black literature.[2] However, while the germinal place of the Philadelphia-based *Recorder* in African American literary history has become more clearly recognized over the last two decades—as texts by Collins and Frances E. Watkins Harper have been recovered—its very real roots in much more unexpected places in Indiana remain unexamined.

Those roots and the complex paths (and intersections) of "our Western boys" are central to this chapter. I focus heavily on Elisha Weaver's transition from a "Western boy" to a Philadelphia-centered editor and, in this, offer new biographical information on Weaver, one of the first in-depth discussions of the Indianapolis-based *Repository of Religion and Literature and of Science and Art*,[3] and the first close reading of Weaver's early work (specifically his travel writing) within the context of the sense of the black West that he helped build in the *Repository*. I pair this reading with the first consideration of a newly recovered antebellum Indiana black author, William Jay Greenly, who published a playlet in the *Repository* and whose short 1858 volume *The Three Drunkards* may be the first collection of plays published by a black author in book form.[4]

But this chapter is also a story of the fragility of black literary communities in unexpected places—specifically the story of the ultimate disintegration of the Indiana base of the *Repository*. After Weaver moved East to Philadelphia to resurrect the *Recorder* (and concurrently began pushing to have the *Recorder* recognized as the primary and official organ of the A.M.E. Church) and after some additional editorial shuffling, the Baltimore-based John Mifflin Brown quoted above became the *Repository*'s central editor. With the *Recorder* in Philadelphia and the *Repository* resettled in Baltimore, Weaver and Brown soon became somewhat-hesitant participants in a debate about whether the church could support two periodicals; by 27 September 1862, a letter to the *Recorder* actually accused the *Repository* of being Baltimore-centered and "so sectional in its circulation." While the *Recorder* bloomed, the *Repository* ceased publication in 1863. This chapter thus examines the arguments swirling around the *Recorder*'s rebirth and the *Repository*'s demise; within this context, it closes with a contrastive reading of recently rediscovered *Repository* texts by early black activist Maria W. Stewart and Weaver's later travel writing for the *Recorder*. Throughout, it focuses on not only the varying conceptions of the West as a site of a version of the domesticated black frontier that John Berry Meachum alluded to in his *Address* (albeit a more radically black nationalist and abolitionist one) but also on two symbiotic forms of black mobility, that of the ever-striving settlers (who were mobile long enough to go West and then *settle* in hopes of building domestic spaces, even domestic centers—in both senses of the word "domestic") and that of itinerant ministers (whose continuing mobility drew connections between various western outposts and eastern civilization, even as it sometimes strikingly reversed the "outpost" and the "civilization"). Both of these forms of germinal mobility allowed a richer and more fully realized sense of black nationalism and uplift discourse than found in the texts studied in the last chapter, and both presage work done by African Americans throughout the nation later in the nineteenth century.

"MAN INDEFATIGABLE"
Elisha Weaver and the *Repository*

As a pioneer not only of the A.M.E. Church but also specifically of black periodicals, Elisha Weaver has nonetheless remained largely ignored: even the massive *African American National Biography* does not include an entry on him, and few studies of black literature, black culture, or even the black press mention him at all. The cultural forgetting of Weaver is part and parcel of the larger elision of many of the African Americans whom Brown referred to as "our Western boys" and who saw textual expression as a key method of both spreading their faith and creating a shared public memory of that faith.

Unfortunately, exhaustive archival research offers us only glimpses into Weaver's earliest years. Weaver himself referred to North Carolina as "our native state" in a 9 March 1867 *Recorder* piece, and a 4 December 1890 *Recorder* article by Bishop Alexander Wayman pointed specifically to Fayetteville, North Carolina, as Weaver's birthplace. Census records also suggest that Weaver was born in North Carolina—in about 1830. His parents' names remain unknown, although he printed a notice in the 28 December 1861 *Recorder* looking for the widow of his uncle David Weaver, who had "moved to the city of New York some twenty-five years ago, from Salusbury [*sic*], North Carolina."

Like his uncle and aunt, Weaver's immediate family seems to have left North Carolina in the late 1830s; by all accounts, he was already in Indiana by the 1840s.[5] Alexander Wayman's 1882 *Cycopedia of African Methodism* says that Weaver "settled in Indiana, where he received his schooling" (177). An obituary of a Lucy Graham published in the 25 June 1896 *Recorder* says that she was "converted Jan. 5, 1841, under the preaching of Rev. Elisha Weaver," and while this date seems much too early (as Weaver would have only been ten or eleven), its placement of Weaver among early Indiana A.M.E. activists is accurate. The more-trustworthy Benjamin Tucker Tanner's 1867 *An Apology for African Methodism* says that Weaver was "brought up at Paoli, Indiana," attended nearby Orange County Quaker schools, and was, "in 1846, teaching school under the auspices of his Quaker friends" (175). Other evidence suggests that at some point in the late 1840s, Weaver sought further schooling—perhaps traveling as far north as Richmond, Indiana, to get it.[6] Regardless, it is clear that Orange County was Weaver's initial "home base" in Indiana.

Studied in some depth in Coy Robbins's *Forgotten Hoosiers: African Heritage in Orange County*, many of the African Americans among whom Weaver was raised (and, perhaps, later taught) were, like Weaver, from North Carolina. Specifically, many were related to slaves freed by a group of Quakers led by Jonathan Lindley (1756–1828), who left Orange County, North Carolina. These early black Indiana residents owned land and sometimes prospered—even in the face of intense individual and governmental racism in early Indiana and the fact that Orange County was far enough south that Confederate scouts actually entered Paoli during the Civil War.

While their southern roots as well as their initial settlement patterns in Indiana (near key rivers like the Wabash and the Ohio) certainly had much in common with other early blacks moving to Indiana, their relative prosperity was perhaps more out of the ordinary. Successive revisions to Indiana's black laws made immigration, settling, and success more and more difficult. By 1860, when the state's population had topped a million, there were only about twelve thousand blacks in Indiana—mainly clustered in the river trade areas, early-metropolitan Indianapolis, and segregated sites like the Roberts Settlement in Rush County. As Emma Thornbrough notes in her landmark study, *The Negro in Indiana before 1900*, "their resources were small and prejudice against them strong" (133). Most who lived outside of urban areas made their living through farming and related labor. Still, select groups were already pushing for fuller A.M.E. recognition by the early 1840s, were organizing Masonic groups by the late 1840s, and were building schools and churches as well as fighting for fuller social and political rights.[7]

Coming of age under the limited protection of area Quakers, Weaver would nonetheless probably have found—as did many antebellum African Americans—that while white Quakers offered much to blacks in terms of education, their sense of race could border on the paternalistic, and their church hierarchy offered few places for African Americans.[8] A young man with both great faith and great ambition, instead of joining the Quakers, Weaver thus joined the African Methodist Episcopal Church (and specifically the Indiana Conference) in 1849; he seems to have begun preaching soon after.

Tanner claims that, in 1852, Weaver "obtained permission of Bishop [William Paul] Quinn and the [Indiana A.M.E.] Conference . . . to go to Oberlin College, where he remained but a few months, less than a year, Bishop Payne having called him into active service" (175–76). Weaver's time at Oberlin—then a young campus celebrated in the black community for its potential to offer interracial secondary and postsecondary education—remains sadly undocumented beyond Tanner's comments. If he attended, he did not stay long enough to be listed in the college's catalog; still, the possibility that, for however brief a period, Weaver sat in classrooms that had hosted A.M.E. luminaries like Brown and David Peck, future politicians like John Mercer Langston (A.B., Class of 1849), writers like George Boyer Vashon (Oberlin's first black A.B., Class of 1844), and even two of John Berry Meachum's sons (who attended between 1839 and 1841) is fascinating.[9]

Better documented is the desire of Quinn and Payne to increase the A.M.E. presence in Indiana, Illinois, and beyond. Called "the indomitable leader of African Methodism in the West," Quinn was stationed in the nascent Ohio Conference in 1833, was integral to the founding of the Indiana Conference in 1840, and was named the presiding elder of Illinois, Indiana, and Missouri in 1841 (Early 21).[10] So impressed were his eastern fellows with his "missionary" work in the West that, "amid a great deal of enthusiasm," they elevated him to the rank of bishop at the A.M.E.'s 1844 General Conference (Handy 163). Payne was perhaps an even greater visionary. Elected a bishop in 1852 and now generally remembered for his massive efforts collecting and compiling church history and for his post–Civil War outreach to southern blacks, Payne made contributions to the black (Mid)West that were just as significant—especially his efforts surrounding the young Wilberforce College.[11] Payne also fought hard for education to be central to the A.M.E. agenda: the same 1844 Conference that elected Quinn a bishop also accepted Payne's recommendations for a standard course of study for all church ministers.[12]

Later described by Tanner as "man indefatigable," Weaver was an important find for Quinn and Payne (175). A skilled orator as well as a strong organizer, he quickly moved up in the church ranks—ordained a deacon and appointed to raise money for missionary work at the 1853 Indiana Conference, made an elder the following year, and appointed to key national committees by the mid-1850s.[13] In 1854, Weaver was stationed at the growing A.M.E. Church in Chicago—still very much a frontier city—

but, according to Payne's *Recollections,* Weaver "was impeached in 1857 by his Board for introducing vocal and instrumental music into his Church" (234).¹⁴ Still popular among the church hierarchy, though, Weaver quickly received a call from a larger church, Indianapolis's Bethel A.M.E.

It was during this period that Weaver began writing for publication, and, appropriately enough, he focused on black mobility. His public debut—he even opened with the lines "For the first time in my life, I sit me down to spend a few thoughts upon paper"—appeared in the 23 February 1856 Toronto-based *Provincial Freeman.* A letter to the editor, his text recounted the racism he encountered when traveling from Chicago to Detroit via Marshall, Michigan. Frustrated by a series of insults on the trains and especially at a Marshall eatery, he concluded that "in order to avoid the insults that our people so frequently meet with, from such landlords who will take your money, and treat you with discord and contempt, let each one prepare something to eat, put it into your pockets or carpet sacks, sufficient to do you the journey, and then you can save your dimes in your pocket." He signed himself "Yours for the cause of justice." It was far from a unique contribution; such letters on transit and business discrimination filled African American and, more broadly, abolitionist periodicals of the time.¹⁵

Weaver's decision to write to the *Freeman* was likely the result of a meeting with the paper's all-but-editor Mary Ann Shadd, who published a *Freeman* piece about Chicago in early February 1855 that—although it misnamed Weaver as "the Rev. Elijah Weaver"—called him "a very energetic man and honest, upright minister."¹⁶ That said, in part playing to convention and perhaps in part demonstrating a larger ambition, Weaver ended his letter to the *Freeman* with "And now, I hope that all papers friendly to the cause of equity and justice will copy this."

Weaver's role in founding the *Repository* was both much larger and much more ambitious than this small request for copying, though it echoed both his commitment to the African American civil rights struggle and to questions of black mobility. A cursory glance at the inaugural April 1858 issue of the *Repository* belies such—and might even lead readers to assume that the magazine was solely Daniel Payne's venture. Indeed, Payne was key to the journal in a number of ways: listed first among the editors (the only bishop among local pastors), his eleven-page "The Christian Ministry" and shorter essay on "Science" made up roughly a quarter of the issue's contents. In addition to frequent later contributions, he clearly gave editorial input throughout the 1850s; as Ronald Zboray and Mary Saracino Zboray have demonstrated in their *Literary Dollars and Social Sense,* Payne actively solicited and even paid for contributions,including a poem from a young Charlotte Forten (43, 54–56). Finally, he served as a prime supporter of the publication within the church hierarchy, and this was probably sometimes difficult, as, after a number of fits and starts, the older *Christian Recorder* had already, at this point, in the delicate language of Payne's *History,* been "suspended for the want of means" (315).

But Payne's large and growing purview within the church was paired with uneven health.[17] Early on (probably before the first issue was even fully planned), he assigned the management of the *Repository* to a small group of ministers named in a smaller note—"published by J. M. Brown, W. R. Revels, and E. Weaver"—that appeared under the longer list of editors (which included Payne, Brown, Revels, Weaver, Molliston M. Clark, the young Alexander Wayman, and S. L. Hammond). Revels's role lessened quickly.[18] The Oberlin-educated Brown, soon to move to Baltimore, wrote the magazine's salutatory as well as the April 1858 issue's featured article on the life of church founder Richard Allen.[19] However, the day-to-day management of the *Repository* fell to Weaver—and called on not only his talents, but also his location. The magazine was published in Indianapolis by the Indianapolis Journal Company's Steam Printing House, probably both because of the Indiana Conference's sway in the planning of the publication and because this printer created an acceptable product for an acceptable price. By April 1858, Weaver was already one of—if not the—leading A.M.E. force in Indianapolis; the issue of the *Repository* published that month noted (perhaps a bit self-servingly) that Weaver's congregation had "recently completed an excellent meeting-house, with a bell and pews. There is . . . good work going on in that church" (47). By the July 1858 issue, it was "E. W." who signed notices explaining publication schedules, future contents, and omissions—even an apologetic note to Payne alerting him (and readers) that a piece Payne had submitted would have to be held due to timing and available space. An unsigned item in the November 1858 issue was even more direct: it simply said, "NOTICE. All communications for the Repository must be sent to Rev. ELISHA WEAVER" (192).[20]

The handful of sources that mention the *Repository* (as well as Weaver's own published accounts) assert that the periodical's circulation grew during his tenure, although the amount and character of subscribers is much more debatable. The most detailed accounting, presented to the 10 September

1859 Indiana Conference and subsequently published in the October 1859 *Repository* claimed that circulation had increased from 500 for the final issue of 1858 to 700 for the October issue of 1859, and the bills listed for printing costs show a corresponding rise from $50 to $61. However, many of the numbers that follow literally don't add up. Weaver presents a city-by-city tally of subscribers—21, for example, in Richmond, Indiana—and lists as the total, 494 (a number close to 500 but far short of 700). Complicating matters further, when added up, the city-by-city numbers actually total 817, far in excess of 494, 500, and 700.[21] If these numbers were trustworthy, the most striking features would be the large number of subscribers—354—listed for Philadelphia and the concentrations in cities where editors had a presence (for example, 56 in Indianapolis, 56 in Louisville, 80 in Baltimore, 20 in Chicago). The sense that circulation in Philadelphia, the center of the A.M.E.'s national organization, would be highest and that other subscribers would be grouped around mostly western local A.M.E. churches that pushed the *Repository* certainly seems logical; however, at this point, we cannot assume any specific ratios.

Whatever the specific mix, though, the fact that the subscription list shows a national audience with significant components west of Pennsylvania does fit neatly with the magazine's content. Many of the pieces in the *Repository*—and some of Brown's comments in his opening remarks— were designed for a general black audience. Theology was the subject of the majority of articles—Molliston Clark's July 1858 "The Capabilities of the Human Soul," Payne's July 1858 "Religion and Piety," and Weaver's April 1858 "New Birth, or Regeneration," for example. Brown's extended series of biographies of "Bishop Allen and his Coadjutors" wove together theology and church history, as did Alexander Wayman's "Lecture on the Rise and Progress of the African M. E. Church in the United States." Literary works and discussions of other topics—like Weaver's own four-part series on "Economy," which argued that individuals needed to manage their work and financial lives carefully and to save actively—often assumed specific senses of A.M.E. uplift theology as givens.

A set of other prominent features would have reminded readers that the journal was largely a western production. While certainly national in scope, Brown's salutatory nonetheless prominently featured the *Repository*'s home region: addressing the *Repository* in the formal third person, he says, "Thou wilt make thyself the intimate companion of all classes. Go thou, then, into every family, and soar not above the humble cabins of thy own native West; visit the frontier settler, and make his home the place of cheer, and make him forget those whom he has left behind—the polished society of the more favored city. Cheer the matron burthened [*sic*] with care, and filled with anxiety to know how to rear the cherub which God hath given her" (1). Further, contributors outside of the editorial board were often identified by place, and while the 1858 volume offers work from more expected places like Philadelphia and Baltimore, it also includes, within its 192 pages, contributions from Mt. Pleasant, Iowa; St. Louis, Missouri; Quincy and Chicago, Illinois; Wilberforce, Ohio; Louisville, Kentucky; and New Albany and Indianapolis, Indiana. Summaries of church activities often highlighted western developments, as in Brown's 1858 report that "this has been emphatically the year of new Churches," which briefly praised developments in Philadelphia and then noted new buildings in Indiana, Illinois, and Kentucky before asserting that the new Quinn Chapel in Louisville (which Brown had a hand in building) "eclipses all. It is the handsomest temple that we have in the West. God bless the little band of that Church" (116). Finally, each issue contained a section—generally at least two full pages—of "Church News"; the vast majority of such news covered efforts in Indiana, Ohio, Illinois, Missouri, and Kentucky—though Baltimore, Philadelphia, and other locales were occasionally included.

All of these texts provided a fairly consistent narrative of the church's work west of Pennsylvania: it was not easy, but it was progressing admirably. The April 1858 issue, for example, talked of how Bishop Quinn "had met with a serious affliction in Cincinnati, Ohio. Some robbers attacked him, robbed him," but also noted that "Under Rev. Edward Epps, at Cleveland, O., we learn that the good Lord has heard the prayer of his people, and the *Church is revived*" and that New Albany, Indiana, "has been blessed under the labors of Bro. and Sister Jackson—about thirty have been *converted, reclaimed* and *sanctified*. Bro. Jackson always leaves a happy state of things wherever he goes" (47). Similarly, the November 1858 issue reported that "Bishop Payne was robbed of sixty odd dollars in Chicago" but also that "Brother Willis R. Revels, of Chicago, is engaged in a great work there" and that "we also received a circular" from a school in Kentucky "that is called the 'Free people's Union benevolent school club of color.'—The branches taught are as follows: Spelling, Reading, Writing, Arithmetic, Grammer [*sic*], Geography, and History. Hurrah for old Kentucky! So far, she is a head [*sic*] of the free North" (191).

The vision of the West offered by the *Repository* was, then, a deeply nationalist and progressive one—in that the region was capable of leading the country toward an idealized, racially pluralistic, Christian society. That the magazine had a strong subscriber base in places like Philadelphia and Baltimore further suggests that its mainly western editorial nucleus hoped to spread the West's promise. A comment in Weaver's multipart report on a visit to Philadelphia is perhaps most illustrative: "Philadelphia is a beautiful city. . . . [However,] I must say, before leaving this part of my subject, that while I love the city, with all its grand appearance, I would recommend that some, if not all, of the great host of idlers to migrate out West, and we can find employment for them if they will roll up their sleeves and wade into it with a willing mind" (117). Much of what may be implied in Meachum's *Address* becomes both more specific and more open in Weaver's language; indeed, rather than embracing Meachum's discriminatory premigratory selection, this passage suggests that the West might even *make* the idlers into better citizens.

This kind of call for a very specific practice of black mobility—the germinal movement related to becoming committed settlers—was one of the centerpieces of Weaver's and the *Repository*'s depiction of black agency; it was a mode that Weaver would later return to as editor of the *Christian Recorder*, especially in his repeated encouragement that the newly freed move not simply north but west.[22]

But Weaver's sense of a germinal, settlement-creating black mobility is deeply dependent on another, second construction of black mobility, one that he praised throughout his time with the *Repository* and that he himself eventually adopted as his modus operandi: the mobility and agency of the itinerant preacher—both in the form of the minister traveling on a set circuit and the true "free agent" moving without a circuit. To say that traveling ministers were the bedrock of African Methodism would be a deep understatement. Like many nineteenth-century congregations and communities west of Pennsylvania (and even in the East), most A.M.E. groups were too small to fully support a minister; even among churches in larger cities, there was regular shuffling of ministers—as all appointments were technically one-year positions. Bishops like Daniel Payne and William Paul Quinn were charged with massive areas that demanded constant travel; it was also not uncommon for ministers to shift conferences—sometimes for political gain and sometimes at the behest of church leaders. Finally, the church was forever undertaking new missionary work (which resulted in Brown's time in New Orleans and, as discussed in the next chapter, in Thomas M. D. Ward's appointment to California). Weaver's longer stays in Chicago and Indianapolis thus made him a bit of an anomaly—although it is clear that, during his time in Indianapolis, he traveled widely throughout the region on church business.[23]

Weaver's representations of traveling ministers—especially in the "Church News" section—were consistently full of praise, in that he saw such work as essential to expanding the reach of the Church.[24] But he also saw such travel as central to building a larger African American community. In his three-part "Visit Down East"—the source of his remarks on Philadelphia noted above—Weaver told of being called to give a sermon as a visiting minister at Philadelphia's Mother Bethel and of how "the Lord seemed to have been in" him. But beyond the Philadelphia congregation, such a moment could also allow him to reach further—through the textual. "It was a glorious time," he wrote, "and, my reader, just imagine that you were there and participating" (117).

At times Weaver's sense of allowing his western—and larger—audience to be "there and participating" took the form of the traditional "sights and sounds" representation of area landmarks and exotica[25]; thus, he told of "having the pleasure of seeing the spot upon which that great man, William Penn, stood and made a treaty with the wild Indians" as well as seeing "a very sharp, grave-looking man, with his spectacles on. That man was Bishop Payne" (117, 66). His account of visiting Washington, D.C., fits this approach even more directly; he says that "we were in the Capitol House, and I saw many of the silver-headed Senators, and members of both houses. I also had the pleasure of going to the Patent Office or building, and there my eyes beheld the image of George Washington, his whole dress, cane, and frying pan, &c." (167). *Repository* readers were certainly familiar with such conventions from not only their secular reading but also other items in the *Repository*—like Molliston Clark's serialized "Observations in Europe," which began in the initial issue, spoke of Clark's 1846 trip to attend the Evangelical Alliance conference, and promised to share "close observations of men and things" (26).[26]

But what is striking from Weaver's very first installment is his focus on individual people. Some of this certainly takes the form of introducing the famous or important—as in the mention of Payne above or in Weaver's extended discussion of meeting the injured Quinn (still suffering from being beaten by thieves) in Richmond, Indiana, and accompanying him East, with every stop becoming an occasion for local folk to run "out with gleeful hearts to see the Bishop," who many thought was dead (65). However, Weaver also spoke almost lovingly of staying with "Bro. George Peterson, a wealthy huckster " and being "received with great cordiality by him and his kind lady, whose house is always open to the heralds of the cross of Christ," and, while staying with "Bro. Brown," of seeing "an old friend, Sister Smith, whose husband is so well known to our people who travel up and down the western rivers, and have received such kind treatment from him" (65). Some of these accounts have an almost rural idyllic quality to them—as if Weaver were writing letters home about seeing cousins long lost but also deeply cherished. He talks, for example, of a cold morning at the Philadelphia Conference meeting when the ministers "had to have a little fire made up in the stoves, but I believe the boys got warmed up, for it seems that they had a very warm time of it, and kept the Bishop busy to keep them right" (118). But perhaps more important, the leveling of the characters here—Brother Peterson and Sister Smith in the same column with some of the most important A.M.E. divines (indeed, depicted as *helping* those divines as they traveled to Philadelphia on church business)—suggests that the West functions as a truly democratic space.

Finally, such accounts position Weaver's travels very specifically. They mark him as a sort of itinerant minister—as, even though he has an established and single charge, he is asked to preach at several of the stops.[27] This itinerancy offers Weaver the powerful role of linking various small communities of African Americans spread across his route from Indianapolis to Philadelphia (certainly a wider reach than most appointments). In essence, he does some of what the *Repository* itself was charged with doing—spreading not just the news, but the "good news." But this power is combined with a simple need for sustenance and welcome from those communities, and thus Weaver's "Visit Down East" demonstrates a symbiotic relationship between the more-mobile itinerant and the settlement of the recently/formerly mobile but now/still eminently domestic African Americans of the West. In short, especially in the West, where ministers were in short supply and where a welcome might be rarer for an African American, both itinerant and community needed each other desperately. Even as Weaver's powerful and continuing mobility separates him from his readers, his text, like his visits, holds the larger community together. Further, Weaver's tone and content consistently remind readers that he is "one of them"; at the conclusion of the four-part series, after telling of an overnight train trip which brings him back to Indianapolis at eight in the morning, Weaver ends with "I went to see my scholars, and they were all glad to see me." Weaver's piece finishes at home—and that home is a school for young African Americans in a promising West.

Weaver takes up this sense of mobility much more directly in his fare-well pieces for the *Repository*, both of which appeared in the October 1859 issue following his national appointment as the General Conference's book steward and editor. In explaining the delay in producing the issue, he actually attributed some of the wait to "our having to pass through the same difficulty that always attends an itinerant preacher in getting ready for his charge" (191). But in Weaver's case, that charge nationalized the kind of symbiotic, church-centered travel at the heart of his "Visit Down East": he would, "knowing that there is no money in the Book Concern to publish any books or papers . . . travel through the length and breadth of our con-nexion [*sic*], and collect money . . . between now and the sitting of the next General Conference, that we may have of a truth, a Book Concern, and be able to issue a regular weekly paper, and a quarterly or monthly, as may be best" (189).

Generally hopeful about his new appointment—as, in essence, a super-itinerant—Weaver nonetheless exhibited some deep hesitation about the conference's other dictate (via the editorial board, on which John Mifflin Brown, now of Baltimore, was the leading voice): to move the *Repository* to the East—either to "Philadelphia or Baltimore." Weaver says "whether it will be for the better remains to be seen. Certain it is, that there is very little difference in price of publication, and if there is any at all, it is in favor of the office where it has been published. It is our candid opinion that it could have been just as well sustained here as elsewhere. I think all our eastern subscribers were satisfied with the place of publication, and those of the west know we were satisfied. It may be for the better, and if so we have nothing to say, still we have our doubts" (192). Though Weaver knew that this news "will meet you with sadness," he expressed hope that his and the magazine's moves would "not be enough to sever your relation and friend-ship with the Repository" (189).

Weaver would certainly not forget the West, and he would keep his senses of both domestic mobility and itinerancy as key modes of defining black citizenship. However, as my discussion of his *Recorder* work later in this chapter shows, the East would become the locus from which he reached out—the center in the face of an ever-growing frontier that was full of more marginal western spaces. His "we" would no long be synonymous with "those of the West," and that shift, along with the others described below, would change Indiana's fledgling place on the black literary landscape forever.

TEMPERATE MOBILITY
William Jay Greenly's *The Three Drunkards*

One of the western "we" who Weaver left behind was William Jay Greenly, a Pennsylvania-born smith who remade himself into an Indiana teacher and who both contributed to the *Repository* and saw his first and only book praised there. While Greenly heavily endorsed the sense of itinerancy that dominated Weaver's travel writing and the *Repository,* he himself represents a phenomenon that differs greatly from the moves from South to North that opened possibilities for Weaver (and, of course, authors of slave narratives) as well as from the moves West that shaped the lives of the (initially) enslaved Meachum and Wash: he was a free African American born in Pennsylvania who chose to come West because of the promise of the frontier. In essence, Greenly was a "settler," exercising the germinal mobility Weaver spoke of in order to create communities friendly to itinerant ministers, based on A.M.E. domestic principles, and emblematic of black potential in the West.

Born in York County, Pennsylvania, on 16 May 1805, Greenly left his initial trade to move to Pittsburgh to take a factory job in September 1827.[28] Pittsburgh's growing black community became especially active in the decades that followed. With both ties to Philadelphia and intellectual powerhouses like John B. Vashon, Lewis Woodson, and, later, Martin R. Delany, it occupied at least the fringes of expected places of black literary activity.[29] As arguably the most "western" of the major urban centers of black life in the Northeast, Pittsburgh soon hosted a cluster of improvement societies and regularly engaged with—and even hosted—national conventions of African Americans.[30]

A skilled tradesman with a social conscience and some education, Greenly worked with several of these groups—the Moral Reform Society of Pittsburgh, the Pittsburgh African Education Society, and the Temperance Society of the Colored People of Pittsburgh and Vicinity, for example. With

Vashon and Woodson, he also, in a notice published in the 18 July 1840 *Colored American,* called for a National Colored Convention in 1841. This last event seems to have shaped his life significantly. The *Colored American's* discussion of the call lists Greenly as a member of a Committee of Correspondence "for the purpose of effecting an interest in this measure among our people in the West." At some point in early 1841, Greenly decided to go far beyond simply "corresponding" and moved his family West—specifically to New Albany, Indiana.[31] Close to both Cincinnati and Louisville, the New Albany area had a growing free black population that allowed Greenly to change trades and become a teacher (the occupation both the 1850 and 1860 federal censuses list for him). This freedom and the sense of broader possibilities offered by the "new" place must also have been quickly and definitively tempered, however, by a reminder of just how far south New Albany was (and just how much formalized racism existed in early Indiana): one of the earliest Indiana records of the Greenly family is the collection of bonds that they, as free African Americans, were required to file by state law.[32]

Like Weaver, Greenly recognized that education and faith could be powerfully linked in the struggle for broader civil rights, and he expanded his participation in the African Methodist Episcopal Church greatly during his time in Indiana.[33] He was, for example, the secretary of the 1853 Indiana Conference Annual Meeting that gave Elisha Weaver his deacon's orders; he served in the same role at the 1854 conference. Decades later, Bishop Payne would refer to him as "an intelligent layman and an excellent scribe" (*History* 313).

Greenly's teaching career was interrupted when he fell ill in January 1856, but, as he wrote in his preface to *The Three Drunkards,* "being very fond of writing," he took "up his pen to write a few lines" during his recovery "on a favorite subject of his; viz: TEMPERANCE" (1). He continued "until he had written thirty-five pages, and then laid it aside for two years"—perhaps recognizing the relative dearth of publication opportunities available for such work (1). In January 1858, perhaps in light of the Indiana Conference's plans for the *Repository* and his own seemingly better financial resources, he returned to the draft, revised sections, and wrote a set of additional short pieces.

It seems likely that one of these short pieces was "Religion and Good Sense, Against Fortune-telling and Conjuration," which appeared in the July 1858 *Repository.*[34] A brief dialogue that can be read as either closet drama or a playlet designed for a church- or school-centered performance, it shares the conversation between Jonas, Joel, Sister Enlew, and Sister Todd, in which Jonas and Sister Todd ineffectively defend fortune-tellers, conjurers, and purveyors of charmed "medicines" against Joel and Sister Enlew's recognition that such forces do the "work of the devil" (94).

Sometime earlier in 1858, Greenly also "came to the conclusion to have" some of his plays—though curiously not "Religion and Good Sense"— "published in book form, by which he might realize something to pay him for his time and trouble" and be of "benefit of those who encourage the improvement of time and talent" (1). The self-published end product was a seventy-page volume that the *Repository* (in a notice probably penned by Weaver himself) told readers to "get and read," noting that it was available from "Mr. Greenly, New Albany, and from most of the preachers" (115).

The vast majority of the volume (fifty-five pages) consists of the title play *The Three Drunkards*, which is divided into eleven "chapters" and follows the struggles with alcohol that shape the lives of its three title characters, Timothy Trusty, Zachariah Dow, and Tom Nimble. Two of the short works that follow the title play also focus on temperance: "Husband, Don't Stay Long" is a three-page soliloquy that describes the thoughts and actions of a wife waiting for her husband to return from a grogshop, and the seven-page "Ira Perkins" features teacher John Allen demonstrating the economic implications of intemperance to the title character—and showing that Perkins has probably wasted "enough to have a handsome little farm" in his twelve years of drinking (66). The final piece, a two-page dialogue between "the Pen" and "the Press," consists mainly of the pen demonstrating its primacy and has no real thematic connection to the rest of the volume—except for its implicit argument on the importance of black writing to developing black communities.

Perhaps disappointingly for modern readers, none of the plays marks characters by race. None places characters in specific and named settings— with the exception of John Allen in "Ira Perkins," who is briefly described as "the School Teacher, who lived in a town in the far West" (62). None directly addresses the broad questions of African Americans' enslavement, civil rights, or role in either the nation in general or the Indiana frontier in specific. Some of these omissions are to be expected in the shorter pieces, which are both exceedingly didactic and thin on characterization and plot. Still, given the concrete links earlier black leaders had made with temperance, moral reform, and both antislavery and civil rights activism—some even published in the very *Colored American* that named Greenly among

Pittsburgh activists—these absences are striking in the longer and more-developed *Three Drunkards*.[35]

Readers looking for a landmark "first" in black letters may be equally frustrated. While internal evidence suggests that the volume may have been published before (that is, earlier in 1858 than) William Wells Brown's better-known play *The Escape*, specific dating may prove impossible. More troubling, perhaps, is the fact that Greenly's play is much weaker than *The Escape*: it carries none of Brown's lively sarcastic humor, skillful character-ization, head-on consideration of contemporary politics, or awareness of oral performance.[36] Strictly speaking, one might even challenge the genre definition of *Three Drunkards* as a play: its novelistic "chapters" contain, in addition to play-style dialogue, long sections of narratorial intervention and prose description and offer little sense of how characters might, for example, move around a stage.

Some of these features may be the result of Greenly's limited reading and experience with the stage,[37] but some are probably also tied to the occasion for the plays. The same A.M.E. Church that witnessed Elisha Weaver's dismissal from his Chicago pulpit for introducing music was—like many antebellum religious organizations—not overwhelmingly supportive of theater. Many Indiana blacks probably also associated theatrical perfor-mance with minstrelsy, as such was widespread throughout the region.[38] It seems most likely that Greenly expected his pieces to simply be read silently—that is, to function as closet drama—or to be presented with a minimum of staging—in, for example, dramatic readings. Chastened by their removal from the genre specifications of performance drama and of the theater generally, Greenly's plays might well have served as fodder for church-related literary and social societies as well as for Greenly's elder stu-dents. (This last seems especially likely, given that, according to a 2 August 1862 *Christian Recorder* letter from his later Terre Haute pastor Thomas Strother, Greenly helped start "quite an intelligent debating club" among "the young men of this place" and that "among the first questions they de-bated, was: 'Has the use of ardent spirits caused more misery and distress than lying and stealing?' which was discussed . . . quite ably.")

Certainly the play's moral lessons are designed for such audiences. The play's first six chapters focus on Timothy Trusty and Zachariah Dow. After comparing their latest drunken sprees (and painful results), they complain about itinerant temperance lecturer Mr. Stiles, who is new to the area and who is quickly convincing their wives to advocate for total abstinence. Tim's participation in the diatribe against Stiles quickly grows half-hearted; by the end of the first chapter, he admits that his "base conduct" has caused his wife to lose both "her former beauty and amiableness" (8). Zack is much more ardently opposed to Stiles, in large part because he wrongly assumes that Stiles is taking liberties with his wife. Still, both are converted by the end of the fifth chapter: Zack, for example, realizes that when he kisses his wife, "it seems to her almost like bussing the bung-hole of a whiskey barrel" and so takes the temperance pledge and joins the "Methodist" church (14). Tim, also now a member of the church, has "got his place repaired," "white-washed inside and painted outside," put in a crop that "yielded abundant," paid his bills, and saved some three hundred dollars. Building from Tim and Zack's conversions, Stiles settles in the town and helps start both a temperance society and a Sabbath school. In essence, in a message central to much A.M.E. theology, the sinners are redeemed and, through much improved behavior and belief, move toward sainthood.[39]

The rest of the play focuses on Tom Nimble and relegates Stiles, Tim, and Zack to supporting roles. Nimble, "a very shrewd boy" and the son of a wealthy farmer, marries Lucy Rice ("a beautiful young lady") and begins a successful grocery business (29). At the height of his success, though, he takes "some brandy" because of a toothache and is soon a confirmed drunkard (30). Though his loving wife discovers his drinking (and resulting gambling) and then attempts to save him, Tom insists on getting "pretty well 'soaked'" each night; "in less than five years he is bankrupt" and "turned out of house and home" (36, 39). Tom reforms briefly twice, and both times convinces Lucy to take him back, even though "sometimes, when under the influence of liquor, he would go home and beat her severely" (40). Stiles, Tim, and Zack attempt to convince Tom to turn away from drinking; however, in part because Tom is jealous of his wife's respect for Stiles (as Zack was), he resists and even physically threatens Stiles. Tom's drunken violence culminates in the murder of his wife, and he is sentenced to hang. After Tom's temperance-centered gallows speech and execution, the play offers a brief concluding chapter—strangely out of sequence—on Tim and Zack's early life.

One could argue that a certain sense of placeless-ness actually aids a story that is as much an allegory as anything (an allegory that clearly values the "trusty" Tim's development over Tom's seeming "nimble"-ness). Part of Greenly's point, like the point of most temperance activists, is that the redemption—as well as the loss—of the intemperate can happen anywhere.

Certainly later black novelists would similarly de-/e-race their characters in temperance tales.[40] Finally, what at first glance may seem an apolitical stance is more usefully understood as a sense that temperance is a kind of uber-issue governing all political choices and more.[41] The play's only mentions of slavery (other than a brief naming of abolitionism among the political questions of the day) come when the narrator says that Nimble has "become . . . a slave to rum and whiskey" and when Tim tells Nimble that he "was once a slave to intemperance" (39, 48). Certainly like many abolitionists, Greenly would link intemperate behavior with slaveholding,[42] but his play does not foreground that linkage.

For all of this, though, given its author, its intended audience of Indiana blacks—probably especially black youth—and especially its consistent reliance on the language of movement and mobility, *The Three Drunkards* is very much a text about what the black West might and should look like. This does not mean that the play considers the frontier in "original" state; Tim and Zack are described as being "raised in the country" but also as the sons of "wealthy farmers," and Tom is also the son of a successful farmer (who sets him up as a grocer). But it does seem likely that the generation before Tim, Zack, and Tom pioneered the area: land is still plentiful enough that Tim and Zack's parents each give them eighty-acre farms; much of the land discussed in the play remains uncultivated; at the time of the play, the area "had neither Sabbath or day schools"; the community relies heavily on the (formerly) traveling Stiles to set up key institutions to aid with the "march of moral and religious improvement" (27, 28). In short, the community described in *The Three Drunkards* looks much like that area around New Albany—Nimble even briefly takes work on "the river" after his business fails (40)—or any number of "newer" towns in Ohio, Indiana, and Illinois. The battle against intemperance in the play is thus conceived largely as a battle over what a community should look like—as when Stiles, speaking to Nimble, argues that "a man . . . jealous of his wife without a cause, is a dangerous man in a community" (47).

In this, it is also a battle between differing conceptions of mobility—the unchecked and ultimately false mobility of the intemperate like the "nimble" Tom and the much more temperate mobility of the itinerant Stiles (whose ultimate goals are tied to the germinal domestic processes of settling). While Tim and Zack are occasionally positioned within this debate, Tom is the play's focal figure in terms of the language of mobility: in describing Tom's initial sneaking to his grocery for alcohol, the narrator glibly says "and away he goes" (31); Zack sees Tom "still pursuing the downward course to misery and ruin" (43); Stiles talks of the drunkard "pulling and hauling your wife about" as he continues "in the path of wickedness" (47, 50); and Tom's gallows speech—where he is finally described as standing still—addresses "men who have not yet tread the drunkard's path" and hopes to help them "to steer your bark safe" (55–56). Tom ends his speech by telling Tim and Zack that "we were once all traveling the same road to ruin together" but that he foolishly "took my own course" even when they tried to save him (56–57).

Certainly among the most dangerous features of Tom's mobility are its anti-domesticity and its slippery lack of goals (beyond intoxication). Repeatedly, Tom's drinking disrupts his household, in large part because it makes him "get tolerable high, and ma[k]e for home—cursing and swearing" (50). At one point, when Lucy tells him that "she only wished he was as good a man as Mr. Stiles, Zack or Tim," Tom, "enraged," flies "at her to strike her" (43). He is "felled to the floor" when Lucy hits him with a chair; temporarily beaten, he "left the house and did not return to it till the next day" (43–44). When his drunken threats later make Lucy run "from the house," Tom's chase leads him to trip and break his arm (51). These scenes are frightening precursors to the play's penultimate chapter, when Tom once again "came home drunk as usual" and, after waiting for Lucy to fall asleep, "went out of doors, and brought in the axe, and struck her one blow in the head and killed her!" (53).

Initially, it appears that Tom has significant mobility, as he comes and goes from his home as he pleases. However, as the play develops, it becomes clear that he is simply bouncing back and forth between home and grogshop, causing destruction at the former, and using up his dwindling resources at the latter. Far from the germinal mobility of the settlers or the symbiotic mobility of the itinerant, Tom actually locks himself into a path to his own destruction and is unable—or simply unwilling—to change his course.

While the character of Stiles is not developed in great depth, what Greenly does show about him places him in clear opposition to Tom and within the tradition of itinerancy Weaver considers. He is introduced as "that great Temperance lecturer that has come into the neighborhood," and he says that Tom's drunkenness "is every moral reformer's business" (4, 48). In confronting Tom, he says that "we don't want to force you into measures. . . . And if you listen, and give your conscience fair-play, we shall gain our point and no one will be injured, but each party and the community benefited [*sic*]" (49). He continues to fight for temperance, even though Zack reports that "I saw Tom Nimble laying in a fence-corner with a gun, watching to shoot" Stiles "as he came out of town" (14).[43] While he is clearly not a minister, he is consistently linked to the church: after Zack's conversion, Zack invites "Mr. Blake, the minister, Mr. Stiles, Tim and his wife" to dinner, and when Stiles decides to stay in the community, he is "elected Superintendent" of the new Sabbath School (26, 28). Most notably, as with Weaver's own spreading of faith via traveling, Stiles's lectures and personal interventions are credited with saving—both from intemperance and for God—Tim and Zack.

That agency, even though it cannot save Tom and Lucy Nimble, holds great promise for helping build the West into a place of black hope, education, faith, and prosperity. Thus echoing the symbiotic pairing of settlers' germinal mobility and religious itinerancy, Greenly's early play offers a black Indiana that allows full citizenship and community-building—albeit in (and perhaps *because* it is in) an unexpected place.

Sadly, it was an Indiana Greenly himself was able to realize only partially. He moved to Charlestown, Indiana—one county over from New Albany—in early 1859, and he attempted to start a black newspaper called the *Prospect*. While the paper received a favorable notice in the *Repository*, it folded quickly, and no issues seem to be extant. He moved to Terre Haute in April 1862 and there became deeply involved in both black educational efforts and the local A.M.E. Church (pastored by the Reverend Thomas Strother).[44] He died, however, on 10 April 1863, was eulogized briefly in the 25 April 1863 *Recorder,* and then was essentially forgotten, along with most of the rest of the authors surrounding the *Repository* who did not move East.

A Different Kind of Travel "Down East"
Philadelphia's *Recorder* versus Baltimore's *Repository*

Among the wickedest ironies tied to the demise of the Indiana *Repository* and the western literary community surrounding it is the fact that the very itinerancy that several of the community's members celebrated in print caused, in fairly quick succession, transfers of several minister-editors out of the area and then removal East of the periodical itself. For both Weaver and the *Repository,* this was far from the kind of temporary "visit" he had written about; it marked a permanent shift with long-lasting implications. Some in the church leadership clearly wanted to use Weaver's sales and editorial talents to tighten the ever-growing A.M.E. community, but the resulting rise of the reborn *Christian Recorder* contributed to the ultimate death of the *Repository.* So did the relocation of the *Repository.* John Mifflin Brown not only moved all *Repository* editorial operations to Baltimore, but also removed the listing of the literary societies of Indiana and Missouri from its masthead. Instead, Brown wrote, the *Repository* would be supported by "all the Literary Societies that will contribute the annual sum of $24 for its support" (21).[45] These removals and the events that resulted from them also indelibly shaped Indiana's place on the map of black literature: while a few small local pockets thrived,[46] it would not be until the rise of the Indianapolis *Freeman* in the 1880s that Indiana would have again a national presence in black literature (and even this popular and important newspaper has been all but ignored by contemporary critics and canon makers of African American literature).

The contest between the *Recorder* and the *Repository* in 1861 and 1862, which remains all but ignored by historians and literary critics alike, began slowly. Initially, Weaver and Brown seem to have hoped that both periodicals could be supported by the Church—as evinced in part by the praise Brown showered on Weaver in the letter that opens this chapter. That letter also includes Brown's statement to Weaver that "your old friend, the Repository, is now out" and that "our subscribers in Philadelphia can get them at your book store." Later, in the 6 April 1861 *Recorder,* Weaver praised the *Repository* as a "valuable publication" that "makes a very fine appearance"; he wished "great success" to his "brother" Brown. Former *Recorder* editor Jabez P. Campbell (who would be elected a bishop in 1864) published an extended call in the 9 February 1861 *Recorder* for the Church to celebrate the "noble" and "blessed" possibilities inherent in having two active A.M.E. periodicals; he was certain that the Church had the resources "to sustain a weekly paper, *and* a quarterly magazine" (italics mine). Campbell echoed these sentiments in a 9 March 1861 follow-up letter to the *Recorder.*

However, doubts about supporting two periodicals were raised quickly. In the 23 February 1861 *Recorder,* Savage L. Hammond (who had served on the *Repository* editorial board under Weaver) offered his concerns about "two little trees . . . planted in the same soil," noting that "one of them ought to be dug up and set at a proper distance" because, if the trees were "too

close together," "one will impoverish the other." Hammond did not elabo-
rate beyond this metaphor, but, in a separate column in the same issue,
Weaver argued that, while "we do not oppose the *Repository*," if "both cannot survive, if one only can be encouraged and supported at the sacrifice
of the other, then we would urge upon all our church-members the higher
claims of *The Recorder*—which belongs to, and is the organ of, the General
Conference of our church—to those of the *Repository*, the mere organ of
the Literary Society."[47]

Weaver's choice to step down from the *Recorder*'s editorship in July 1861
in favor of A. L. Stanford did little to change the terms of the argument.
During Stanford's short tenure, for example, W. D. W. Shureman of Borden-
town, New Jersey, wrote in the 14 September 1861 *Recorder* that he viewed
"the *Christian Recorder* as the voice of our people—as the representative
of the Church." Given that Weaver's decision to leave the editorship was
motivated in part by his upcoming western tour as book steward (during
which he would solicit subscriptions for the *Recorder*), his shift may have
even fanned the flames a bit. To complicate matters further, an extended
debate in both the *Recorder* and the *Repository* over the place of Bishop
Willis Nazrey (whose move to Canada had caused one of Weaver's major early committee appointments and continued to befuddle the church
hierarchy) exploded in pieces from Brown, Willis Revels, and, ultimately,
Nazrey himself and split the periodicals further. While the *Repository* was
often condemnatory toward Nazrey, the *Recorder* was more even-handed
and sometimes even pro-Nazrey.[48]

By the beginning of 1862, after Stanford's resignation and the return
of Weaver to the editor's chair[49] the *Recorder*'s reception of the *Repository* was noticeably chillier. The 25 January 1862 *Recorder* included a letter
from Ebenezer Williams reporting that the New England Conference had
passed a motion naming the *Recorder* as its "organ for various publications"
alongside a report on a meeting between Payne, Brown, and a handful of
Baltimore-area ministers that "resolved that the *Repository* should be kept
in existence" but shifted to monthly publication. In the 15 February 1862
Recorder, Weaver tersely reported that the literary societies of the Indiana,
Missouri, Baltimore, and New England Conferences had been removed
from the *Repository*'s masthead and "they have reduced the number of
pages to twenty."

Henry McNeal Turner—who had attended the January *Repository* meeting—attempted to heal the breach with a 1 March 1862 *Recorder* letter that

argued that Hammond never "intended to convey so radical an idea as what has gained prevalence among the people" and that "it was never the intention either for the Recorder or the Repository to antagonize each other" because "we need both the Recorder and the Repository." But Weaver's subsequent comments on the *Repository* were much thinner than his past praise—he could only give "it but a hasty glance" (though he could "voice for it as containing its usual acceptable store of good things") in early March 1862, and later in the month claimed that he had only "scanned it over slightly." He did read closely enough, though, to take offense at its comments on the *Recorder*'s handling of the Nazrey debate—which several in the church began referring to as the "Episcopal debate." As that debate—and especially Brown's outspoken condemnation of Nazrey—continued, Campbell, who wrote a long and measured piece that was fairly supportive of Nazrey in the 22 February 1862 *Recorder,* shifted to Weaver's side in the *Recorder/Repository* debate. In a 5 April 1862 letter to the *Recorder,* Campbell argued that "the Editor of the Christian Recorder has done himself much credit in the management of the Episcopal discussion" of Nazrey—while Brown and the *Repository* had "gone so far out of the good and right way."

While both Weaver and Brown limited their negative public comments during the summer of 1862, they often found themselves competing directly against each other for subscribers and church dollars—as at the Indiana Annual Conference of 1862, where both pressed their cases for support. The conference ended with a lopsided resolution—published in the 6 September 1862 *Recorder*—that its ministers "would pledge ourselves anew to encourage the publication of our church organ, the *Christian Recorder,* subscribe for it ourselves, according to our abilities, even at the sacrifice of some worldly comforts—and also patronize the *Repository.*"

Curiously, members of the Indiana—and, more broadly, Midwest—*Repository* base had been fairly silent in the print debate up to this point. But on the heels of the Indiana Conference's clear leaning toward Weaver, the 27 September 1862 *Recorder* included a stinging "INQUIRY" that was signed only "FROM THE WEST":

To the Rev. E Weaver:

DEAR SIR: — Will you please answer the following questions?
1. The *Repository,* as sometimes seen in your paper, and often in the Annual Conference, in connexion [*sic*] with the *Recorder*—is it or

is it not the *property* of the general connexion [*sic*] of the A.M.E.
Church?

2. If it is the property of the connexion [*sic*], why is it not under the
jurisdiction of the General Editor and Book Steward?

3. Why is it so sectional in its circulation?

Weaver, as both general editor and book steward, took it on himself to
provide a lengthy answer. He first recounted his view of the founding of the
Repository—that "in 1857 the Indiana Conference Literary Society felt the
need of some kind of religious periodical" and "I introduced the subject in
our Conference—that the members of the Literary and Historical Society
respectively take our own money out of our own pockets and publish a
quarterly magazine. But that in no sense whatever was it to interfere with
the publications of the general concern." Taking a brief swipe at Payne—
who wanted the *Repository* to continue, seemingly at an equal level of
support—Weaver asserted that Payne and Molliston Clark (who was to be
the initial "Executive Editor") failed to establish the periodical and so that,
with Brown and Revels helping, "I would publish it myself in the city of
Indianapolis." He then offered a brief summary of his move to become the
General Conference's book steward, emphasizing that "I revived the *Christian Recorder* to its present size, and have kept it in the field ever since."

In answer to the perhaps-planted and certainly pro-*Recorder* questions
of the "Western Inquirer," Weaver succinctly said that "it was never intended that the *Repository* should interfere with the organ of the Church"
and that "the *Repository* is not the property of the general connexion [*sic*]."
The reason for its current Baltimore-centered sectionality, Weaver said, was
thus obvious—the answer to "the third interrogatory I will leave you to
judge from the answer to the other two questions." In short, Weaver asserted, the *Repository* was now solely a publication of Brown's Baltimore
group, an almost-rogue journal not sanctioned by the General Conference,
not under the book steward's (i.e., Weaver's own) careful supervision, and
certainly not of the West anymore.

Weaver was at a distinct advantage in this debate, given the *Recorder*'s
weekly publication schedule and more extensive circulation—as well as
Weaver's place in Philadelphia. Still, Brown took enough umbrage at this
"disposition to revive an old feud, which I had hoped well nigh died out"
to write directly to Weaver. In a long letter published in the *Recorder*'s very
next issue, he claimed a much larger role in founding the *Repository* than

Weaver's account granted him, and he noted that, while the publication "was not authorized by the General Conference" it "is approved of and supported by nearly every member of that body."

Brown then answered the "third interragatory" both angrily and perhaps a bit disingenuously:

> I scarcely know how to answer this . . . because "Inquirer" doesn't define what he means by "sectional." Does he mean that it circulates in a *certain defined district?* Or does he mean that it is *partial?* If the former, I deny the allegation, and the latter, I deny that also. The Repository is not confined to any one region. It circulates as far East as Massachusetts, and as far West as Iowa, and North as far as New York, and South as far as Virginia. If he means that it is partial, then its partiality consists of attending to its specified duties, viz.: extension of *Religion, Literature, Science, and the Arts.* . . . If he means that the "Repository" does not circulate in his *immediate household,* it is his fault and not ours.

Then Brown took aim at Weaver. Reminding readers of Christ's criticism of John for stopping a man for "casting out devils in thy name" because "he followed no[t] with us," Brown claimed, "Much less approvingly did the Son of God speak to his beloved disciple than did our General Book steward to Mr. 'Inquirer.' By what authority have you, Rev. Sir, and your friends, directly and indirectly, in private and in public, aimed death blows at the existence of the 'Repository[?]'" Nonetheless, Brown ended with this simple sentence: "We are no enemy of the Recorder."

Weaver's extended reply in the 25 October 1862 *Recorder* dismissed Brown's arguments in depth, asserted that the "Western Inquirer" was not his surrogate, and offered an extended discussion of how the *Christian Recorder* was founded, written into the A.M.E. *Discipline* of 1856, and clearly marked as the organ of the A.M.E. Church. But a brief note in the same issue from A. T. Hall of Keokuk, Iowa, was more telling: it included a postscript asking Weaver to "Please inform me through the Recorder whether the *Repository* is living or dead. I subscribed and paid for one year at our Conference, and have not yet received a single number."[50] Weaver occasionally mentioned the *Repository* later in 1862 and into 1863—even bestowing a bit of praise[51]—but these notes were short, were almost always tied to material lauding the *Recorder,* and did not deign to engage (or even include) any suggestion that any contest between the two periodicals continued. Weaver also—generally without mentioning the *Repository* directly—included material that suggested that the old *Repository* community was on his side, including a 10 January 1863 letter from none other than William Jay Greenly, who said that he had been a *Recorder* reader for some fifteen months and that he was enclosing "fifty cents, due on my subscription" for 1862—and promising to send his full subscription fee for 1863 soon. The *Recorder,* Weaver's silence shouted, had won; the *Repository* was, for all practical purposes, done.[52] It should also be noted, however, that, while most did not attack the *Repository,* a steady stream of letters "from the field" praising the *Recorder* appeared throughout 1861 and 1862, including several from the West, like W. J. Davis's letter from Muscatine, Iowa (which was published in the 6 April 1861 issue) and J. M. Wilkerson's letter from Leavenworth City, Kansas (which was published in the 7 December 1861 issue).

This long and polarizing debate, the growing intensity of the Civil War, Weaver's progress with the *Recorder,* Brown's increasing attention to the South (and especially to work with the newly freed), the massive difficulties Brown seems to have had in getting subscribers, and Brown's alienation of some former subscribers (and even editors and contributors like Revels and Strother) all took a toll on the *Repository.* Although no issues after January 1863 are listed in Bullock's *Afro-American Periodical Press* or WorldCat, evidence suggests that the *Repository* limped on through 1863.[53] After that, operations were suspended completely. The Baltimore Conference—not so much because it was anything like the periodical's "owner" as because it was now Brown's home conference—made a last call for ministers "indebted for the Repository" to "settle such bills by the 1st of June, 1864" in order to move "toward liquidating the debt on the Repository" (qtd. in Bullock 44). And while, according to a 6 August 1864 letter to the *Recorder* from "Look Inn" of Baltimore, Brown was contemplating "a resurrection of the old Repository," no such resurrection ever happened.[54]

Weaver's victory could certainly be read as a narrative of the Northeast's dominance within black literature, and the slow embrace of the *Recorder* by western readers may well be emblematic of those readers choosing what they felt was the most West-friendly of the two now-eastern periodicals. It should also be read, though, as a lesson in how external factors (including conflicts in church leadership) could crush nascent black literary communities in unexpected places—or, at least, force those communities to engage with and *in* more expected places. The remainder of this chapter thus uses a close examination of some of the more Baltimore-centered content in Brown's *Repository* to explore why—beyond Weaver's Indiana ties and Brown's clumsy maneuvering with western constituents—western readers might have been drawn away from the *Repository*. It then examines how Weaver's own later *Recorder* travel writing might have reached out to the West—even though, while it still idealizes the itinerant, it marks him as an eastern leader spreading the "good news" to the West instead of as a son of the West.

"A Wandering Gypsy"
Maria W. Stewart and Baltimore's *Repository*

The recently recovered *Repository* work of Maria Stewart—a lecture on "The Proper Training of Children" published in the January 1861 issue and especially a serialized short story titled "The First Stage of Life" published in the April, July, and October 1861 issues[55]—effectively embodies many of the *Repository*'s shifts after Brown took over the periodical. Stewart was never a part of the same *Repository* community as Weaver and Greenly. A woman who never joined the A.M.E. Church, Stewart added to these differences in gender and denomination a key difference in location: she never visited Indiana and, indeed, never seems to have been West of Pennsylvania.

Both of Stewart's *Repository* texts were clearly written in Baltimore, where Stewart settled circa 1852. Scholars have traditionally seen this period (as well as the several years prior in Williamsburg, New York) as large gaps in a biography bookended by, on the one side, her 1830s Boston lectures, *Liberator* publications, and *Productions of Mrs. Maria W. Stewart* (1835), and, on the other, the Washington publication of her 1879 *Meditations from the Pen of Mrs. Maria W. Stewart,* which was financed by her husband's long-withheld War of 1812 pension.[56] Stewart's exodus from Massachusetts and New York (not ideal locations, but still among the more liberal free states) to Maryland (the same slave state Frederick Douglass's autobiographies located as a center of cruelty) may initially strike some as surprising—perhaps even unexpected. However, we need only remember the title of Leroy Graham's 1982 study *Baltimore: The Nineteenth-Century Black Capital* for an explanation. In part because the large and lively black community in Baltimore created opportunities for Stewart to work as a teacher—albeit sometimes in straitened circumstances—and to explore her growing Episcopal sensibilities, she stayed there for several years.[57]

Gender probably also shaped her decision. Initially widowed and likely bereft of any extended family connections—and then seemingly single by choice for the rest of her life—Stewart might not have seen westward migration as a viable option, given her strict sense of morality, the broader culture's consistent questioning of and attacks on single black women without community roots, and/or the pragmatic recognition of the kind of black community she needed in order to teach.[58] Finally, Stewart had chosen to cast her lot with the Episcopal Church, a denomination deeply tied to the East and to the "civilized"—so much so that some A.M.E. members asserted that black Episcopalians were pompous and exclusionary.[59]

While the recovery of a lecture given by Stewart in 1860 and published in 1861 complicates Carla Peterson's hypothesis that Stewart's shift from Baptist roots to Episcopalian membership was based on Stewart becoming "convinced at this point of the incompatibility of speaking publicly and being a lady," Peterson is likely quite correct in seeing Stewart's shift as "indicative of her determination to hold on to her achieved middle-class status" (58). In giving her lecture within the walls—perhaps even from the pulpit—of St. James Protestant Episcopal Church as part of a women's literary festival, Stewart arguably found a site for weaving together public speech and middle-class aspirations in a way that was socially acceptable for even an unattached black woman leaning toward Episcopalianism. But this was clearly done on her terms. Within the African Methodist tradition, while there was certainly nothing like gender equity, there *were* a number of opportunities for women's public speech and writing that Stewart chose not to take; for Stewart to attend St. James was to separate herself from Baltimore's A.M.E. community specifically and African Methodism more generally. Certainly, western readers might well have seen Stewart's Episcopalian label and views as a bit foreign; while several were undoubtedly familiar with such from their ties to the East, a successful black Episcopal church was not established in Indianapolis, for example, until 1900 (Thornbrough 372).

However, the relationship between A.M.E. Church's Baltimore clergy and St. James was actually, at this point in time, surprisingly strong—probably in part because Baltimore's A.M.E. churches were dominated by clergy who were extremely friendly to Bishop Payne's calls for a highly literate (and even scholarly) ministry as well as more formal services. Among those who worked in key roles in the larger A.M.E. nexus between Baltimore and Washington, D.C., during the late 1850s and early 1860s were *Repository* editorial board member and later bishop Alexander Wayman and future *Recorder* business manager and bishop Henry McNeal Turner, as well as George Thompson Watkins, son of educator and activist William Watkins and first cousin of Frances Ellen Watkins Harper.[60] The positive relationship even filtered into the A.M.E.'s *Christian Recorder*: a 20 July 1861 letter from Wayman, for example, praised St. James's school and especially the church's rector Harrison Holmes Webb ("a fine scholar and iminent [*sic*] theologian"); Webb was similarly lauded in a 10 November 1866 *Recorder* piece as "purely a self-made man and a very able one, too" who "has a sound mind" and whose sermons were "full of logic and profound theology."

But while Wayman and even Turner may have been friendly with area black Episcopalians, easily the central figure among Baltimore's A.M.E. clergy in such a relationship was the *Repository*'s own John Mifflin Brown. Brown's biography suggests that he would have been especially suited to bridging an A.M.E./Episcopalian denominational gap: as a youth, before joining the A.M.E. Church, he attended Philadelphia's St. Thomas Protestant Episcopal Church, the city's bastion of black Episcopalians; the historian Stephen Glazier describes him as "more of an Episcopal than a Methodist by temperament" (1: 628). Brown's leaning shaped his criticism of Willis Nazrey as well as a host of subtle content shifts in the *Repository*. He certainly interacted with Stewart's pastor Harrison Webb, and that interaction probably included invitations to events like the festival that hosted Stewart's lecture.

Whether Brown served as the conduit for the *Repository*'s publication of Stewart's lecture—or whether that conduit was another A.M.E. minister like Wayman, an Episcopalian like Webb, or even one of the women involved with the festival—the acceptance of a three-part short story like "The First Stage of Life" would have involved direct interaction between lead editor Brown and author Stewart. That interaction was probably shaped by a set of factors. First, given Stewart's prefatory prayer on working as a writer, her lack of reconnection with white abolitionists (especially Garrison) until the late 1870s, the lack of serialized fiction in the newly reborn *Recorder,* the failure of most black start-up periodicals of the period (like Greenly's short-lived newspaper), and the heavily political and fairly secular nature of the fewer long-lasting black periodicals (Douglass's papers, the *Anglo-African*), the *Repository* may well have seemed like Stewart's best hope—and perhaps one of her only hopes—for publication.[61] Further, in addition to the fact that the *Repository* did grant significant space to women authors, Brown may well have had a somewhat more enlightened view of women authors than Weaver held at this point.[62] Some of that enlightenment may have come from that fact that when Brown served as principal of the church's Union Seminary in Ohio, his assistant was Frances Ellen Watkins.[63]

Stewart's lecture probably wouldn't have greatly surprised readers used to Weaver's approach to the *Repository*. Though it was tagged as being delivered "in St. James' Protestant Episcopal Church, Baltimore," referred to the audience "we" as "the citizens of the State of Maryland," and spoke of "as much need of pious missionary labor in different parts of this city as there is among the Hottentots or the wild Hindoo" (159–60), it fell squarely within practice established during the *Repository*'s first two years of occasionally printing various addresses given by women before small groups— especially literary societies.[64] Stewart's lecture did address the West—but only as a side piece of her construction of a Puritan ideal (complete with references to Plymouth Rock), which talks of how the "native Indians . . . gave vent to their unholy tempers," resulting eventually in "millions of their race" being killed and God's decision "to drive their posterity on our far Western borders"—a position those used to Weaver's constructions of the West might have received ambivalently at best (161).

"The First Stage of Life," however, is like nothing that had previous appeared in the *Repository*. First, of course, the periodical had not featured serialized fiction—or even serialized narrative beyond a handful of travelogues like Weaver's and Clark's; it certainly never featured work that experimented with narratorial voice and characterization in the ways that "The First Stage of Life" does. Second, nothing like the piece's autobiographical preface—reflecting on how hard it was for a black woman to become a writer[65]—appears anywhere in the full run of the periodical. Third, its protagonist—the young, black, and soon-to-be-orphaned child Letitia— represents a voice completely absent in the *Repository*'s pages. As the story follows Letitia through her difficult and confusing youth, it shares the ambiguity of setting that Greenly's book of plays demonstrates. Still, while its setting is unspecified, it is clearly a tale of a settled area near an urban center: in its discussion of Letitia's first experience of night, it refers to "the light of the lamps" on the streets and talks of her how "her mother desires to go to the city" nearby "to die" (162, 163).[66]

Two features of the story are most strikingly divergent from the West of Weaver and Greenly: its ambivalence about the itinerant ministry and its response to an almost-unchecked mobility. The story's only minister makes a very brief appearance. After the death of Letitia's mother, Letitia sees, amid "a very large number of men, all dressed in black" and a crowd of "women, all dressed in black," a "tall man" who "stood up" and had "a gown on: he must have been a minister." He leads the group in a hymn and a prayer, but Aunt Sally—the caretaker of both Letitia and her mother—fears him and tells Letitia "that the tall man spoken of previously, was her cousin, and that he wanted to carry her off" (164). Though Letitia later learns that he was "a distinguished man of God," Sally's fears (which the narrator seems to share) lead her to hide Letitia, in language certainly suggestive of a rewriting of the Christmas story, "up in the hay, in the box under the manger" (164). When Letitia cannot be found, the minister "was obliged to go and leave her" (164).

Aunt Sally's subsequent behavior, though, suggests that Letitia might actually have been better off with the minister, even though he temporarily serves as a locus of fear. After the death of Letitia's stepfather, with whom Sally seems to cohabitate, Sally wanders aimlessly with Letitia in tow—in essence becoming "almost a wandering gypsy" because she "had not a settled home"—and teaches "Letitia all kinds of naughtiness, and became very unkind and cruel to her" (165). Reminiscent of Tom Nimble's goal-less and false mobility of addiction, Aunt Sally's intemperate movement victimizes both Letitia's physical being and soul; ultimately, it leads her to leave Letitia "in the street, without home and without friends" (165). Even when a kind family takes her in, the narrator reflects that Aunt Sally's "gypsy" movement has made Letitia "almost a ruined child, she was so bad" (165). What is radically different from the texts studied earlier in this chapter is not the condemnation of intemperate mobility; rather, it is Stewart's dismissal of the itinerant as a saving force. No itinerant Weaver or Stiles rescues Letitia, and, while the narrator asserts that she eventually becomes "a good girl . . . like a tree planted in the house of my God," the narrator never tells *how*— never suggests any human agency, much less the saving and symbiotic work of the itinerant minister and a group of settlers (165). Indeed, Letitia's progress seems to be simply an example of God's unknowable will.

While the distinctive and challenging features of Stewart's story alone obviously didn't turn western readers from the *Repository,* combined with the deep cuts in the amount of coverage of western churches, the marked increase in eastern contributors (especially those, like Stewart, from the larger Baltimore area), and the exodus of western editorial board members (either from the periodical or from the West) arguably combined with

Brown's increasing hostility toward some western groups (like the Indiana Conference) to push the periodical into what the "Western Inquirer" rightly recognized as a sectional base very different from its origins. The columns of the *Christian Recorder,* including the lists of new subscribers the paper began publishing in its acknowledgments columns, suggest that western readers increasingly turned to the A.M.E's official organ. The *Repository,* as noted above, would die, John Mifflin Brown would move on to other projects, and Stewart would attempt to build a new life in Washington, D. C.

"A Western Tour"
Elisha Weaver, Itinerancy, and the *Christian Recorder*

Two features of Weaver's early stewardship of the *Recorder* contributed to its embrace by readers in the West: Weaver's physical travels to the West and the sense in the paper that, if not nationally germinal, the West was still deeply important. Stanford's move into the editorial chair was neatly timed to support Weaver's "Western Tour" to drum up support for the A.M.E. publications under his control. In the 13 July 1861 *Recorder,* Weaver announced that he would "hold meetings, by Divine permission" spread over July and August in Lewiston, Huntingdon, Pittsburgh, and Allegheny, Pennsylvania; Columbus, Xenia, and Cincinnati, Ohio; Richmond, Indiana; and Bloomington and Chicago, Illinois—this last, the site of the Indiana Conference's Annual Meeting, at which Weaver would speak for the Book Concern and the *Recorder.* We know from his letters to the *Recorder* that he rearranged his schedule to add visits to Altoona, Pennsylvania, and Indianapolis prior to the conference—and Springfield and Brooklyn, Illinois, on his way to another added stop in St. Louis, Missouri, for the Missouri Annual Conference, where he secured praise and recommendations in support of both the *Recorder* and Book Concern.[67]

Simply to have a member of the A.M.E. hierarchy who was not a bishop specifically charged with overseeing the region tour these locations would have been seen as a reaffirmation of the church's commitment to the West; that it was Weaver making the trip specifically meant that it was in some ways a homecoming.[68] The tone of Weaver's travelogues on his "Western tour" emphasized this all the more, in part because Weaver again employed several of the techniques he had used in his *Repository* "Visit Down East" and "Church News" columns. His letters back to the *Recorder* certainly accounted for "sights and sounds." He commented in the 24 August 1861 *Recorder*, for example, on how, "as I traveled along west of the mountains, through the western part of Pennsylvania, and through the States of Ohio, Indiana, and Illinois, I don't know that I ever saw better crops." In the 14 September 1861 *Recorder*, he spoke of how readers should "just imagine the greeting and shaking of hands" on his welcome to St. Louis, where the Reverend John Turner's congregation treated him to "watermelon, ice cream, cake, &c." He wryly added, "I think I hear some of my readers say, Were you not afraid to be out so late at night, when the city was under martial law? Oh, no! For it is as much as the authorities can do to keep down the *secessionists*, without interfering with free colored people who are trying to serve God." Also in the 14 September issue, Weaver told of how he witnessed "the funeral procession, with the body of General Lyon," a "day of serious solemnity," led by "Mr. Frank Paul, a colored gentleman who was waiting on" Lyon "at the time of his death, and had been attending him for some years previously."[69] He also reported on the vicissitudes of traveling in a racist society—including an account (published in the 3 August 1861 *Recorder*) of trouble on the trains around Pittsburgh, where he saw fellow black passengers "subjected to insult and disrespectful treatment" that made "my very blood boil within me in commiseration." Weaver also again focused heavily on naming names and on linking the prominent—including many of the leading A.M.E. clergy in Pennsylvania, Ohio, Indiana, Illinois, and Missouri—to the "plainer" congregants, with liberal mention of visiting old friends.

Such approaches were certainly consonant with Weaver's broader treatment of the West in the *Recorder* prior to his trip—and arguably far more attractive to westerners than Brown's uneven coverage and Stewart's dismissal of itinerancy. Most notably, Weaver had quickly established a fairly consistent practice of heading his Philadelphia-area news "City Items" (as in, for example, the 20 April 1861 issue) and of then including a much broader section titled with a variation of "News from the Churches"—as in the 25 May 1861 issue, which reported on Springfield, Illinois; Indianapolis (which Weaver parenthetically referred to as "our old home"); and San Francisco, California.

But there are also key differences between Weaver's *Recorder* treatment of the West and his earlier *Repository* work. While he ranges in tone, many of his letters to the *Recorder* offer a kind of minutes-like reporting of church visits and especially of the annual conference meetings.[70] While he certainly comments on individual congregations, his reports are much more brief, emphasize the number of congregants unfamiliar with the Book Concern or the *Recorder,* and report on how willing congregations are to support such. (In travelogues later in 1861, Weaver would actually begin reporting specific amounts collected from individual congregations.) In essence, though they often maintained the vestiges of letters home noted above, Weaver's texts also emphasized repeatedly his much more official functions. His formal position was marked even further by items like a 13 July 1861 piece from Weaver about "some scamps making a living under the garb of the *Christian Recorder*"—specifically "a person who represents himself" as a *Recorder* agent, who collected significant funds under this pretense from a group of "white friends," and who was most definitely *not* "appointed by me. I have made no such appointment." Weaver closed by reminding readers that all true agents carried "certificates of appointment."

And while the West was certainly writ large in Weaver's travel accounts of July, August, and September, his "Western tour" was neither his first nor his last venture of the year. Prior to going West, he described his "Visit to the New York Conference" in great depth in the 15 June 1861 *Recorder.* Soon after reporting in the 14 September 1861 *Recorder* that he was "once more, through the blessing of God, returned home," he described, again in depth, "Our Visit Down South"—a trip to Baltimore and Washington, D.C. (including, ironically, a visit to Brown's church)—in the 16 November 1861 *Recorder.* In the same issue, he published his "Programme" for an upcoming "Eastern Tour," which would take place later in November and early in December and include Princeton and Newark, New Jersey; Brooklyn, Harlem, and Bridgeport, New York; New Haven, Connecticut; Providence, Rhode Island; and New Bedford and Boston, Massachusetts. His accounts of all of these trips, which appeared throughout the rest of the year in the *Recorder,* duplicated and refined the rhetorical strategies found in his earlier columns.[71]

The implicit message to the West and to the former *Repository* community in these columns was decidedly mixed. On the one hand, the West was essentially placed on equal footing—same coverage, same rhetoric—as other regions; on the other, it was no longer the immensely powerful germinal place of the *Repository*'s depictions. Similarly, while Weaver early and continuously reaffirmed the importance of the itinerancy—noting, for example, in the 15 June 1861 *Recorder,* "We were kindly received, and made to feel at home. *Itinerant ministers are brothers*" and repeatedly telling stories that center on tropes of hospitality—all must have recognized that Weaver's charge had changed deeply.

As much as Weaver would praise his "old home" in Indianapolis, he was no longer a western minister; now he was a national figure based in the East—an itinerant preacher of faith, literacy, and the literary who was willing to work with any free black community he could reach through pen or pulpit. And in inhabiting that position, he had come to reify the very centrality of the urban Northeast to early black literature that the *Repository* had so actively, if briefly, challenged from the unexpected places in and around Indianapolis, Indiana.

Chapter 3

THE BLACK WEST
Northern California and Beyond, 1865–1877

"I wish that you could . . . cause your valuable journal to make its permanent residence at the *White House*," wrote "P. K. C." to Philip Bell in a letter published in the San Francisco *Elevator* on the first day of 1869, "so that the correspondence from Japan found in its columns . . . may have effect. . . . What a pity that Reporters and everything connected with the relationship of this country to the United States should be so amiss, *without eyes*." "P. K. C.," who was identified elsewhere in the *Elevator* as black expatriate Peter K. Cole, argued specifically that Secretary of State William Seward, for all "his years" and "his mental powers," was steering the United States on the wrong course: "he cannot, does not conceive or know what great benefit Japan is to the United States." In short, Cole asserted, "the United States government" must be brought "into a closer connection with Japan, and that speedily."

Cole's White House desires were certainly fueled by the fact that he was the author of the "correspondence from Japan"—over a dozen extended letters published in the *Elevator* between mid-1867 and mid-1870.[1] However, beyond self-interest, Cole also evinced a consistent and honest desire to see the country of his birth expand relations with the country in which he had found a new home. Writing mainly from Yokohama, Kanagawa, and self-consciously describing what his 22 May 1868 letter referred to as "the preludes to the final scenes in the last act of the opening of the entire Japan, " Cole asserted that revisions to U.S. policy needed to be based on firsthand observation and deep understanding. He undertook to provide both in his long letters to the *Elevator*—letters that, in his words, were also part of a clear effort to "elevate the people" through the literary forms of travel writing (29 November 1867 *Elevator*). The tone and content of Cole's letters certainly evince an attitude that the historian James E. Hoare finds common among Kanagawa's nineteenth-century foreign community: Cole and many of his colleagues in Japan often "thought of themselves as being the representatives of a superior society" (6).[2] In this, Cole slipped regularly into what Helen Jun refers to as "Black Orientalism"—that is, "the discursive production" by African Americans "of an utterly foreign, premodern, alien Oriental in opposition to a rational, modern Western subject" (1049). As such, he asserted both that "the enterprising faculty of the American people is a something so puzzling to the people of this Empire that it will be a time before they will recover from the wonder" and that "the impossibility of stopping the onward march of civilization" was alternately fascinating and frightening to "both prince and peasant" in Japan (29 November 1867; 22 May 1868).

Nonetheless, Cole's depictions of Japan—including his comments on the small black expatriate community there—offer a much more complex sense of "Black Orientalism" than has previously been suggested; in this, Cole's letters also present both a case study in the conscious creation of African American literature from an extremely unexpected place and an entry point for a more in-depth consideration of the larger and still unexpected black literary community surrounding San Francisco, of which Cole was a member (albeit a physically distant one). In addition to studying Cole, this chapter thus begins to introduce the diverse group that made up black literary California through examining, briefly, William H. Newby and Philip Bell, and, in more depth, Jennie Carter and Thomas Detter. That introduction will demonstrate the richness of this specific unexpected place, a richness tied to the fact that black San Francisco's literary community was more long-lasting, more connected to eastern publishing venues and simultaneously more independent of them, and much more prolific than the communities studied in previous chapters. (While there is much left to be said about the black literate and literary communities in St. Louis and Indiana, there are books to be written about black California.) Within the specific parameters of this study, black literary San Francisco is especially intriguing not only for its size, diversity, and impact, but also because its authors offered significant revisions to the conceptions of black locations and mobility considered in earlier chapters. Some of these revisions were tied specifically to California and the black West as places, though many more flowed from the shifts made possible by the Civil War and especially the hope of Reconstruction. Bathed in both these hopes and the conflicts surrounding them, the writers discussed in this chapter articulated a sense of the West as a center of black citizenship, a sense long lost in African American literary study.

"COLORED SOCIETY IN YOKOHAMA"
Peter K. Cole's Japan and (African) America

Some of the roots of Peter Cole's conception of Japan—and his desire to stay there, at least for a time—must have come from his circumstances; his biography, while hazy and partial, suggests that Cole traveled not simply in the United States but around the world. However, Cole's very mobility—when placed in the dual contexts of the governmental inadequacy in recording nineteenth-century African Americans and the destruction of many San Francisco public records in the massive earthquake of 1906—makes him one of the most difficult authors in this study to track. The few modern references to Cole say, generally without citing sources, that he was born in 1830 in New York and later lived, taught school, and lectured in San Francisco when not traveling internationally.[3] Bibliographers occasionally (and correctly) add that Cole authored *Cole's War with Ignorance and Deception*, a pamphlet published in San Francisco in 1857 that consists primarily of a public lecture he gave on the state of black America (with some emphasis on education) and a fragmented account of his disagreements with the San Francisco *Mirror of the Times*, the far West's first black newspaper. Only a few scholars have noted that he was the "P. K. C." who authored the *Elevator* letters on Japan.[4]

The birth date generally given for Cole is almost certainly wrong, though the assertion that he grew up in New York City is correct. In the final pages of *Cole's War*, Cole briefly praises New York activist Charles L. Reason and then makes a set of claims: that he studied with Reason for "ten years," that Reason and Henry Highland Garnet were "at the time . . . studying . . . in the same public school with myself," and that "William H. Day, now Editor of the *Aliened American*" was "my classmate and bosom friend" (50). Though Cole does not name it, the only school all of these men had in their background was New York City's famed African Free School. Garnet, the eldest of the three, was a student at the Free School from about 1825 until about 1828, although, after time at sea and a crippling injury to his right leg, he enrolled in the related Phoenix High School for Colored Youth in New York in 1831.[5] Reason began his studies at the African Free School in the late 1820s and was so skilled in math that the school hired him as a part-time instructor in 1832 when he was only fourteen years old.[6] Day was only at the African Free School briefly before being "adopted" by the white J. P. Williston and taken to Northampton, Massachusetts, circa 1837.[7] Given this confluence and Cole's specific reference to Day as his "classmate," it seems more likely that Cole was born in the early or mid-1820s, studied with Reason in the 1830s and perhaps the early 1840s, and knew Garnet only as one of the older students in the relatively small black school system.

At the African Free School, Cole would have learned—as per a notice in the 11 January 1828 *Freedom's Journal*—"Reading, Writing, Arithmetic, Geography, and English Grammar," among other subjects that were "calculated to fit" students "for usefulness and respectability." He would have been part of an incredibly germinal location for black leaders; in addition to the figures mentioned above, other African Free School students included Ira Aldridge, Samuel Ringgold Ward, Alexander Crummell, and James McCune Smith. But Cole, like all of these future leaders, was also in the midst of an object lesson on racism and reform. The Free Schools were originally founded by the New York Manumission Society, which often treated African Americans patronizingly and paternalistically. Many members of the Manumission Society had colonizationist leanings; indeed, according to some accounts, one of the period's leading Free School administrators, Charles C. Andrews, resigned in late 1831 because his pro-Liberia stance clashed with parents' ideas. (Other accounts argue that Andrews actually resigned when parents' protests over Andrews's caning of a student who had referred to a black visitor at the school as a "gentleman" threatened the school's enrollment.[8]) Black leaders in New York regularly clashed with the Manumission Society's politics even as they recognized that the Free Schools offered a level of educational access that was incredibly rare during the early years of the nation.

Cole's parents or benefactors would have been participants in this daily negotiation of politics; a young Cole may even have known Albro Lyons—the student who was caned and who later become an important New York abolitionist.[9] Finally, given New York City's ties to the sea trade and immense growth, Cole would have become acquainted early with the possibilities and limitations of black mobility in the 1830s and 1840s. New

York City's comparatively small but also multifaceted black community housed African Americans from many regions of the country and was the base for several early impulses toward black textual presences, including black America's first newspaper, *Freedom's Journal*. The students surrounding Cole almost certainly knew of this publication, as the editors donated copies of the paper to the Free School in the late 1820s.[10] Many of those involved with the founding of the *Colored American* in the 1830s had ties to the Free Schools, and Cole was likely a reader of that paper, too.[11]

How, why, and when Cole came to California remains as much of a mystery as most of his biography; he does not seem to have been a participant in the eastern convention movements of the 1840s and 1850s, and he is not mentioned in black newspapers like the *Colored American* or Frederick Douglass's later *North Star*. His 27 September 1867 letter from Japan talked of being "a destitute traveler from the soil of Mexico" and of being helped on arriving in San Francisco (on an unspecified date) by community activist and second-hand furniture and clothing dealer Henry C. Cornish.[12] Cole was definitely in San Francisco by early 1857, when his lecture on "Comets" was disparaged by the 30 May 1857 *Mirror of the Times* in an article that suggested that Cole could "employ his time much better in lecturing on some subject that he knows something about" (qtd. in Cole 10). Unfortunately, only a few issues of the *Mirror* are extant, and so *Cole's War* (which was biased against the *Mirror*) is the only source on what seems to have been a flurry of public insults and counter-insults.[13] Whoever Cole was arguing with, it is clear that he was interacting with some of San Francisco's most educated and most active literary African Americans; in addition to Anderson and Newby, Reverend John Jamison Moore, Thomas Detter, and a host of black California luminaries were, for example, part of the relatively small 1857 San Francisco convention.[14] Further, the centerpiece lecture in *Cole's War* was delivered on 11 August 1857 at St. Cyprian's Church, which would soon become the basis for San Francisco's Bethel A.M.E. congregation and effectively launch the west coast career of future A.M.E. bishop Thomas M. D. Ward.[15] Like many of these figures, Cole also clearly saw print as a central forum for public argument: *Cole's War* shares pieces seemingly rejected by the *Mirror* (signed "Retepo Seloco") and asserts that the audience at St. Cyprian strongly urged Cole to publish his lecture for the betterment of the community.

However, Cole's place must also have been in some ways marginal— or perhaps his lectures, his arguments with the *Mirror,* and/or his long-winded and often-confusing *War* marginalized him; Cole's 27 September 1867 *Elevator* letter talks of "the great conventional struggle of 1857, when the volcanoes burst over my head, and heaved forth their sulphurous spite." He appears in the 1858 San Francisco city directory—listed as a teacher— but does not appear in subsequent directories. In a similar vein, while Cole is mentioned in the 2 October 1862 *Pacific Appeal*, he is generally absent from the paper, including reports of its founding; while he is noted in the 17 November 1865 *Elevator*, he is again absent from both the few early extant issues of the paper and later discussions of its founding.[16]

How and when Cole settled in Japan remains unclear: he was there by May 1867, when his first *Elevator* letter (no longer extant) went to Bell, and by his 20 September 1867 letter to the *Elevator*, he was clearly familiar not only with the country's language, economics, and expatriate community but also with its complex political circumstances. Cole would have been among the first Americans to settle in Japan, as Commodore Perry's "Black Ships" had only come in 1853, and the dictates of the "Convention of Kanagawa"— held under the shadow of Perry's returned armada in 1854—had only begun to force the nation to open itself to "barbarians." The Pacific Mail Steam-ship Company (which initially came to prominence during the Gold Rush) had only begun offering the first consistent route between the cities of San Francisco, Hong Kong, and Yokohama in 1867.[17] Cole's letters do not specify his occupation. While some of Cole's praise for the Pacific Mail steamers makes him look almost like an employee, he also offers some criticism and seems to have had no background in shipping per se. He probably worked as a trader, as he regularly mentioned the prices of various goods and talked in some depth about processes tied to silk production.

Cole's choice to write for Bell in the late 1860s was probably partially connected to the *Elevator*'s place among the (very few) black newspapers in the West; his extended travel writing simply would not have found a place, for example, in the competing San Francisco black newspaper, the *Pacific Appeal*, which, at some points in the late 1860s, fell to being little more than an ad sheet built around bits of Masonic material and a smattering of news. Cole also seems to have known Bell reasonably well, as Bell, several years Cole's senior, had also attended New York City's African Free Schools and already attained local prominence in New York by the 1830s. They certainly knew each other during the 1860s, and Cole wrote, for example, in his 29 November 1867 letter, that he was sending his work to Bell in part as "a simple turn of gratitude for your many past kindnesses to me."

The intent of Cole's letters and their sociopolitical contexts are much clearer than Cole's biographical circumstances. Written during the early years of Reconstruction, most of his letters were published prior to the passage of the Fifteenth Amendment. This meant that, in addition to appearing next to debates about the best way to gain black male suffrage, Cole's work was published alongside complex and often negative discussions of California's Chinese American population, who fear-mongering racists argued would get the vote with (or soon after) black men. Black press representations of this other Asian—and Othered Asian—group shaped the reception and content of Cole's commentary on the Japanese. Arnold Shankman rightly reports that "from 1880 to 1935 almost every time the Chinese were mentioned in the black press, it was in connection with intrigue, prostitution, murder, the sale of opium or children for money, fan tan games, lotteries, smuggling, superstitious practices, shootings, or tong wars" and accurately traces these later depictions to those of the 1860s and 1870s (15). For California blacks in specific, Chinese immigrants presented "serious job competitors" as well as deeply "foreign" additions to broader American discussions over race including debates over suffrage (8). While a few *Elevator* correspondents (like Jennie Carter) attempted to greet Chinese Americans with some open-mindedness, as Shankman concludes, "Even Philip Bell . . . who tried to see positive elements[,] reluctantly concluded that the Asians were people whose 'habits, customs, modes of living, manner of worship (faith or religion it cannot be called) are all at variance with our ideas'" (5). This meant that there was a large-scale shift from antebellum depictions of the Chinese and Chinese immigrants "as an exotic, curious spectacle," in Helen Jun's words, to, again in Jun's language (building from the work of Nayan Shah), "'a way of knowing' Chinatown as an alien space of filth, disease and contamination" (1049, 1051). In turn, as Jun argues, the black press in California "consistently narrated the cultural and moral underdevelopment of the Chinese in an effort to distance blacks from the dangerous implications of anti-Chinese Legislation that occupied the political discourse of California" and to create opportunities for the practice of "performing heteronormativity" in depictions of African Americans and so also stronger positions for blacks vis-à-vis American citizenship (1058, 1054).[18]

Cole certainly used his depictions of the Japanese to perform his own kind of herteronormativity: he consistently—as in his 10 January 1868 *Elevator* letter—referred to "the Americans here" without any kind of racial

distinction and did not talk in any depth about "colored society in Yokohama" until his sixth letter (21 February 1868). He uniformly positioned
himself among "modern" westerners, and he engaged in a range of stereotypes—from referring to a representative of the Japanese soldier class as
"a two sworded man" to listing a series of "the evil characteristics of the
Japanese," which ranged from the assertion that they were "deceptive in
the major degree" to the claim that, "like all Eastern nations, the Japanese
are unboundedly lascivious, they have no idea of such a thing as common
decency in speech before the female sex" and "at no time are either men
or women ashamed of exposing their nudity to the four winds" (31 July
1868, 24 June 1870). Cole also occasionally abused the Chinese immigrants
living in Yokohama in ways similar to the black press's attacks on Chinese
immigrants in the United States—noting, for example, that "just as you
see the Chinaman in California, just as he is here: coining money by any
means in his power, and sending it to the flowery land, to be exchanged for
an import to Japan of rice and counterfeit dollars" and that "the Chinese,
although they have had for many years the benefit of European instruction
. . . are not up to the Japanese in daily European advancement" (24 June
1870, 20 September 1867).

But the distinction Cole draws in this last comment illustrates how far
some of his remarks fall from the rubric of "Black Orientalism."[19] Beyond
simply distinguishing between the Japanese and both the Chinese and Chinese American immigrants—albeit in deeply Eurocentric, paternalistic,
and often stereotypical ways—Cole offered a range of much more positive
comments about Japan. Several fall under the general rubric of travel writing and are reminiscent of both the "sights and sounds" approach discussed
in chapter 2 and the antebellum sense of China "as an exotic, curious spectacle" Jun notes (1049). He repeatedly waxed rhapsodic over "the beauty of
the scenery"—from "the valley streams of cool water" to the "profusion of
verdure, noble forests, and manifold plants, thousands of which are as yet
unknown to the students of botany in the Western world"—and claimed,
for example, that "Flowers of a thousand different hues, fruits of a manifold
variety, singular in all their aspects, taste and prolificness [sic], are to be
found in this second Eden of the East" (6 December 1867). In his 29 May
1868 letter, he even included a poem he composed "in praise" of Mt. Fuji—
part of which tells of how the mountain is "Covered with living green, /
Tufted with moss clad coats, / Like a thousand beauties seem." Cole also

praised the "common people" of Japan—again, in a Eurocentric rhetoric of quaintness—as, in his 31 July 1868 description of the inhabitants of the town of Haramachida, which had "the appearance of cleanliness throughout" and was both "genial" and "ready at a moment's notice to see the stranger alighted."

However, at other moments, Cole offered a more egalitarian—if still racially inflected and massively generalized—sense of the Japanese. In his 10 January 1868 letter, he called the Japanese "a quick, clear-sighted people." In a section entitled "Their Analogies to the Foreigners" in his 27 May 1870 letter, he not only marked *himself* as one of the "Foreigners," but asserted that the Japanese "eat, drink, sleep, dress, buy, sell, borrow, len[d], cheat, steal, and dissemble upon the same principle as the foreigner does" and argued that "the Japanese is a man fitted for an excursion from pole to pole, without fear of meeting an impediment." While the same column referred to a racially essentialized "representative" Japanese man as having "a tongue so oily, that an electric eel would find it difficult to pass over it," Cole also found the Japanese "deeply thinking even to within a hair's breath of infinity" and asserted "my sincere regard for a people so progressive." Cole even noted, in his 22 May 1868 letter, that he could "fully imagine the feelings of the [Japanese] Princes and their retainers, when seeing the foreign [Euro-American] ministers and their attendants passing over the time-honored highway to the palaces of the Mikado. The very thought of foreigners daring to attempt what they deem a sacriledge, was more than doubly sufficient to stir up all that murderous courage for which the haughty retainers of Tosa are so justly celebrated."[20]

Cole's wider and more-conflicted representations of Japan and the Japanese may have been the result of a range of factors, including his own almost-unique position as an African American man in a nation that, while he was there, was in the midst of a painful transition. Set in motion in part by Perry's forced opening of Japan's borders, two centuries of rule by the Tokugawa ended after the Boshin War of 1868 and 1869, moving power to a group tied to the imperial court of the teenaged Meiji emperor in what is now known as the Meiji Restoration.[21]

It is tempting to think that *Elevator* readers would have been struck by the visual proximity of Cole's comments on the "reconstruction" of Japan (under a new government and in a newly internationalized context) and items about African Americans' work during Reconstruction (including the battles for suffrage). Cole's second column ran next to a letter supporting U. S. Grant for the presidency and a report of several Emancipation Day celebrations; his sixth, next to a piece headed "Knowledge is Power," on a newly formed black debating society and a report on Peter W. Cassey's San Jose Phoenixonian Institute (California's only secondary school for blacks); his "Notes By the Way," next to Jennie Carter's column on the struggles of San Francisco African Americans for equal access to education; his twelfth, two columns away from a reprinting of the full "Emancipation Proclamation" and next to a large ad for San Francisco's celebration of the sixth anniversary of the Proclamation; his fourteenth, next to a report on black activist James E. M. Gilliard's lecture on "The Future Condition of the Colored Americans," which was delivered to "a large and appreciative audience, composed of both blacks and whites" and was "one of the most brilliant lectures that the public has been favored with."

Beyond the simple visual proximity caused by the *Elevator*'s layout, both Cole and Bell drew some tentative connections between these "reconstructions." Cole's 21 February 1868 letter—the letter that ran next to "Knowledge is Power"—reported that, in considering the shifts in the Japanese government, Americans should remember that "the very methods of civilization exemplify themselves with war"—rhetoric certainly similar to black press depictions of black participation in the American Civil War. His 1 January 1869 letter—the twelfth, so close to the "Emancipation Proclamation"— argued that "our changes from civilization to barbarism are as fast as our progress to the development of greatness. Search history, search ancient, search modern—search to-day's history, and tell the world if to-day's barbarisms may not excel the refinements of this wonderful age." Bell himself "commended" Cole's fifteenth (17 June 1870) letter to readers, saying that "it takes a philosophical and cosmopolitan view of affairs in Japan" and that "the innovations recently introduced, and the progressive spirit of the Japanese, are indications that Japan, like America, is fast losing caste prejudice, and adopting a more humanitarian policy."[22] And instead of opening his 24 June 1870 letter with further discussion of Japan, Cole chose instead to offer extended commentary on the passage of the Fifteenth Amendment as well as deep praise of Senator Hiram Revels.

Arguably, then, on multiple levels, Cole's letters from Japan were also about shaping an African American identity in the United States and especially in the West. Certainly some of Cole's contribution to building that identity came from his significant revisions to "Black Orientalism" and his tentative linkages between Japan and the United States. Some also came implicitly from the narrative positions that Bell constructed for him—and that Cole himself fashioned. In Bell's words, Cole "writes from personal knowledge and experience" and was an "attentive correspondent"; his letters, Bell said, "will well repay a careful perusal" (27 September 1867, 21 August 1868, 22 May 1868). One of Cole's most extended accounts of Japan—his fourteenth letter (27 May 1870)—talks of his "ample opportunity for obtaining a general knowledge of all that appertains to" the Japanese. That letter also says, "It will require the most competent journalist to sum up the data before him of the more than eventful past of the country. My recollection of that past is ever before me." Beyond thus being "the most competent journalist," Cole argued that he could give lessons in diplomacy to American politicians: Cole's comments on Secretary of State Seward opened with "I would say to the Hon. Secretary of State" and proceeded to lecture him not only on what should be done with Japan but also on diplomacy generally. In short, all of Cole's letters—as well as Bell's editorial comments—positioned Cole as an expert.

Beyond all that might be gained from placing a black Californian in the role of foreign policy expert, Cole's commentary also considered—briefly, but also thoughtfully—the formation of black communities that were centered on intellectual elevation within the limits of black expatriate-hood. Cole talked about American and European expatriates in his 17 January 1868 letter, noting that "our every day life is the same the year round . . . getting up and going to the counting-room, inspecting silk, and tasting tea. We are a small community. . . . Few and far between are our enjoyments. Hunting, boating, or riding, after the day's toil is over, sum up our merry pastimes." However, he would not mention the races of his compatriots until his 21 February 1868 letter, when he briefly asserted that "this is the most lonely place for anything like company among intelligent colored people that can be found in all the East. Nothing like a literary man in the whole settlement."[23]

Some of Cole's comments shared a similar sense of homesickness—as, he claimed that when he was writing his *Elevator* letters, "my mind is filled with pleasant ideas, thoughts of my own land, my home, my friends" (29 May 1868). However, Cole's last extant letter (24 June 1870) shifted this sentiment into something closer to full-blown nationalism, reborn (or born) in the black expatriate community in Japan of the pride and hope embodied in the Fifteenth Amendment: "several of us, colored men here, think of turning our steps ere long to the prolific field of labor in the United States. We feel that we cannot sit, tamely looking on and see you preparing to reap the benefits to be derived from the great cause of freedom, without lending a hand in the good work." Aware that some readers might find a Johnny-come-lately quality in the expatriates' return to the United States, Cole continued: "Perhaps many will say, why did we not stay at home and lend a helping hand when needed. . . . I will tell you why. In being where we have been and being where we are in this wide world, we can bring you a knowledge of how mankind is ruled in other spheres, [and] from this knowledge, we will help you to deduce facts for important legislation." In short, Cole promised to help internationalize the black community just as it was fully entering public politics, and he asserted that such international- ization would be a key piece of a political consciousness based on "patience and perseverance, liberal ideas, and that general knowledge that springs from the deep-rooted principles of sound education."

Cole's early letters implicitly—and occasionally explicitly—suggested that his international mobility helped him gain expertise that would posi- tion him as both a national and international citizen and, in turn, through the literature he was creating, help him "elevate" other African Americans. However, his final letter shifted these basic assumptions. Perhaps, it sug- gested, the Fifteenth Amendment would give enough real potential that a black free agent, an internationally mobile African American, would be drawn home; further, it recognized that Cole and his compatriots had not only the kind of mobility it would take to return to the United States but also a wide worldview created by carefully exercising such mobility. That worldview, Cole argued, would be of real value to African Americans in ways beyond the textual.[24]

Given the dearth of information on Cole's post-1870 life, it remains unclear—and probably doubtful—that he was ever to fully share that value in the United States. However, beyond offering a sense of the potential of black literary production in an extremely "unexpected place"—nineteenth- century Japan, published through the still-unexpected conduit of San Fran- cisco—Cole's letters give a template for how one might turn black inter- national mobility into a domestic force within the unique circumstances of the Reconstruction. In this template, black San Francisco became not just a place of settlement, but also a very real entry point to a much wider world.

Building a Black Literary California

In retrospect, Cole's clarion call embodied much of the hope of the Re-construction—hope that remained largely unfulfilled, but was nonetheless central to the self-definition of the black literary communities in northern California and the larger black West. To gain a fuller sense of this unexpected place in nineteenth-century black letters—the place that created Cole's chances to write about Japan—the remainder of this chapter first offers a sense of black attitudes toward (and moves to) Gold Rush and post–Gold Rush California and, in this, a discussion of the early history of San Francisco's black press—a history which is introduced through brief comparative study of two of its founders, William H. Newby and Philip A. Bell. The chapter then turns to a more in-depth consideration of two of the extended community's leading figures, Jennie Carter and Thomas Detter.

Historians regularly point out that there had long been a black presence in California—from the mixed-race groups working with Spanish conquistadors to the Danish–West Indian William Leidesdorff, a key figure in early San Francisco. But the first time African Americans came to the territory in significant numbers was during the Gold Rush.[25] During most of the late 1840s and early 1850s, black newspapers regularly carried information on California; the richest accounts arguably appeared in Frederick Douglass's various newspapers. While more positive reports on the "California Gold Mania," as dubbed by the 6 October 1848 *North Star,* ran regularly, there were also pieces like the 3 August 1849 *North Star*'s "Danger of Gold Seeking!" which bluntly told readers, "Let no man flatter himself that gold is to be gathered without toil and peril" and recounted the vices of mining towns. In this same vein, the 12 October 1849 *North Star*'s "Other Side of the Story" asserted that, while there was "much gold" in California, "in most cases a man can clear but little beyond his board, while the labor is the hardest and most exposing kind." California also figured prominently as the end goal in an 1851 series (mis)titled "Sketches from California" and authored by longtime Buffalo activist Abner H. Francis.[26] (While much of the series was mailed *from* California, it focused much more on Francis's journey *to* California and so said relatively little about the new state—and even less about the African Americans Francis found there before deciding to move further North.)

Francis does assert, in his 30 October 1851 installment, that "Truly, San Francisco is one of the great wonders of the world,"[27] and such claims certainly set the stage for increased African American migration to California (and the West generally) as well as for the germinal work of William H. Newby, to whom a grateful community (that included Peter Cole) presented a gold pen at the 1857 San Francisco black convention. Born in 1828 in Virginia to an enslaved father and a free mother, Newby grew up in Philadelphia, where he was active among the black community's literati (including participating in the Library Company of Colored Persons).[28] He worked as both a barber and daguerreotypist before moving to California in 1851. He threw himself into building black San Francisco through both Masonic and broader political activism, helped found the San Francisco Athenaeum (a literary and debating society) in 1853, and was a driving force behind the conventions held by California African Americans in 1855, 1856, and 1857. His involvement in the 1857 efforts was cut short when he decided to take a position with the French consul to San Francisco, Guillaume Patrice Dillon, who was being transferred to Haiti; Newby's leaving was the occasion for the gift of the gold pen.[29] Newby's major literary efforts in California—beyond the Athenaeum activities—centered around his work with the *Mirror of the Times*. Although, as noted above, only a few issues of the *Mirror* are extant—thus forestalling any in-depth discussion of the ways in which it articulated a sense of the unexpected place of a black literary California—the paper was a key element in the memory of black California's beginnings (as constructed by the later *Pacific Appeal* and *Elevator*).

Nonetheless, some writing of note by Newby has survived: the columns that he wrote for *Frederick Douglass's Paper* under the playful pseudonym "Nubia." As the paper's "San Francisco correspondent," Newby wrote over a dozen "Nubia" letters in the mid-1850s, and all are consciously designed to satisfy what Newby called in his inaugural 22 September 1854 letter "your great interest in all that concerns the welfare of 'our people.'" While the topics of the letters ranged widely—California politics, San Francisco commerce and banking, Chinese immigrants, and even the possibility of annexing Hawaii—they all attempted to construct black San Francisco and the black West generally as places of great promise. Early in his first letter, Newby claimed that "you can have no idea of the progress made by the colored people in this city within the short space of two years"; in his 15 June 1855 letter, he said proudly that "the colored people of this city and, I believe, throughout the State are not surpassed anywhere for energy and enterprise."

Newby's approach relied heavily on representing black San Francisco as a highly civilized location. Some of this work was done comparatively and emphasized eastern ties: when he discussed Thomas M. D. Ward in his 22 September 1854 letter, for example, he spoke not only of an "eminently qualified" minister, but also of the nephew of Samuel Ringgold Ward; when he wrote of J. H. Townsend, his partner in the Athenaeum and (later) the *Mirror*, he marked him specifically as "a regular graduate of one of the Eastern Colleges"; when he considered the city's reading activity, he praised the *Liberator* and especially *Frederick Douglass's Paper.*[30] But as willing as he was to reach the East, Newby first and foremost trumpeted his own community: the Athenaeum, which, according to his 22 September 1854 letter, had collected over 800 volumes and had 70 members; the number of blacks "engaged in mercantile pursuits" who, per his 15 June 1855 letter, "have stores on the business thoroughfares, and are doing good business"; the "colored Masons of this city," who, per his 27 July 1855 letter, "seem to outstrip their brethren in the Atlantic States, in the way of beautiful Lodge Rooms."

Newby was certainly not universally positive about African Americans' experiences in the West. His very first letter noted that "we suffer many deprivations. . . . We have no oath against any white man or Chinaman. We are debarred from the polls"; his 4 May 1855 letter was much more blunt: "The colored people in this State are made the beasts of burden." He recounted in some depth both larger struggles for equal treatment (as in the question of schools) as well as individual struggles (like the abuse the Reverend John Jamison Moore experienced at the hands of other San Francisco educators).

Nor was Newby uniformly laudatory of black westerners themselves— especially in his later letters. His 28 September 1855 account of a com-memoration of British Emancipation, for example, complained that those present spent too much time in "entertainments," especially dancing: "The Negroes, as a race, are remarkably fond of dancing. Let us throw aside these senseless graces and frivolities, and expend the time, and money in improving our minds and dignifying our characters." In the same letter, he worried that the 1855 convention meetings would be "consumed in idle and unprofitable discussion." In his 26 October 1855 letter, he claimed that, while he had "no disposition to speak lightly of religion," it was "almost a matter of impossibility to get together a respectable attendance of colored people in this city, when the object . . . is not to hear a Methodist sermon."

He added that he was "constrained to say that our religious fanaticism has done more to retard our elevation than all other causes combined."

Finally, he was also fully participant in the derogatory rhetoric of anti-Chinese "Black Orientalism"—noting, for example, in his 22 September 1854 letter, that Chinese American immigrants "exhibit a most grotesque appearance" and that "their habits are filthy, and their features totally devoid of expression"; in his 6 April 1855 letter, he claimed "that they are filthy, immoral and licentious." In this, per Jun's analysis of this discursive field generally, Newby's representation of the Chinese immigrants served to emphasize blacks' "normal" and positive character; in his 22 September 1854 letter (ironically soon after the abusive language cited above), he even suggested that the Chinese immigrants "have not friends, unless it is the colored people, who treat every body well, even their enemies." In short, Newby was using his textual presence to attempt to make San Francisco a more expected, more accepted place for African Americans; while his contribution was cut short by his (attempted) move to Haiti and then by his ill health, his work certainly shaped the later black literary San Francisco. Remnants of the *Mirror* group—most notably, Peter Anderson—were key in setting up San Francisco's next black newspaper, the *Pacific Appeal,* which was founded in 1862.[31] And that community was central in bringing west perhaps the single most important figure among the black San Francisco literati: Philip Alexander Bell.

Like Newby, Bell spent his formative years in the urban Northeast in one of the centers of both eastern abolitionism and free black activism, and this undoubtedly contributed to his clear sense of black self-determination (to be achieved in part through print culture and in part through mobility). Born circa 1807 to free black parents in New York City, Bell—as noted above—attended the city's African Free Schools. In an age where smart, young, politically minded men of color often chose the ministry—a career centered on oral performance—Bell confronted a problem that would taunt him throughout his life: a persistent stutter. Previous scholars often explain his turn to writing as a response to his stutter, but Bell actually worked to hone his oral skills, too.[32] Bell's turn to the textual came more from the fact that he saw the written word as something more lasting and, perhaps in the end, more powerful in giving "publicity to our thoughts" (5 October 1839 *Colored American*). He thus became one of the earliest New York supporters of William Lloyd Garrison's *Liberator:* he was formally appointed an agent of the paper in February 1831, and a letter to this effect appeared in the 12 March 1831 *Liberator.* He regularly corresponded with the paper, earned special praise for his success as an agent in the 28 December 1833 issue, and was mentioned in the paper over three dozen times in the early 1830s.

This work, paired with his efforts in organizations like the New York Philomathean Society, early activism in the Colored Convention movement, speeches to groups like the Anti-Slavery Society of New York, and deep community ties made Bell a natural fit for the group that formed the New York *Weekly Advocate*—soon renamed the *Colored American.* As the *Colored American*'s first "General Agent," sometime-editor, and sometime-assistant editor, Bell worked closely with both Samuel Cornish (a Delaware-born minister and boot maker who had established the first two black newspapers—*Freedom's Journal* and the *Rights of All*—in the late 1820s) and Cornish's partner, the *Colored American*'s traveling agent, and later Cornish's successor, Charles Bennett Ray (a Massachusetts-born minister who studied briefly at Wesleyan University before racism forced him out).[33]

Bell weathered Cornish's decision to leave the paper, as well as several shifts in its governing structure and publication schedule. He also continued to develop close friendships with a number of New York black activists, but he was uncompromising in his politics. He engaged in a public fray with Peter Paul Simons, a would-be writer for the *Colored American* who asserted that color prejudice had resulted in his submissions being rejected; Bell maintained, in a 13 January 1838 piece, that Simons was simply a bad writer, a "liar," and a "fool." This attack led him into direct conflict with David Ruggles, then-secretary of the New York Vigilance Committee. Bell sparred with Ruggles and with Gerrit Smith's New-York Anti-Slavery Society in the pages of the *Colored American* in late 1839 and 1840—at one point (in a 5 October 1839 column) boldly telling prominent white abolitionist Smith that "we think we know what course should be pursued to benefit the colored man better than any of our white brethren; our experience tells us that they are not pursuing the right course, and while we so think[,] we shall always freely and without reserve give publicity to our thoughts." These battles seem to have culminated in Bell's resigning from a formal role with the *Colored American,* although, in part because he and Ray were friends, Bell continued to write occasionally for the paper.

He also continued to be active among New York's free blacks.[34] By the time the financially strapped *Colored American* folded in December 1841, Bell had been operating an "intelligence office"—a kind of employment agency—for a number of years, and he continued to be involved in both local and statewide struggles for African American rights. He became especially active in founding New York's "Committee of Thirteen," a group that included longtime activists like James McCune Smith, George T. Downing, and William J. Wilson and that called for a statewide anticolonization convention in 1852, organized several anticolonization meetings in New York City, raised money to aid fugitive slaves, met with Hungarian revolutionary Louis Kossuth during his visit to the city,[35] and even sent money to other similar groups (including the Philadelphia Vigilance Committee) to support their efforts. He served as one of the vice presidents of a marathon anticolonization meeting held at New York's Abyssinian Baptist, and he was regularly asked to serve as secretary for a range of organizations and for gatherings like a July 1853 meeting that featured William Cooper Nell and a young John Mercer Langston.

In part because of this work, in part because Frederick Douglass had grown to respect Bell, and in part because Bell valued Douglass's efforts (especially his attempts to fill the vacuum in the black press created by the failure of the *Colored American*), Bell began writing for *Frederick Douglass's Paper* with some regularity in the early 1850s. Most of Bell's columns were published under the pseudonym "Cosmopolite," and, while they certainly exhibited some of the polemic tendencies of his efforts in the *Colored American,* they were more wide-ranging.[36] Bell's writing as "Cosmopolite" also allows us to trace his growing connections to the West and to California specifically. Bell undoubtedly had closely studied the *Colored American* letters of the white Augustus Wattles[37] and the black "Augustine" (the Pittsburg-based Lewis Woodson, who had interacted with William Jay Greenly) on the (mid)western frontier possibilities for enacting black uplift and perhaps even a black nation. Bell probably also read a range of coverage of the Gold Rush, and he knew several of the few thousand African Americans who moved to California. Among the articles in *Frederick Douglass's Paper,* James R. Starkey's 27 May 1852 letter might have been of especial interest to Bell: it recounted attending a meeting of Bell's Committee of Thirteen (who Starkey referred to as "men of stout hearts and lofty purposes"), described his passage from New York to San Juan and then on to California, and said that he wished that the committee was with him because "a few bombs thrown" by them "would have quite a renovating affect." Given Bell's consistent support of the black press, his writing for Douglass's papers, and his avid reading, it is very likely that he also saw

Abner Francis's letters. Bell also formed a friendship with William Newby: in his 20 June 1863 sketch of Newby, Bell identified Newby as "Nubia," said his columns "added brilliancy" to Douglass's paper, and noted that he and Newby had become acquainted when Newby stopped in New York in late 1857 on his way to Haiti and had corresponded regularly thereafter.[38]

As early as April 1855, Bell was quoting from letters from a friend in Portland, Oregon, in his columns for *Frederick Douglass's Paper*.[39] In a piece published in the 31 August 1855 *Frederick Douglass's Paper,* Bell shared extracts from "a batch of letters from California" including one from "Robert B——s" (Robert Banks, who would later write for the *Elevator* as "Il Roberto") and another from "J. H. T." (Jonas Townsend, soon to be editor of the *Mirror*). But the most interesting of the "batch" was attributed to "Cosmopolite, Jr., a perfect chip in ever respect"; the historian Rudolph Lapp identifies "Cosmopolite, Jr." as Bell's son Zadock.[40]

It thus seems likely that his son as well as friends and acquaintances like Newby and Townsend encouraged Bell to come to California. Bell himself was fairly silent on his reasons, but by mid-1860, he was settled in San Francisco, where the federal census-taker listed him as fifty-one years old and a native of New York.[41] Given his rich background, Bell was an obvious choice for a leadership role when the community decided to found the *Pacific Appeal,* and, along with Peter Anderson, he was key in producing its early issues.

The first issue of the *Appeal,* with Anderson as "proprietor" and Bell as editor, noted that the paper's title meant that it would "enter the field boldly, fearlessly, but with dignity and calmness to *Appeal* for the rights of the Colored Citizens of this State." A brief look at the contents of the first issue—from a series of petitions (especially on the right of testimony) to a laudatory piece on the San Francisco Literary Institute (a successor to the Athenauem)—alerts readers to a sense of California and the larger black West that echoed and expanded upon the complex hopes asserted by Newby in *Frederick Douglass's Paper*. But Bell also argued that the *Appeal* marked the maturing of a growing history—both his own and the state's. He noted his own work with "that father of Colored Editors, the late Rev. Samuel E. Cornish," as well as his experiences with Charles Ray and James McCune Smith of the *Colored American,* and he reminded readers that his colleague Peter Anderson had been "one of the founders and a contributor to that pride of Colored Californians, '*The Mirror of the Times*.'"[42] Several columns in the next few issues treated previous California conventions and activities; these historical works include an extended discussion of the *Mirror* in the 7 June 1862 issue.

Far from Newby and Francis's tentative discussions of pioneers, Bell was arguing that the *Pacific Appeal* and black Californian efforts of the early 1860s were direct successors to not only the community work of black westerners in the 1850s, but also to eastern efforts to create a national black press and, through it, a national black literature. Tutored by the founder of the first black newspaper (*Freedom's Journal*) and schooled in the offices of the *Colored American* by key black activists, Bell could "enter the field" not only "boldly, fearlessly" and "with dignity and calmness" but also with history on his side. Bell's assertion that black California was a place with real history, though, came to fullest flower in a series he initiated under his penname "Cosmopolite." Early in the *Appeal*'s existence, feuding between Anderson and Bell forced Bell from the editor's chair, but he continued writing for the paper occasionally and began a series titled "The Colored Men of California" in the 23 May 1863 issue. Featuring biographies of pioneering figures like Francis and Newby, as well as Thomas M. D. Ward and Jennie Carter's future husband Dennis Drummond Carter, the series emphasized, per its introduction, that African Americans "have been among the pioneers of civilization" in the state and beyond. Bell knew he was treading into an unexpected place—"the acquirements and abilities of colored men in California are not generally known, and where known are not fully appreciated, nor publicly acknowledged." He also knew that such work was deeply necessary, as "we have men among us who would shine in any sphere, and shed luster on any position, however high." While he humbly claimed that he would "not enter the field of history, not attempt biographical memoirs of individuals," he did both regularly throughout the series, in large part to show "our readers . . . that ostracised [*sic*] and persecuted as we are, we have among us men, who in any community, would be recognized as representative men."

Bell repeatedly returned to this sense of the region's promise, history, and place in national struggles in his later *Appeal* pieces, and it became central to every issue of the *Elevator,* the weekly newspaper he founded in early 1865. While a (desperately needed) full-length study of the *Elevator*—like the similarly absent and needed full biography of Bell—is beyond the scope of this study, a brief examination of the various prospectus documents Bell published in the earliest extant issues of the *Elevator* clarifies his extension of the concept of a black literary West and outlines the context in which members of his *Elevator* group—including Cole, Carter, and Detter—wrote. Bell asserted, in a paragraph under the title "Our Name" published in several issues including the 5 May 1865 *Elevator*, that "our Name is indicative of our object; we wish to elevate the oppressed of all nations and of every clime to the position of manhood and freedom. We wish to place all mankind on a level; not by lowering them to one standard, but by elevating them in virtue, intelligence and self-reliance on a level with the most favored of the human race. We are levelers, not to level down, but to level up." Playing on both one of the latest technological advances and his own metaphor of mobility to define his sense of the textual as an aid to rising,[43] Bell implicitly and explicitly argued that the West—and the nation—needed a textual leveler and that San Francisco was well positioned to provide such.

But if his metaphors of rising offered a next step in the process of germinal mobility that had brought blacks to the West (and that Newby had advanced), the paper's motto described where the community should stand. In the same 5 May 1865 issue (in a snippet titled "Our Motto"), Bell said, "We claim full 'Equality before the Law,' we desire nothing more, we will be satisfied with nothing less." This motto certainly played with the word "before," suggesting both that blacks needed to receive equal treatment when standing *in front of* the law, but also that blacks might need to take their equality temporally *before* the law caught up to that higher ideal. In this, Bell's sense of equality was deeply tied to the ability to move within the public sphere. While he dismissed "social equality"—by which he meant forms of social intercourse like friendship and courtship—as "a bug-bear, a hideous phantom raised by political necromancers to frighten the people from their duty," he offered a broad canvas of the sectors where equality must happen: "We do not expect, because we trade with a merchant, to visit his house, and mingle with his family; nor do we invite him to our house, and make him a welcome guest; neither can worshiping in the same church, riding in the same car, or voting at the same ballot box, make men associates."

To gain "equality before the law," Bell argued (as he had in the *Colored American, Frederick Douglass's Paper*, and the *Pacific Appeal*), the black West and the nascent black nation needed the textual. His vision demanded a wide approach: "We do not," he wrote in "Our Position" (which followed the pieces above), "confine our correspondents to our own peculiar views." Bell did not confine them to his San Francisco location, either: he published writers from "Private L'Overture" (J. J. Spellman) in New York City to Peter

Cole in Japan, writers spread throughout the state of California, and writers throughout the larger West—from Thomas Detter in the Idaho Territory to a group of correspondents in black British Columbia. While Bell himself traveled throughout the state and recounted several of these trips in the *Elevator*, he grew to view his correspondents as extensions of the paper's itinerancy. To further deepen the well on which he could draw, Bell worked as an agent for the New York-based Hamilton family (especially their *Weekly Anglo-African*) and later for William Still's landmark *The Underground Rail Road*, he fostered exchanges with black newspapers across the country (not only bringing eastern and southern clippings to his western readers but also ensuring that items from California appeared in eastern papers like the *Christian Recorder*), and he served more and more as an elder statesman of black journalism (aiding younger editors through advice and fostering the growth of correspondents toward editing their own papers).[44] He even included material on white periodicals, and seems to have developed at least a cordial relationship with the San Francisco-based *Overland Monthly* (which aided white writers like Bret Harte in building careers).[45] In short, he worked not only to place black California on the literary landscape, but also to assert that it might be a literary center.

"ALWAYS FAITHFUL"
Jennie Carter and Germinal Mobility

Though she was a major figure in the black literary California that Bell worked for, Jennie Carter was essentially written out of African American literary history until 2007, and even now most of her early life remains in shadow. Born circa 1830, she claimed to have lived in New York, New Orleans, Kentucky, Wisconsin, and Illinois before coming further west in the early 1860s. After the death of or separation from her first husband, a Mr. Correll, Carter married Dennis Drummond Carter of Nevada City, California, on 29 August 1866.[46] Dennis Carter, a musician and music teacher who had played in Frank Johnson's Philadelphia-based band for several years before moving to Gold Rush California, was well connected within northern California's black community. The earliest mention of Jennie Carter after their marriage demonstrated her interest in the public literary and appeared in a short, recently discovered item in the 19 December 1866 Nevada City *Daily Transcript*: at a performance of various town bands and choruses benefiting her husband's musical and music education efforts, "Mrs. Carter" offered "a humorous poem on reconstruction, in which the 'city dads' received sundry hits about the condition of the side-walks, and other city matters." While this poem does not seem to survive, certainly the play on "reconstruction" might have been picked up by some in her audience; some might even have considered, beyond the "humorous," the ways in which a national rebuilding might be tied to the local and deeply domestic shifts in and around those "side-walks"—on which African Americans hoped to walk equally.[47]

Carter sent the first of what would total over seventy pieces to the *Elevator* in June 1867, and it implicitly argued that both the *Elevator* and her own texts would be literary agents in domesticating the West and so also culminations of the germinal mobility like that considered in the earlier chapters of this work. Writing under the penname "Mrs. Ann J. Trask," she told editor Bell that, "I have been a reader of your excellent paper for some time, and thank you for your efforts on behalf of our people." But, she added, now that "our children and grandchildren are readers, and to encourage reading," Bell "should have in each number a short story for them" (3). The repeated "our" was a marker of shared blackness, but also a marker of location, for while Bell regularly included national items, he placed a clear emphasis on the black West and specifically black California. Carter's columns quickly went beyond juvenile stories, and even she noted—at the end of her second column—that "I commenced writing for children, and have wound up writing for everybody" (5). That said, her earliest columns focused heavily on advancing domestic principles—helping children (and adults) deal with death, color prejudice, and anger. She advocated observing "three things. . . . First, keep your head cool and calm. Second, keep your feet dry and warm. Third, keep your heart free of anger" (7–8). When these early letters spoke about specific locations—including her own portion of Nevada City, which she renamed "Mud Hill"—they emphasized the potential to generalize Carter's comments beyond specific locations. Bell's own editorial notes did the same: in her 13 September 1867 column, for example, Carter wrote of the generic but local "Mrs. A." and condemned her gossip and tale-telling; Bell appended a postscript that reads: "We have such people in San Francisco. In fact, wretches of that kind can be found anywhere" (9).

However, even though she continued to hope that the lessons in her letters would be generalizable to a large variety of locations, Carter began talking more and more about specific places. In this, her 17 January 1868 *Elevator* letter represented a pair of key shifts: she offered both a series of telling pictures of the land around her home and a close description of that home. A bit mockingly, she told readers, "In Nevada City, there are Cayote [*sic*] Hill, Lost Hill, Aristocracy Hill, Hangman's Hill, Piety Hill, with Tribulation Trail leading to it"; given the "unceasing rain" and snow they had experienced, she said, "every one of these are mud hills to-day" (20). After this heavily equalizing statement—naming all of the neighborhoods that marked class and racial stratification in her hilly community "mud"— she said that "Mr. Trask has a mud hill of his own, covered with peach trees, and among them a brown cottage with six rooms, and there Mrs. Trask lives. The first room is furnished with a melodeon and contra basso; the second with a trumbone [*sic*] and cornet; the third with a violincillo [*sic*] and a bugle; the fourth with a guitar and two canaries; the fifth with a violin and dog; the sixth with an old fiddle and cat. So you see we live in style, which no doubt all will be pleased to hear, as a person's surroundings determine the amount of weight they are to carry in this world" (20).

While certainly not the "neat" cottage of the mid-nineteenth-century domestic idyll—a fact emphasized by Carter's repeated earlier jokes about her lack of housekeeping ability[48]—this home *is* domesticity's ideal of comfort: the Carters live surrounded by the music and animals they love, but have not fallen into the materialism Carter's last ironic words condemn. They are settled—properly—as a result of their germinal domestic mobility.

In stark contrast to her humor in this section of the letter, though, are her words about the area landscape: "Were you ever in the Sierra Nevadas? Now is the time to appreciate their beauty, covered as they are with their mantle of white, the tall pines casting shadows when the sun shines. From some of the peaks can be seen the Sacramento Valley, now presenting a grand appearance of one vast lake" (20).

A clear sense of the results of sentimental, germinal mobility emerges from all of these passages—despite their differences in tone—and these values were central to Carter's conception of the West. Carter saw the region as filled with natural potential, but also as a battleground between true domestic settlers and those who would separate the lush Sierra Nevadas into boundaried and stratified hills because they valued possessions and rank more than beauty and harmony. Carter ran this thread through several of her later columns. Consider her 15 January 1869 account of her trip from

Nevada City to Sacramento via the tiny town of Colfax. She confidently asserted that "the scenery is unsurpassed, and would please the eye of the artist. Bear [R]iver and the road winding up the hills like the old Roman Labyrinth . . . a small streak of silver, and the road just passed like a long serpent"; the "many beautiful towns" that "dot the line of the road from Colfax to Sacramento" were also wonderous, as "all of them" were "centres of civilization to their inhabitants" (55, 56). However, the stands along the way that sold food and liquor—"what the male part of our company called 'smiles,' (and to me a misnomer—better call it tears)"—raised the specter of intemperance and ruin; while the small towns all contained "some happy homes, if you can judge by the exterior," she noted that they also held "some aching hearts too, to be read from the signs where they dispense 'smiles.' . . . While many are 'smiling' there, in lonely homes sit women and children in tears" (55–56). Similarly, in a series of letters on San Francisco published in the summer of 1868 "to give . . . my impression of this great city," Carter moved between recognizing "native talent" and expressing concern over how African Americans in the city were "cut up into factions and cliques" (38). In each case, Carter saw the intemperate (widely defined to invoke those greedy for status, power, money, and lascivious pleasures like alcohol consumption) as a threat to the black West—a threat she hoped her texts could expose and thwart.

Carter saved her praise for locations that seemed to model her sense of a black western domesticity that resulted from a version of germinal mobility that did not forget its roots. The small town of Oroville, whose "people . . . are imbued with taste," drew some of her most glowing comments because of "the improvements made, the regularity of the Streets—the comfortable yards full of fruit trees and flowers" (74). California on a larger scale, Carter argued, suffered because "the neatness and thrift of New England farming is entirely overlooked. The money making, an ever restless feeling that actuates people of every pursuit in California is a great drawback to the prosperity of the country. When farmers come to California to remain permanently, purchase small farms, build good houses and barns, substantial fences, set out plenty of fruit and ornamental trees, adding year by year improvements, having schoolhouses easy of access, churches within reasonable distances; then this state will surpass every other in the Union" (74). Carter had similar praise and raised similar questions about Carson City, Nevada, which she visited in late 1873. She wrote that she found "Carson beautiful for situation, surrounded by mountains whose sides channeled, broken and abrupt brown and grey, make a formidable defence [*sic*] to the beautiful valley in which this city is located" and that she could "imagine no more pleasing picture in early spring when nature puts on her dress of green tha[n] this valley and city" (113). She also praised the new stone state buildings, which she suggested would "be as enduring as the mountains," but she nonetheless noted that "the rushing spirit of the Pacific Coast is apparent" in Carson City, "where building [is] for the present and no heed for the future is taken, consequently many cheap buildings are to be seen here" (114, 113).

Her sense of the West's potential was perhaps best embodied in her 15 January 1869 description of Sacramento:

In Sacramento, some of the company (thinking of our Granite mountains left behind,) said "What a sea of mud." Not so thought I, but what a city of "ants;" how they labored through the floods and flames, and made their "hills" on the low plains, and oh the dirt they have carried, load after load, until they can say to the waters, "Thus far shalt thou go and no farther." I can compare them to the coral insect who commenced his work under water and toiled on year after year, century after century, until at last a beautiful island rose from the depths of the sea. And so they labored on through all discouragements, being weak, yet fainting not by the way; and they have their reward, a beautiful city above the floods. And how it would gladden the hearts of their ancestors in Eastern homes to see the beautiful gardens as I saw them on the 1st day of January, 1869, filled with rose bushes in full bloom. (56)

Having settled into her own "Mud Hill" to see roses blooming amid a nearby black community in which she found "the public spirit . . . pervades all hearts" led—along with the Emancipation Day celebration at Sacramento that offered the occasion for this column—to "an uplifted heart, and bowed head" (56).

Carter was well aware of the multiple factors that could destroy this ideal—or even stop communities from ever coming close to it. She was unrelenting in demanding personal responsibility and in linking germinal mobility with temperance (and, like Greenly, saw temperance not simply as an issue tied to alcohol but as a way of life). Her 9 April 1869 account of a walk she took on her birthday is most instructive. She visited "a region round Mud Hill that I have not explored" (65). She found a solitary "miner's cabin, situated in one of the most romantic places imaginable—sheltered between two large hills, and nearly surrounded, with one by its south side open, and a creek whose running waters made ceaseless music" (65–66). There she met a "feeble old man" who told of coming West to find gold, turning to gambling for entertainment in the winter, turning to "Old Bourbon" as he gambled, and drunkenly losing all he had gained—even though he had a family back East that he was responsible for supporting (66). Too ashamed to contact his family again and addicted to both "cards and whiskey," he claimed that "I shall never hear from or see them again, for whiskey has nearly done its work"; he could only "hope" to "die here" (67).

Carter's next letter advanced these arguments even further: coming upon a group of girls who were talking about what would happen when they were grown and married with children, she recounted how one said, "my children shall never drink whiskey," startling Carter so much that she "involuntarily turned to view the face" of the girl (68). There, she saw "what God had never designed should mar the face of childhood—sadness—unutterable sadness!" (68). The girl's parents, Carter learned later, came "to California from Connecticut seven years ago, both endowed with superior mental and physical constitutions, with high hopes and considerable money," but fell victim to "champagne suppers" (68). The mother's death and the father's fall into being "a confirmed drunkard" left the girl and two siblings "without a protector" (68).

But Carter was unwilling to oversimplistically ascribe the failure to reach the promise of the black West to intemperate individuals alone. As she continued to write for the *Elevator,* she spoke more and more about sociopolitical limits imposed by the dominant white culture, in which intemperance was writ large. The 13 March 1868 *Elevator* published her account of two young free African American cousins in Virginia—one of whom was taken into slavery when his parents and grandparents died and the other of whom was taken by his mother to Philadelphia in hopes of remaining free. The column ended by praying that the free Philadelphia cousin would one day see his (now formerly) enslaved Virginia cousin again. Indirectly commenting on the hundreds of "Information Wanted" ads being placed in black newspapers across the nation by family members trying to reunite with relatives sold away during slavery, Bell appended a note to the end of this column, saying, "The above is not a tale of fiction. We can vouch for the truth of it, although we have never heard of it until the present time.

We know the survivor of the cousins . . . the one who escape the grip of the slavemongers" (29). Bell did indeed know "the survivor": it was Dennis Carter, and thus Jennie Carter's tale of the love between the two young boys, a love savaged by slavery, was also a story of how, while the mobility of escape had saved her own husband, it had been denied to a child about whom he cared deeply.

Carter's 25 December 1868 column—perhaps one of her most stunning—again took Dennis Carter as its subject and began with her trademark veiling of the important in a depiction of the minute (and even briefly humorous). What began as a joke about a husband convinced that he was taller than he really was quickly turned: "'Six feet two inches'; so said Mr. Trask to an inquiry in regard to his height. I told him I thought he was mistaken; he said not, for he was measured, and had his measurement recorded at Harper's Ferry in the summer of '51" (53). Her husband was located at Harper's Ferry because of the immense mobility he gained through his role in Frank Johnson's famed touring band, but, as Carter next describes, that mobility was deeply threatening to white southerners: along with other band members, Dennis Carter "was asked who he belonged to, if he had any scars upon him, and then measured, and told he would have to stay over night as no colored person could travel after 4 o'clock P.M." (53). Forced, in essence to register in a way similar to that Polly Wash, John Berry Meachum, and Cyprian Clamorgan faced in St. Louis, and that Greenly family members experienced in New Albany, Carter rebelled: "He stood up, and in his wrath I guess he was six feet three inches, he pronounced curses upon that State. They then threatened him with the lash, and he told them to proceed, that the first one who laid hands on him should die. And their courage was no greater then than years after, when John Brown, with a handful of men frightened the whole State, for they told Mr. Trask, they knew he was a free nigger, he was so independent; and they have long ere this suffered all the curses Mr. Trask pronounced upon them." His mobility, threatened—indeed, even his very chance of going "up," challenged—Dennis Carter fought to raise himself an inch. That he did rise was confirmed by the column's conclusion: "Born free, living in Philadelphia, associating with men and women, respected as a gentleman, the insult will *never* be forgotten. And when anyone asks him his height he will say six feet two inches, and think of that occurrence" (53).

Carter's later columns consistently articulated the ways in which broader social policy and institutionalized racism continued to limit black

germinal mobility, especially in the West; in short, she often suggested implicitly, the insults carried out against her husband before the Civil War
were still present. She voiced strong dissent on California's inequities in
education, roundly criticized the failures of the mixed-race board who was
charged with founding the Livingstone Institute (planned to be the first
black secondary school in northern California), regularly drew connections between current Democrats and the anti-Lincoln/pro-slavery Democrats of the 1850s and early 1860s, condemned factionalism in the black
community, recognized that whites' attacks on Chinese Americans looked
in some ways like their attacks on blacks, and argued forcefully to expand
the railroad system (which she saw as a democratic endeavor that would
allow greater germinal mobility).

Like Cole and many of her contemporaries, she prayed especially for the
ratification of the Fifteenth Amendment. She saw California's refusal to support the amendment[49] as a marker of "intelligent people . . . gulled by lying
politicians," but also as a deep moral failure of the West—because she could
"never forget those near and dear to us, who so bravely died, and never can
. . . be reconciled to traitors" (80). Lest her readers misunderstand just what
was at stake in gaining the vote, she cast such in terms of specific movement forward: "Will not we awake one of these days and hear the welcome
cry of the Fifteenth Amendment [as] an established fact? Shall we not see
our men walking boldly up to the polls by that Act, saying, 'I am a man in
God's image, and a free man with his privileges" (80–81). When she heard
that Georgia had ratified the amendment (and that Iowa would soon fin-
ish the process), she wrote that "I can't keep still, no use trying" (84). She
called for a statewide celebration at Sacramento, and asked "every town,
village, city and mining camp in the State" to "send her new-made citizens
with banners, transparencies, and torches" in a grand "Procession . . . the
grandest and best California has ever seen" (84–85). That massive exercise
of mobility—coming to Sacramento and marching down its streets, just
as she imagined black men would march to the polls—would allow "the
mountains [to] greet the plains" and let "San Francisco join with her sister
cities" (85).[50] Carter's greatest fear was that the race would—because of its
own choices, because of external forces, or because of a combination of
both—stand still or even move backward. "This state of things," she argued
passionately, "cannot exist" (70). "We must be aware," she asserted in her
7 May 1869 letter, "that the 15th Amendment is the last thing that will be
done for us by the so called 'ruling powers,' and if we remain inactive our

children will curse our apathy when we are slumbering in our graves, and wonder why we did not bestir ourselves when action was so much needed, and its effects would have been so telling" (69).

Carter did such work after having shifted her penname permanently from "Mrs. Trask" to "Semper Fidelis"—Latin for "always faithful." Each and every column she wrote with this penname—including those discussed above—thus ended with the assertion of her continuing faithfulness to the cause of black elevation.

In her calls for a grand procession, Carter was articulating a kind of postgerminal, postsettlement mobility. She was talking about the kinds of ever-vigilant, ever-rising movement (and the character of a movement) that would be necessary once African Americans were in the West in order to ensure the continuance of the kind of domestic settling she had begun to find with Dennis Carter. What is noticeably absent from this struggle is the figure of the itinerant: there is no Stiles or Weaver, no individual person marked as traveling from town to town to help ensure that those nascent communities became proper centers of faith, domesticity, and nascent black nationalism. This absence is even more striking given Carter's ties to the Reverend Thomas M. D. Ward and the paper's connections to both Ward and the Reverend John Jamison Moore, both ardent supporters (and sometime-practitioners) of itinerancy.[51] That said, the *idea* of an itinerant force linking communities over space (and even over time) was integral to Carter's worldview.

That force was the textual—and was embodied specifically in the *Elevator*. With the mobility of elevation writ in its very title, the *Elevator*, Carter argued, could spread both the news and the "good news" to every community where it had subscribers. Read in this light, her very first letter not only articulates the paper's spread to "children and grandchildren," but also asserts its duty to reach those populations (3). Carter repeatedly spoke of the power of the textual—as when she asserted that "my books are my fortune . . . and I treat them as dear friends, use them kindly" (80).

The representation of herself as a reader is no accident. She commented regularly on finding information through reading, and she prayed that others would recognize as much power in the act as she did—as when she told Bell (but also told readers) in her 7 May 1869 column that "I have read your earnest appeal to our people on the subject of organization, and I earnestly hope they will not let it pass unheeded" (69). She also spoke—directly and concretely on several occasions—of receiving letters from readers and shaping her columns around such (30, 88, 91). Because of this exchange—and the *Elevator*'s power in allowing it—even after she told readers that she was "afflicted with rheumatism, and find writing more painful than anything else I do," she continued to send columns to the paper (91). So deep and faithful was her commitment to the *Elevator* that, in response to a call to support the paper from area ministers and activists, she wrote a 7 February 1868 letter under her own name soliciting aid for the *Elevator*—specifically from other women readers like herself—because she (half-jokingly) found nothing in Thomas Ward "or Rev. J. J. Moore's theology to prevent women giving as the 'Lord has prospered them.'" For the next several issues, the *Elevator* ran Carter's letter—generally under the heading "Mrs. Carter's Plan"—with a list of those who contributed; a Sacramento woman calling herself only "Mary" even wrote in, "lamenting" that Carter had had to make her plea because she felt that subscribers should have simply stepped forward on their own, as "the communications of our venerable sister, 'Semper Fidelis,' are alone worth the price of a subscription" (25n4).

Certainly Carter's interest in spreading the word of (and through) the *Elevator* was motivated in part by her desire for broader communal sociopolitical activism (of the type for which Bell urged "organization"); within this, she also, of course, hoped to spread her messages of temperance and education. But Carter was not interested solely in making the news and commentary of the day mobile. Rather, she saw a key function of the *Elevator*—and several of her own columns—as making *memory* mobile, and, through such spreading and sharing, ensuring that the black readers of the *Elevator* did not forget just what "rising" meant. Her columns about her husband's experiences, of course, addressed these issues—as did a number of letters that described slavery in Kentucky and New Orleans, celebrated local pioneering efforts and town-building, depicted Emancipation Day festivals, and offered (seemingly) autobiographical accounts. Such history, Carter felt, would keep black mobility ever germinal—rather than allowing the race to fall into the land of rootless mobility writ in figures like the "feeble" old miner she met on her birthday.

This philosophy was most clearly embodied in a pair of texts Carter sent in the summer of 1872 after the release of William Still's *Underground Rail Road,* a book that carefully recorded and narrated Still's years aiding fugitive slaves (as well as the escapes of other fugitives around the nation). Philip Bell was the Pacific Coast's main agent for the book—which was sold on subscription—and he actively marketed it, published excerpts from it, and even seems to have encouraged correspondents to write about it. Carter's initial response, which began with the expected notice of the "pleasure I enjoyed in glancing at Mr. Still's book," fit neatly with Bell's push to get what, in essence, was a history of one kind of black elevation (through the exercise of the mobility of escape) into black western hands (104).

But Carter then broadened her scope considerably, asserting that *The Underground Rail Road* "had awakened many incidents in my mind of escapes from slavery in another road not named in this book, and which if written out would make a volume of thrilling horror, and with now and then a note of joy" (104). "Oh!" she exclaimed, "how often have I wished someone competent would write out the history of the 'Underground Railroad,' from the Mississippi River to Chicago; for hundreds of slaves escaped from Missouri, and if not retaken before reaching Chicago, they found asylum in Canada" (104). The rest of this 17 May 1873 column, as well as her 19 July 1873 letter,[52] certainly celebrated the ways in which Still's texts—and the specific memories it articulated—were traveling west. However, she also expanded the story to reflect the ways in which those in the early West aided the enslaved in taking their mobility, and she thus turned a South-to-Northeast story into a more fully national story.

Carter's two Underground Railroad columns also, though, specifically placed *her* as an agent of change and as a mobile free woman in the northern Midwest. The later column spoke of how she set up a community meeting to aid a fugitive who had been directed to her door by the "President of the anti-slavery society of Chicago" (106). But the 17 May column involved Carter much more directly: she wrote of how, resting in a chair in front of her home in Wisconsin just north of the Illinois line (and holding a baby that represents one of the central mysteries of her biography),[53] she closed her eyes for a moment; on opening them, she saw "a woman with scarcely clothing to cover herself and a baby not three months old, and both nearly famished. She told me to hide her quick for her master was in town. . . . Six long weeks she had been on her way from Canton, Mo., traveling only by night and all the time in fear of pursuit, living as best she could by milking cows; hungry and nearly naked, with feet bleeding she came to me" (104).[54]

Carter "believed the Lord had led her to me"—certainly a rewriting of the agency removed from a slave by a master—and knew she had to act quickly and decisively. She hid the fugitives in her cellar for three days, and then, carrying her own infant, hitched up her buggy, hid the mother and child in it, "rode out of town, just at evening when it was dark," and "drove twenty-eight miles to a Quaker family . . . who would care for" the fugitive mother (and her child) "as she cared for her baby; for to save it from the [slave] trader she endured everything but death" (105). Carter ended her tale with a reminder of just how much power the *Elevator* had to extend the memories of mobility in Still's account—and how far those memories could themselves travel through the textual: "none to this day knew what a ride I took that night with my baby in my arms and the mother love in my heart going out towards that homeless mother and baby" (105).

For Jennie Carter, the textual could function as the itinerant, traveling from community to community, collecting and preserving the black stories so essential to establishing a doubly domestic agency in the West—telling even those stories that "none to this day knew," but that nonetheless *mattered*.

Unfortunately, like so many authors in this study, we do not yet know Jennie Carter's full story, including that of her later life. The last of her columns found to date appeared in the 19 December 1874 *Elevator*. In an object lesson of just how the existing archive may limit the full recovery of black literature in unexpected places, the California Newspaper Project has found only five issues of the *Elevator* published after this date and prior to Carter's death on 10 August 1881; none contain references to Carter or work by her.

"How checkered has been life"
Thomas Detter and the Black West

Described as a man with "a nervous, restless disposition" in a 6 August 1891 *Christian Recorder* obituary penned by former Californian James H. Hubbard, Thomas Detter not only made the trek west from his birthplace in (or near) Washington, D.C., but also traveled throughout California, Nevada, the Idaho Territory, and the Pacific Northwest. He worked as a mason, a shoemaker, and a barber prior to coming to California in 1852 when he was about twenty-three years old; there, he quickly joined the convention movement among California's African Americans and, per the above, was involved in the meetings that led to the founding of the *Mirror of the Times* (for which he may have written, though the few extant issues do not contain contributions from him). While barbering would remain his central trade in the West, he also mined, preached, created hair tonics and medicinal remedies, argued persistently for African American rights, lectured, and wrote for both the *Pacific Appeal* and the *Elevator*.

His senses of both the black West and of black mobility are multifaceted and often contradictory, in part because he never settled into the kind of (post)germinal domestic mobility so central to Jennie Carter's life and writing. Detter's literary oeuvre is thus both messy and complicated—but nonetheless deeply instructive on the issues that faced the literary in the black West. In a 26 November 1870 letter to the *Pacific Appeal*, he asserted that most of his hope in California had long since left him:

> Eighteen years ago I . . . beheld the "City of Hills," [San Francisco] far in the distance. Its stately edifices and towering domes lent enchantment to the view, which the sunlight of autumn afforded. To our right the far off hills were dressed in the beauties of Nature; dotted with herds of browsing cattle, which indeed presented a lovely scene to the adventurer as well as to the romantic. Strange emotions filled my soul as we neared our destination. Little did many of us contemplate the reverses and misfortunes California had in reserve for us amid the shifting scenes of life. We looked only to the sunny side of life and for glittering gold. How checkered has been life since that day. Hope has withered and our energies have often been paralyzed by terrible blows of adversity and misfortune.

Ironically, this letter came at the moment when Detter seemed most settled, as he was living in Nevada with his family, working toward a license to preach in the A.M.E. Church (which he would receive in 1871), and probably beginning to work on *Nellie Brown, or the Jealous Wife with Other Sketches*, which, since its recovery in 1996, has been recognized as the first book of fiction published by an African American in the West and as a volume containing one of the earliest pieces of black extended fiction (the title novella). However, by the mid-1880s, his wife and son were dead, his second wife was mysteriously omitted from all records tied to him, and he was readying himself to leave the West for Louisiana, where he would die in the summer of 1891.[55] No extant texts by him from this later period have yet been discovered.

By the time Detter began contributing to the *Appeal* in the 1860s, his senses of the West (including black potential there) and of black mobility were already painfully fractured, and his later newspaper writing—primarily for Bell's *Elevator*—exhibited, sometimes simultaneously, moments of great hope, incredible promise tied to western mythos, deep frustration, and painful anger. His 13 June 1863 letter to the *Appeal*—in the wake of the Emancipation Proclamation and sent from Lewiston in the Idaho Territory—initially, for example, echoed the historical arguments for black rights found in the work of figures like William Cooper Nell: "We have been wronged and outraged in this Christian land. Colored men have been identified with this country in all its struggles for liberty, and the time again [has] come when they are called upon to battle a domestic foe, whose object is to sap the foundation of the Government and to perpetuate slavery." He continued, "Our manhood, though crushed, still lives, in spite of American prejudices. Our hopes, often blasted, are today as elastic as ever." But his 13 February 1864 letter sent to the *Appeal* from Walla Walla, Washington, and titled "Reflections on Life," began with, "Misfortunes and reverses attend the history of all men's lives. They try the souls of men. We are truly creatures of circumstances. In the fearful struggles of life[,] hope often sinks in the souls of many to rise no more."

His early *Elevator* columns were similarly bifurcated between a radical sense of black agency (almost reminiscent of some of Martin Delany's writings) and a level of despair that asserted that not only the white majority but perhaps heaven itself was limiting black elevation. His letter from Idaho City published in the 13 October 1865 *Elevator*, for example, said that "time brings many changes," but that, even though "two hundred thousand brave colored men with strong arms and loyal, willing hearts fought nobly in the defense of the Republic," African Americans were "still denied the franchise," arguably because "the social bug bear . . . deters many from dealing justice for us." Similarly, in his 27 December 1867 letter, he asserted that though "Ethiopia continues to stretch forth her hand unto God," the "North needs reconstruction upon a just and equal basis" as much as the South.[56] Detter even danced between the Republican and Democratic parties in hopes to move arguments for suffrage ahead.[57]

Detter evinced similar splits on his sense of pioneering in western locations. His 22 May 1868 *Elevator* letter (printed next to Peter Cole's eighth letter from Japan) asserted that "a mountain life is indeed romantic, as well as novel," but also said that "its best times are always ahead. The changes a man has to undergo are often sudden, deceitful, and discouraging." In his 26 February 1869 *Elevator* letter from Silver City (in the Idaho Territory), he considered the massive emigration from California and the Idaho Territory by those hoping to profit from Nevada's silver strikes using this language: "This burg is being fast depopulated. Every one seems to have the fever—hence I must follow suit. Such is life in the mountains. . . . I know not whether I will better my condition by going, but I am determined never to surrender to adversity, until the last hope has withered. I have often fought him long and hard—often he has had the best of the conflicts."[58] And once he arrived in Nevada, he sent a letter published in the 19 March 1869 *Elevator* that recognized that while "every passenger car that arrives comes packed with adventures," "board here is ten dollars per week, flour eight dollars per hundred," and that "whiskey mills and restaurants are as thick as fleas on a dog's back. . . . We have ten hurdy houses where the disconsolate congregate to while away their leisure hours, and gaze upon the fair but frail daughters of Eve." Detter concluded that rather than mine, he would barber, as "I have been struggling long and hard to make it stick; it is up one side and down the other with me."

Throughout the late 1860s, Detter saw the textual as the one great hope for black improvement, as its itinerancy was ultimately both more focused and more useful than his (and especially the nation's political) wandering about. Like Carter's work, his 22 May 1868 *Elevator* letter asserted that "all" should "unite in sustaining" the *Elevator* because it "has battled nobly for our rights," "brought the news across the snow-capped Sierras," and was part of "The Press," which "is the lever that moves the world; it moulds public sentiment; it is the beacon light of civilization—a scourge to unjust rulers, and a terror to corrupt politicians. It is the messenger of the universe—the world's text and spelling book." To back up his claims, he organized a fund-raising drive for the *Elevator* in Silver City that sent "liberal donations" noted in the 4 December 1868 issue. And in his 29 January 1869 column "A Voice from the Mountains," Detter asserted that the black press could serve to remind everyone that "though far away, even upon the borders of civilization, we believe in the security to men, of life, liberty, and [property], and hail the glad day that brought freedom to millions of the enslaved."

Given the power Detter recognized in the textual—and his sense of the textual's itinerant ability to draw connections between diverse peoples, which was, at least in the 1860s and early 1870s, similar to Jennie Carter's— it is no surprise that he turned more fully toward writing after his years of working with California's black press. In late 1871, he self-published *Nellie*

Brown with the San Francisco printing firm of Cuddy and Hughes.[59] It is also no surprise that Detter advertised his new book in the *Elevator*—describing the volume as "Stories of Southern Life founded on facts" and as "sketches" that "have a strict moral tendency, and inculcate principles of virtue and propriety" and that "contain characters drawn from life, and are written in chaste and appropriate language." Detter's ads in the 27 April 1872, 4 May 1872, and 18 May 1872 *Elevator* promised that *Nellie Brown* would be "for sale at the Book Stores and at this office."

What browsers at Bell's *Elevator* office and other locations would have found between *Nellie Brown*'s covers might, though, have been more surprising, especially if they picked the book up expecting Detter's activist articulation of black rights or his sense of writing for and of the West. While five of the eight short "other sketches" that are mentioned in the title (which run only a few pages each) consider the West and African Americans as their subject—and show some of the same complex splits noted above—the bulk of the book, per the ad, contains "Stories of Southern Life." In these southern stories, as Dan Moos asserts about the title novella, most black characters are minor and "are caricatured as docile, servile, single-mindedly religious, and dull" (91).[60] Outside of Detter, who is the speaker in the five brief western sketches, the black character with the most agency in the volume is arguably Jane Gray, the heroine of the longest "other sketch," a short story titled "The Octoroon Slave of Cuba." Gray, who has been raised to think she is white even though she is of mixed race, manages to foil the machinations of her Cuban husband, who has kept her long-lost sister Louisa as a slave concubine. She frees her sister and the enslaved woman who cared for her in her youth, but she also keeps both her husband and her caregiver "ignorant" of her "relationship . . . to Louisa" and cautions her sister, "Do not reveal that I am the daughter of a Negro woman or the sister of a slave. It would blast my hopes forever in this life. It would leave a stain upon me that could never be wiped out. You know the prejudices that are entertained against persons in whose veins course the slightest mixture of African blood. I have moved in the first circles of society and have been the guest of the wealthiest families of my State. I was educated to believe I was of the purest Saxon blood. How humiliating it would be to me to be rejected and scorned because of my origin" (103, 97–98).

"Nellie Brown" itself goes farther afield from Detter's base in the black West: all of its main characters are white, and the bulk of the novella takes place in Virginia. Frances Smith Foster rightly classes it as "domestic fiction" and specifically as "divorce fiction." The story centers on Nellie Brown, whose jealousy makes her fall prey to a trio of women who, out of both spite and greed, lead her to file for divorce from her husband. That evil trio—Mrs. H., Aunt Polly, and Martha Lovejoy—is initially angered by a supposed slight from a virtuous widow (whose name is never given). Soon after, Mrs. H. concocts a story of how Nellie Brown's husband is having an affair with the widow. In cahoots with Aunt Polly and Martha Lovejoy, she accepts significant sums of money not only from Nellie Brown but also from Joseph Oldham, who once courted Nellie and hopes to marry her after the divorce. As the novella continues, the women are exposed as "the vilest of the vile" within the novella's dated moral framework: Mrs. H. has "been divorced three times"; Aunt Polly—who is "the best fortune-teller in the State" and always carries "a greasy pack of cards"—has been married five times, but has sometimes taken "leg bail instead of a bill" of divorce because "the world is wide"; Martha Lovejoy has only been divorced once, though she remarried "three weeks to the day she was divorced" (75, 17, 19, 62, 38).

Though Mrs. H. definitively asserts "I hate the Widow," all are profiting by their acts: Aunt Polly says that "money is what we are after" and, at another point, that "business is business. . . . We make our living by it. We should have no sympathy" (40, 65). "The beauty of it," Aunt Polly asserts, "is that we have not only got her [Nellie Brown] under our control, but we are bound to make money out of the affair" (40). When they are exposed at the divorce hearing, the trio crumbles, and Nellie Brown makes a tearful plea first to her husband to take her back (he does) and then to the widow to forgive her for maligning her character (she does). Within this framework, as Foster rightly observes, "Divorce is a central concern, but the text is more concerned with assailing improper marriages, jealousy, and remarriage after divorce than it is with the propriety of divorce itself" (xviii).[61]

While Moos correctly suggests that "the multiple voices found in *Nellie Brown* make Detter difficult to pin down," Foster's explanation of Detter's approach—including his emphasis on white characters—also makes sense: she recognizes that "part of the reason for these elements has to do with the genre with which Detter was experimenting" and part was tied to the fact that "Thomas Detter lived and worked on the western frontier. The same kind of adventurous or rebellious spirit that drove settlers to the frontier and particularly to the mining camps put traditional family values at risk. The highly disproportionate number of men clearly threatened the wedlock ideal" (xiv). This latter observation, though, can be enriched when placed in dialogue with what we know of Detter's columns and specifically his split senses of both black mobility and western potential. Further, as with the un-raced characters in William Jay Greenly's *Three Drunkards,* we can recognize that Detter's southern/eastern white characters might nonetheless be designed as models for his black readers to interact with from a racialized distance.

"Nellie Brown" clearly begins to gender "good" mobility; one of the first things we learn about Brown is that he "was a large cattle-dealer; his business required his absence from home for weeks" (4). This mobility is necessary to support his family—wife Nellie and two children—as well as a handful of slaves. The novella's initial conflict comes from the fact that Nellie Brown never learns to accept her husband's mobility: "though amiable and loving," she "was not free from the sting of jealousy, and not slow in temper when aroused" (4). Nellie Brown's condition worsens when she decides to take on the kind of mobility she (mis)reads her husband as having: she repeatedly leaves the house (generally for Mrs. H's residence) and then begins a romantic correspondence with Oldham. Mrs. H., Aunt Polly, and Martha Lovejoy, repeatedly tell her, "If you are not happy, seek your own happiness," and "Make up your mind, thoroughly, to seek your own happiness, regardless of the praise or condemnation of others" (16, 36). Her husband counters that Nellie is "treading in the path leading to perdition," that her "advisors are leading you to shame," and that, as the divorce hearing comes to pass, "your name will be heralded from city to city, and from village to village" (42). As a result of this public and improper mobility, he asserts, Nellie Brown's "character will become food for the vultures of society" (42). In short, Nellie Brown, the trio of "advisors," and Oldham exercise the kind of "rebellious spirit" that could "put traditional family values at risk."

The novel concludes by allowing readers to watch as the evil Mrs. H. "rushed for the door" of the courtroom after being exposed only to be caught and then fall "to the floor as if shot with a rifle ball"; we then see Nellie Brown cry out as she "advanced to her husband and threw her arms around his neck and kissed him, with tears rolling down her cheeks" (77, 78, 83). Detter thus leaves no doubts as to his sense of a very limited, marriage-centered place for women.[62]

But while Detter's sexist conclusions vis-à-vis mobility and morality may seem far from, say, Jennie Carter's, his book does share the sense of the textual as itinerant. In his prefatory remarks, he addresses his readers directly: "*Readers*—The design of this work is to show the unhappy results of jealousy and misplaced confidence, and the wicked designs of corrupt parties. Man and woman were created for a noble purpose by their Creator; but how often do we see families that have lived long happily together rent in twain by such malignant characters as Mrs. H., Aunt Polly, and Martha Lovejoy. . . . Such characters are to be found in all communities, like hungry wolves hunting down their prey; they often paralyze the hopes of the good and just, cause doubts, gloom and despair to overhang their pathway, where the radiant sunlight of happiness has long beamed" (1).

Assuring readers—in an echo of his *Elevator* ad that "this work is perfectly chaste and moral in every particular"—Detter was asserting the power of his book (perhaps like Greenly's Stiles or Elisha Weaver) to enter into "all communities" and to provide aid and moral elevation (1).

The Black West and Neglect

The reasons for the death—and eventual forgetting—of the black literary community centering around the San Francisco *Elevator* are multiple and complex. Certainly some of its destruction was, like the death of the literary community in Indiana, tied to the loss of leading figures. Detter, Mifflin Wistar Gibbs, and sometime-assistant editor of the *Elevator* James E. M. Gilliard left, like Weaver and John Mifflin Brown, for the East. Jennie Carter, Peter Anderson, and Philip Bell died, respectively, in 1881, 1879, and 1889. The *Appeal* published only a small handful of issues after Anderson's death before folding. The aging Bell was swindled out of his ownership of the *Elevator,* which, it turned out, could not last long without his driving power. He died in poverty after watching the paper he built collapse. Thomas M. D. Ward and John Jamison Moore became national figures, and both ended their lives in the East. The heart of black San Francisco's literary community shrank, and, while murmurings were beginning in black communities in places like Oakland and Los Angeles, such would not rise in volume until the twentieth century. And as the early black historians of the Nadir began their work, while some—especially I. Garland Penn—attempted to remember the West, most focused their work on the South and the urban Northeast.

But just as important to the loss of the textual center surrounding black San Francisco was the demise of Reconstruction, and, with it, the hopes of many African Americans for legally empowered germinal mobility. California became not only a less attractive destination for many blacks, but also a less possible one, as economics, social power, and legal regression drew more and more limits around African American potential.

Chapter 4

Beyond Philadelphia

The Reach of the Recorder, *1865–1880*

As the *Elevator* was rising in the West, the Philadelphia-based newspaper that Elisha Weaver had resuscitated was arguably becoming the most important black periodical in the nation. With the active support of an ever-growing church (including a cadre of ministers who recognized the textual as a key vehicle for African Americans), Weaver could report, in the 30 December 1865 *Christian Recorder,* that the A.M.E. Church's flagship paper had not missed a single issue in his years at its helm. Weaver argued that part of the reason for this success was that he had made the *Recorder* "a paper adapted to the wants of the times"; certainly, his broadening of the paper's secular content, attention to politics, facilitation of a great number of black voices on the Civil War, and desire to place the *Recorder* "among the first-class reading papers" in the nation demonstrated such. But, much like the itinerant ministers he had so greatly praised in his earlier writing, Weaver saw the *Recorder* as the glue that held the A.M.E. Church together. The paper, he asserted "goes into the hedges, the highways and the valleys. It goes to the widow, the farmer, the merchant."[1]

In short, Weaver claimed, "it is utterly impossible for the Church to reach all her members without" the *Recorder* because African Americans, like all of "the people of this world," "move forward ninety percent faster than they did a half century ago." Thus, it would be "impossible for the Church to keep pace with the progressive world without" the paper, because "it informs ministers from one end of the connection to the other." These sentiments echoed assertions Weaver made in his "New Year Greeting" published in the 7 January 1865 *Recorder,* where he argued that the

Recorder had caused "a marked change among our people," in that it has "given" them "a keen appetite to read and to hear from our people in all parts of the country"—even though, in the language of his 30 December 1865 piece, "a large proportion of our people have been denied and deprived of their right to education, for years and years, and therefore were not sufficiently educated to appreciate literature with so keen a relish as those who have enjoyed the privilege of study." The *Recorder* stood as an ever-present reminder "that colored men, wherever they have the least chance," are as capable "of intellectual improvement . . . as any of their white friends." This reminder led Weaver to make repeated calls to expand the reach of the paper even further—as in his instruction in the 1865 New Year's greeting "to have all our subscribers consider themselves the agents for this paper, and try to get as many cash subscribers as possible."[2]

However, Weaver's successes with and ambitions for the *Recorder* may have complicated his role in the A.M.E. Church. He seems to have repeatedly called for additional resources and support and, as in the debates over the *Repository* discussed in chapter 2, made some enemies among powerful clergy. While he managed to hold on to the editorial chair with the exception of Stanford's brief work in 1861, in early 1866, a meeting of all of the A.M.E. Church's bishops extended Weaver's appointment as the conference book steward but appointed James Lynch as the *Recorder*'s editor. Weaver reported this development in the 3 February 1866 issue, in which he also, in a separate item, asserted that he had only asked for an "assistant"—whose duties he would determine—but that he "did not ask our beloved Bishops to appoint an editor." Maintaining that splitting the offices of book steward and *Recorder* editor would improve working conditions and productivity for both, the church hierarchy essentially ignored Weaver's arguments, and the individual area conferences took the bishops' directive as a given. Thus, for example, the report of the Baltimore Annual Conference, published in the 12 May 1866 *Recorder,* referred to Lynch as the *Recorder* editor and included resolutions that recognized that the *Recorder* "was resuscitated six years ago, by Rev. Elisha Weaver, and brought to a high degree of success" but also that "in view of the onerous duties which the joint office of the General Book Steward and Editor imposed, Rev. James Lynch was appointed Editor." "Such division of labor," the report concluded, "has been conducive to great improvement in the character of our Church organ." Ironically, these resolutions were offered by none other than Weaver's old adversary John Mifflin Brown.[3]

As book steward, though, Weaver was never far from the *Recorder,* and when Lynch went out "into the field," Weaver ran the paper—taking the chance, for example, in the 29 December 1866 *Recorder,* to offer an annual summary in "The Last Number of the Recorder for 1866" because "after our Bishops had appointed our brother, the Rev. James Lynch, as editor, we had hoped to be excused from saying anything to the readers of the *Recorder* in the way of a New Year's editorial. But we are disappointed. We had no idea that Brother Lynch would remain away during the holidays, which, to our mind, is the most important part of the year, in which the condition of the paper ought to be defined, and remarks made as to its probable success during the upcoming year." Weaver also took it upon himself to pen "A Happy New Year" message that made such "remarks" and was published in the 5 January 1867 *Recorder.*

By June 1867, Lynch had submitted his resignation. He maintained in his 8 June 1867 "Valedictory" that he felt a calling to move South to aid the newly freed, and he claimed that "Between myself and the General Book Steward, who was formerly the editor, though he has steadily maintained the illegality of my appointment, which displaced him, there is the best of feeling [—] no friction whatever, and nothing that would prevent us from going like yoke-fellows into the next General Conference." "Yoke-fellows" or not, the 15 June 1867 *Recorder* said simply that, given the fact of "Rev. James Lynch, having peremptorily resigned," the "former editor, Rev. Elisha Weaver, will resume his old chair."

Weaver's victory, though, was only temporary; the bishops seem to have been definitive in their desire to separate the two offices—and seem to have become much more focused on specifically removing Weaver. At the 1868 General Conference, they appointed Benjamin Tucker Tanner as the *Recorder*'s editor and Joshua Woodlin as the general book steward. Elisha Weaver was out. His "Editor's Farewell," published in the 20 June 1868 *Recorder*—only a month after the conference—must have been a bit tongue-in-cheek in asserting, of Tanner and Woodlin, that "those two brethren will be as one man." Weaver said that "we shall take work in the New York Conference, at least this year," and he wished the paper well.[4]

Holding the editor's chair until 1884, Tanner would increase circulation, make a name for himself both as a writer and as a leader in the black press, and succeed in bringing in more regular and extended contributions from a range of ministers as well as from well-known figures like Frances Ellen Watkins Harper (whose three serialized novels—along with several poems—appeared during Tanner's sixteen-year tenure as the paper's editor).[5] In 1884, he left the *Recorder* to found and edit the new *A.M.E. Church Review*, and in 1888, he was elected a bishop of the church—an office his predecessor Weaver may well have aspired to but never reached.[6]

Throughout these editorial shifts, the *Recorder* continued to represent itself as a truly national paper. While it carried significant Philadelphia news, it continued and expanded the practices (described in chapter 2) of soliciting contributions from throughout the country. Lynch—in his 8 June 1867 "Valedictory"—even worried that "ministers and others, feeling at home in their Church Organ, as indeed they should, frequently write page after page about matters that would interest nobody beyond their own neighborhood: such as accounts of exhibitions, concerns, festivals, &c. The names of all the leading participants therein, are generally mentioned in order that they may be encouraged when they behold them in print. The editor finds himself in possession of enough of this kind of matter every week to fill up the entire paper. The kindness of his heart says, 'gratify these brethren and friends.' His judgment says, 'abridge, condense, omit, and make up a paper that will suit the majority of your readers.'" Tanner did not comment often on the *Recorder*'s reach; instead, he seems to have taken it as a given, as can be seen in part from the contents of the first few issues he edited: a piece on Montana in the 25 July 1868 issue, reports on Colorado and Utah in the 1 August issue, a discussion of San Francisco in the 8 August issue, and material on North Carolina in the 15 August issue, among several other national items and an expanded regular collection of "News of the Week." One of Tanner's unnamed supporters, in a 20 June 1868 piece titled "The New Editor," argued that "If twenty years hence, our Church shall be able to produce a paper, to equal 'The Methodist' [or] 'The Independent;' if fifty years hence we can match 'The Nation,' we may take courage, and boast of our common humanity with the world."

The literature of the *Recorder* during this period—often consisting of letters (the genre, of course, that Jennie Carter and Thomas Detter participated in so actively) but also including poetry and an increasing amount of fiction—certainly embodied the *Recorder*'s desire for a national reach. It also, though, highlighted some of the difficulties implied in Lynch's complaint. Julia C. Collins's 1865 serialized novel *The Curse of Caste*, for example, is a novel of tremendous mobility—spanning not only both the North and the South but also Europe.[7] But in terms of considering a real *black* mobility, it is almost regressive: there are no black male characters with mobility, the heroine Claire gains her mobility only because her perceived whiteness creates an opportunity not open to blacks (becoming a governess/teacher in a southern family), her black mother's single move (to the North as the wife of planter's son and Claire's father, Richard Tracy) essentially kills her, and the mass of black stories are southern stories of slavery and immobility (with the exception of the story of Claire's caregiver Juno, which is largely that of a free black in the North). Frances Ellen Watkins Harper's 1869 serialized *Minnie's Sacrifice* shifts this ground, with a title character born in the South and raised as white in Ohio (where she gains a Quaker education) who returns south to teach as part of the efforts to aid the newly freed. This means that, in ways largely unaccounted for by contemporary critics, Minnie is both of and very much *not* of the South—and, regardless, is also very much part of the missionary northern efforts to send educators to the newly freed that were praised alongside the novel in the *Recorder*. (While certainly fitting with the missionary rhetoric surrounding her character Minnie, Harper's own movement from her adopted home of Philadelphia around the nation as a lecturer [and not simply on a North-South axis] might actually offer a broader female revision of itinerancy—one not available to earlier figures like Maria Stewart.)[8]

However, in part because of a pervasive and erroneous sense that black writers were less active during and immediately after the Civil War and Reconstruction, until recent attention to Collins and Harper, many scholars simply ignored the *Recorder*. No scholar has specifically attended to the fact that the newspaper was regularly publishing work from "beyond Philadelphia"—sometimes far beyond. Such work was often not only composed in unexpected places but also focused on subjects far from Philadelphia-mediated stories of the slave South (or, in Harper's work, the mission South of the newly freed). This chapter studies three examples of *Recorder* writers working within this much more complex sense of location, one which suggests a Philadelphia-based *Recorder* that was a sort of hub for writing for, from, and about more unexpected places: the letters of Sallie Daffin, the contributions of Lizzie Hart, and the serialized novel *John Blye* by "Will." In this, the chapter differs from the rest of this study in several ways. It nominally focuses on perhaps one of the most "expected" locations for black literary activity, Philadelphia—a center of early African American activism, educational opportunities, and church-related efforts (including publication).[9] However, the chapter's actual focus is on ways in which authors from a much wider range of locations—from Norfolk, Virginia, and Clinton, Tennessee, to Morrow, Ohio, to Cumberland County, New Jersey—used Philadelphia as a publishing conduit to tell stories of both their own locations and of the nation. In some ways, this means that this chapter focuses on a theoretical place—"beyond Philadelphia"—rather than the much more concrete locations of, say, St. Louis in the 1840s and 1850s, or Indiana in the late 1850s and early 1860s, or northern California during Reconstruction.

In other ways, though, one might argue that this chapter is really about several separate locations of black textual performance, as the *Recorder* community "beyond Philadelphia" was much less cohesive, consistent, and region-specific than even, for example, the *Elevator* group studied in chapter 3. Conceived in either way—or both ways—this chapter thus asserts that the writers considered here shared their sense of their own unexpected locations in order to both place those locations on the map of black literary sensibilities *and* to build a definition of a (black) nation that was, in essence, centered on the voices from the margins. In many ways, then, this is a chapter about creating a different sense of a "center"—one that makes the *Christian Recorder* a venue for the margins. It also suggests a reconsideration of the study's title: as not simply locating additional places of black literary activity, but as rethinking our assumptions about "expected" places like Philadelphia.[10]

Thus, while Sallie Daffin's initial place and *Recorder* writings look very much like northeastern (and specifically Philadelphia) -centered missionary epistles, this chapter traces her (at least temporary) awakening to the possibilities of other locations for black (textual) activity that might shape the nation. Lizzie Hart essentially assumed that a young African American woman from a place like Morrow, Ohio, had a duty to use the textual to not simply document her place but to define the nation as it fought and came out of the Civil War. And William Steward, who this study reveals wrote *John Blye* under the pseudonym "Will," created a title character who not only assumed that his unexpected place suited him for a nation-defining and nation-building role, but also created an international mobility a writer like Peter Cole could only dream of.

"EXACTLY IN HER OWN PLACE"
Sallie Daffin and Postwar Mobility

Now best known as one of the northern black women who came South to teach newly freed African Americans, Sarah Louise "Sallie" Daffin is regularly if briefly mentioned in histories of black education after the Civil War.[11] Still, very few consider Daffin's body of contributions to the black press—mainly the *Recorder*—and, to my knowledge, no scholar has discussed Daffin in any depth as a *writer*.[12]

While we still know relatively little about Daffin's early life, it is clear that both her deep desire and the unique circumstances brought about by the Civil War allowed her a kind of mobility inaccessible to most activist women of earlier generations. Daffin's opportunities in her youth—however circumscribed by racism—also represent an example of why we generally perceive blacks in the Northeast as having more chances at literacy and the literary. Born in about 1838 in the Philadelphia area, she was the daughter of Cecelia Daffin.[13] The elder Daffin was born in the District of Columbia and seems to have migrated to Philadelphia in the early 1830s—perhaps after a stay in Connecticut. She seems to have worked as a dressmaker and a laundress; she is almost certainly the "Ceclia Daffney" listed in the 1847 Quaker census of Philadelphia as a "washer" living at 232 Lombard.[14] Of the six people living in that household (five female and one male), four were listed as native to Pennsylvania, and five were listed as over fifteen years old but under fifty years old.

The rest of the information provided by this census—which names only the head of the household, but still provides fascinating demographics on the household's members—is particularly telling when placed in dialogue with later census listings and a biographical sketch of Sallie Daffin written by *Recorder* editor Benjamin Tucker Tanner. It is likely that the one male noted in the household was her brother John Daffin, who is listed with the family (all under the surname variant Dauphin) in the 1860 federal census of Philadelphia as a twenty-nine-year-old "master barber" born in Connecticut (764). Cecilia Daffin's husband and Sarah Daffin's father—whose name remains a mystery—is not included under any census listings for the family: under the "remarks" field of the 1847 census, the census taker noted that Cecilia Daffin "was wronged out of about $600:—left by her husband." In addition to John Daffin, Sarah's elder sister Harriet was also surely living with the family in 1847—and may be the "dressmaker" listed as one of two "children under 20 years employed," as she would later carry this occupational listing in the 1860 federal census.[15] The other two residents—likely boarders—were among those between fifteen and fifty and were likely born in Pennsylvania; they may well have also been the two in the household listed as "at service." Given that almost all records agree that Daffin was born after 1832, she is almost certainly the one member of the household noted as "under 15 years"; she is also then, almost certainly, the one member listed as "at school."[16] Finally, she is likely the "apprentice" listed among the "children under 20 years employed."

All of these details mesh with Tanner's report that Daffin "was placed in school when but a child of six, and kept there until she reached her year eleventh; when she was called away from books to learn the art of dressmaking" (447). The 1847 census also makes it clear that the Daffin family was deeply concerned with literacy: the listing for the household noted four members who "can read," three members who "can write," four "members of beneficial societies," and six members who "attend religious meetings." The household was also stable economically—listing two hundred dollars in personal property and no "incumberance"; while the 1850 federal census does not provide such information on the Daffin family, the 1860 census lists Cecilia Daffin as holding fifteen hundred dollars in real estate and one hundred dollars more in personal property.

Cecilia Daffin's origins remain hazy—but also deeply fascinating, in part because the 1847 census lists one member of the household under the "born slaves" category and the census taker made an unreadable notation under the "by whom manumitted" column. We can, however, draw a clearer sketch of Sarah Daffin's youth in the bustling city of Philadelphia—as a child and then a young woman active in a literate community of free blacks who were pushing into the middling classes, tied deeply to the African Methodist Episcopal Church, and at least on the edges of circles that included figures from Charles Reason (of the New York African Free Schools, who was, for a time, principal of the city's Institute for Colored Youth) to Frank J. and Mary Webb, and from William Still to, for a brief time, a young Frances Ellen Watkins.[17] It is no wonder that Daffin, whom Tanner notes spent "eight years" learning "the art of dress-making" and who is listed in the 1860 federal census as a milliner, felt the pull of the textual. Tanner says "she was not exactly in her own place. Different thoughts filled her mind, than studying how to make the dresses suit . . . the gay coquettes of the city of brotherly love. . . . Her thoughts were upon books and work, not the work of the needle, but of the brain and heart" (447). Tanner says that "she thought even of going as a missionary to dear old Fatherland, Africa" (447). Perhaps because she was the youngest in her family, perhaps because the Daffin family was growing toward stronger economic footing, perhaps because Cecilia hoped such would raise the family's class status, and perhaps, too, because of both Sallie Daffin and the family's zeal for literacy and faith, Daffin seems to have continued her schooling in piecemeal fashion after her primary education.[18] However, in 1858, Daffin enrolled fully in the Institute for Colored Youth.

Described by Tanner as "that model of Quaker munificence" and by Weaver as ranking among "the best seminaries of learning wherein colored youth may acquire a thorough and classical education" the institute was, like the New York African Free Schools, a beacon of early black secondary education (447; 21 June 1862 *Recorder*). Begun in theory in 1832 through a bequest from Quaker Richard Humphreys and now Cheney University of Pennsylvania, the institute offered classes for a small group of students in the 1830s; the 1840s saw it close its doors on occasion, and also, again on occasion, shift into a small apprenticeship program and a "farm school." However, the school rose to prominence after Charles Reason answered an ad like that which appeared in the 27 May 1852 *National Era* requiring "satisfactory references as to moral character, literary acquirements, and ability for the government of such a school. . . . A colored man would be preferred, qualifications being equal." Before leaving the institute in 1855 to return to New York, Reason increased enrollment from 6 students to 118, improved the school's financial standing, began bringing in nationally known visitors for lectures, hired some of the best educated African Americans in the city as teachers, and helped James M. Bustill (nominally the school's librarian) build a collection of several hundred volumes that 450 black residents—233 men and 217 women—used in 1854.[19] The "male department," which, per a notice in the 7 October 1852 *National Era,* included subjects from composition and history to algebra and chemistry, was soon complemented by a "female department"; one of the best moves Reason made as principal was supporting the hiring of Sarah Mapps Douglass to superintend that department.

A Philadelphia native and a relation of the prominent Bustill family, Douglass was one of the organizers of the Female Literary Association of Philadelphia, a key member of the Philadelphia Female Anti-Slavery Society, and a longtime educator.[20] Though she endured an unhappy marriage to Reverend William Douglass from 1855 until his death in 1861, Douglass—along with her cousin Grace Mapps—nonetheless helped make the institute into the flowering center of Philadelphia's free black community and pushed parents to become more active in their children's education.[21] The institute quickly became a locus for Philadelphia's educated elite: Jacob C. White Jr. and Octavius Catto were among Daffin's near contemporaries.[22] The institute's public exams and graduates' accomplishments were regularly reported in the *Recorder*, and its headmaster after Reason, Ebenezer Bassett (who came in 1857 and was only a few years Daffin's senior), was lionized in the *Recorder*.[23]

Daffin succeeded mightily at the institute: she received two prizes awarded by the Literary Association of Philadelphia's Bethel A.M.E. Church—one for an essay titled "Temptation, and the Tempter"—as well as, in Tanner's words, the institute's "first mathematical prize offered to the female pupils" (447). She seems to have authored her first widely distributed text—an obituary of A.M.E. stalwart Jabez P. and Mary A. Campbell's young son Gerrit Smith Campbell that appeared in the October 1859 issue of the *Repository of Religion*—while still a student at the institute.[24] She graduated in 1860, with, again in Tanner's words, "torch in hand," and "she did not subdue the flame as many do, but she prepared to carry it long, and keep it bright" (447). Part of the flame she carried was that of supporting the institute; in September 1861, she was elected to the Executive Council of the school's alumni association—of which Octavius Catto was president (28 September 1861 *Recorder*). More broadly, though, her commitment to educating black youth led to her initial forays outside of Philadelphia. Like many of her fellow graduates—male but especially female—she was engaged as a teacher soon after graduation. She began at a small school in Chester, New Jersey, where an unnamed correspondent for the 18 May 1861 *Recorder* described her as "an interesting and useful young woman." She was back in Philadelphia teaching at the Bethel Sabbath School in late 1861, when, with two other teachers, she was chosen to write resolutions mourning the death of the Reverend Walter Proctor that were published in the 21 December 1861 *Recorder*. Over the next two years, she would teach in small schools in both New Jersey and Delaware. By 1863, she was on a longer-term appointment in Wilmington, Delaware; Wilmington resident Frisby J. Cooper wrote—in a letter published in the 25 July 1863 *Recorder*—that "Miss Sallie L. Daffin has been in our midst. It appears as if there is a fresh impetus given to the cause of moral and intellectual improvement, and for her moral and mental worth, I have need but to say, that she is almost idolized by our entire people."

However, while, according to Tanner, the people of Wilmington "offered" her "the greatest of inducements," Daffin "gave them a decided, 'No,' and torch in hand, she started for the gloomy South, made doubly gloomy by the smoke of incessant battle" (448). While Daffin's letter of application to teach for the American Missionary Association (A.M.A.) as part of their efforts to aid the newly freed (in the areas of the South under Union control) does not seem to be extant, she did send A.M.A. agent George Whipple a letter dated 14 March 1864 that noted that she had arrived in Norfolk, Virginia, and was ready to begin teaching. She arrived none too soon: always a regional hub, Norfolk was flooded with "contraband" and then officially newly freed African Americans from throughout the region.[25]

Daffin's earliest *Recorder* work actually appeared before she moved South. Her two essays "Example Better than Precept" (published in the 30 May 1863 issue) and the short "Affectation" (published in the 1 August 1863 issue) both read like the kinds of addresses centered on virtue and written by institute students (as well as Oberlin and Wilberforce students) that the *Recorder* occasionally published throughout the 1860s.[26] Both offer general commentary on improving what the first essay describes as "the social and domestic circle." Both self-consciously demonstrate literary literacy: "Affectation" quotes Cowper, and both quote from the Bible. While "Example Better than Precept" interestingly marks the revolutionary John Brown as a "great man," neither comments on contemporary events or speaks directly of or to African Americans.[27]

While no direct analogy should be drawn, a comparison between Daffin's path—especially after publishing these texts—and that of Maria Stewart suggests the broader parameters of Daffin's mobility. Certainly, Daffin had greater advantages in her education—especially in the secondary schooling gained through the Institute for Colored Youth, an institution unlike any available to Stewart. While Daffin moved into teaching directly after her graduation, Stewart married, attempted to create a career as a lecturer and writer, and then seems to have fallen into teaching as the only profession that would allow her an intellectual life. Both, though, would have seen their teaching careers limited by the nexus of geography and propriety. Daffin's pre-A.M.A. mobility was limited to a fairly close orbit of her family's home in Philadelphia, and she might well have been moved toward marriage—as her unwilling teacher Sarah Mapps Douglass had been—if she continued teaching in the North for much longer. She might have been able to fashion an intellectual career around—or even in spite of—such a marriage, again, as Douglass did. But she would likely have only found mobility in widowhood (as both Stewart and Douglass did) or in a mobile husband.

Daffin's Norfolk and post-Norfolk *Recorder* letters—especially when placed in dialogue with the seemingly more-private letters she wrote to the A.M.A. officials (a pair of which were nonetheless published in the *American Missionary*)[28]—offer a much wider sense of mobility, albeit one still tied to domestic virtue. They began—and one thinks of Tanner's claims that Daffin once considered doing missionary work in Africa—as the letters of a "missionary" sent from the field. This was certainly a posture encouraged by the *Recorder* and by the A.M.A. (through its very name as well as its practices). However, by the time she had left the A.M.A. and gone much further afield geographically, she sounded at times much more like a resident of an outpost writing to remind urban Philadelphians (and residents of smaller black communities across the nation) that literacy and the literary could happen anywhere that there was both will and faith. While she would step back from this stance—settling in Washington, D.C., as a teacher in the early 1870s—Daffin's letters of the later 1860s nonetheless represents a key facet of the *Recorder*'s reach well beyond Philadelphia.[29]

Several of Daffin's letters combine lively reportage of conditions in Norfolk with deep reflection on the newly freed people she was working with.[30] Initially, Daffin's language emphasized their differences; in her first letter from Norfolk, published in the 16 April 1864 *Recorder*, she noted that "in visiting those poor creatures who have but recently emerged from the 'Prison-house of bondage,' we are frequently astonished at the meek, Saviour-like disposition which characterized many of them." Daffin continued, saying, "Although there is much physical suffering" among "those poor creatures," "it is seldom we hear any murmuring."[31] Later in the same letter—again using a "we" that separated the free northern teachers from their newly freed students—she said that "our hearts are often made to ache when we are obliged to turn them from us, without the means of alleviating their wants."

She wrote comparatively little about the place itself; though she talked briefly of the interiors of schoolrooms and said much about the people and the war surrounding them, it is clear that to her—at least initially— Norfolk was a conceptual space, a missionary field, rather than a concrete location. That "we" and the accompanying sentiment marks many of the now-published letters by white teachers beginning their work with freed-people. Certainly some of Daffin's own "we/them" positioning was rhetorically designed to call on the charity of her *Recorder* readers, as when she asked in the same letter "that some of our kind friends at the North will exercise that benevolent spirit which has always characterized them in such cases, and send us something toward supplying the wants of these dear unfortunate ones" because "there is many a garment cast aside by our friends of the North as useless, which, if we could but get, would be a means of comfort to the Freedmen of this place, and would bring joy and gladness to many hearts." Like many of her sister writers employing the rhetorics of sentimentalism, Daffin hoped that her readers, from their (albeit sometimes only slightly) better positions would exercise their agency on behalf of their less-empowered fellows.[32]

Daffin certainly saw this distancing (and her initial *Recorder* letters generally) very much within the framework of domestic duty. She opened her 16 April 1864 letter by recounting her promise to essentially be a Christian recorder of her "missionary" work: "The promise I made you when in Philadelphia, to correspond with the 'Recorder' has hitherto remained unfulfilled, in consequence of the many arduous duties which necessarily devolve upon all those who enter the missionary field of labor."[33] The staff of the *Recorder* saw her letters in a similar light, heading the first "An Important Letter from a Teacher of the Freedmen." Perhaps to shore herself up and perhaps to remind readers at home of just how important her work was, she also penned an extended essay on domestic duty that the *Recorder* published in its 25 June 1864 issue under the simple title "Woman."[34]

Daffin's need to rely on the discourses of domesticity and to separate herself as subject from the newly freed objects of her deep and loving concern, however, shifted the longer she stayed in the South. Part of this change came from the fact that, per a piece published in the 20 August 1864 *Recorder* that she cowrote with Mary Louise (Lewis) Brown (the wife of John Mifflin Brown, who accompanied him to Norfolk), "the din of war is constantly sounding in our ears, the battle-cry is re-echoing sadly through the avenues of our hearts, and we are daily, yea, almost hourly, beholding our husbands and friends leaving their 'loved ones at home,' to participate in the great drama of the day." Daffin came to a new understanding of how "thousands of our *brave boys,* experiencing all the fearful horrors of war" and especially the "hundreds of our sick and wounded soldiers . . . brought into our midst" were fighting in a common struggle. In a letter published in the 17 September 1864 *Recorder,* she recounted meeting "among the wearers of the blue cloth, one who was a pupil of mine in Mount Holly, N. J. His name is Maurice Games."[35] She then added, "How little did I think, when I bade him good by[e] at that place, that we would next meet in Virginia soil!"

The "we" of Daffin and Brown's 20 August 1864 appeal was very much moving toward the cross-sectional: "the ladies of the several churches in this city, and in Portsmouth, have organized societies for the relief of our soldiers, and we have felt it our duty to assist in bearing the burden." By the end of their letter, it was those in Philadelphia who were separate from those on or near the battlefield: "Could you, dear friends, but with *us* stand around the couches of the ill and dying, and witness the expressions of joy and gratitude beaming from their countenances, as they receive some little delicacy from the hands of the ladies, you would not for a moment hesitate to contribute your mite toward a cause so noble" (italics mine). Her letter mentioning Games published in the 17 September 1864 *Recorder* said that "*our* city is now guarded by colored soldiers" (italics mine). A letter published in the 8 October 1864 *Recorder*—similarly said, "And now, Mr. Editor, before I close, let me beg that *our* Northern friends will not forget our poor soldiers. . . . The ladies of several Soldiers' Relief Associations of this city and Portsmouth, are doing what their limited means will allow, and *we* ask you to lend us a helping hand in this hour of need" (italics mine). Daffin's carefully cultivated, northeastern- and urban-based missionary mobility was shifting; she was rhetorically marking herself as, if not a settler, then an itinerant member of a much larger community centering on the newly freed.

Concurrent with this change, Daffin seems to have also grown into a richer sense of the newly freed men, women, and children as *people*—and in this, her letters present a rare counterpoint to some of the published accounts by white authors.[36] Simply put, her pupils touched her deeply. Her 4 July 1864 letter to the A.M.A.'s George Whipple said, in part, "it is astonishing that these children and their parents[,] many of whom have been subjects all their lives to the 'driver's whip' and have been 'incapable of supporting themselves,' should so readily yield to the genial influence of mild persuasion and by their actions indicate an independence that would do credit to many of our most refined and intelligent minds." The final clause comparing the newly freed to Philadelphians differs massively from her letters of just a few months before: the newly freed men, women, and children have gone from "poor creatures" to independent beings (almost) like her and her fellows from the Institute for Colored Youth.[37] Her letter published in the 17 September 1864 *Recorder* said that while "most of the schools have been closed since July," the "interest hitherto manifested by the pupils has not diminished. So earnestly have they entreated me, that I would not refuse their request, 'to keep my school open during the summer.'" Proud of her students—and trying still to be properly humble—she told the *Recorder* readers that she found "their progress . . . commendable, and their conduct meritorious; and I think, in both these particulars, they will favorably compare with any of our Northern pupils, who have had more excellent advantages."

She also grew to understand even more completely just how slavery had attempted to sunder the bonds of family and how, nonetheless, many of her pupils kept hoping: "Every day or two," she wrote in her 17 September 1864 *Recorder* letter, "we meet instances of the re-union of those whom the monster, slavery, had separated for years. Only a few days ago, I saw a woman who had just received a letter from her son, who had been sold away from her six years [before]. Another, while passing along the streets of this city, met her husband, who, some time since, had escaped from the '*Rebs*,' and joined the Union army. He had obtained a furlough to come here to look for his companion. What a joyful meeting it was!"

Daffin never completely equated herself with the newly freed people, but she soon came to the conclusion, expressed in a letter to the American Missionary Association, that "none can so fully experience the strength of their [the freedpeople's] needs, nor understand the means necessary to relieve them as we who are identified with them" (qtd. in Morris 462). Her public letters evince more and more of a sense that the newly freed were joined with her, standing with her—in a very different place than the urban North. "At Ropewall," she wrote in her letter published in the 26 November 1864 *Recorder,* "we have assisted in organizing a Sunday School, which we hope 'ere long will be in a flourishing condition. It would probably amuse some of our Northern city friends, to see us seated upon boards raised from the floor with bricks, with a little company of eager listeners around us, anxiously waiting for the words of knowledge to be imparted to them; but it is pleasure to us to feel that, even besides many inconveniences, we are able to perform some humble part in the establishment of the Redeemer's kingdom." She signed herself, "Truly yours, for the elevation of our race,

SALLIE."[38] In a 2 June 1864 letter to Whipple that was published in the July 1864 *American Missionary,* Daffin simply said, "Throughout the four years I have been engaged in teaching, I have never spent a month more pleasantly and seldom with as little trouble as I have the last" (173).

Daffin's growing identification with the newly freed seems to have contributed to a growing sense of place as well. Daffin saw her fellows literally die around her: "I regret to have to announce," she wrote in a letter published in the 8 October 1864 *Recorder,* "the demise of another of our teachers at Hampton, Miss Day." She also reported that, "Yesterday Miss E. G. Highgate left here for her home in Syracuse, N. Y., in care of Miss C. C. Duncan, being afflicted with that terrible malady, 'aberration of mind.'" Daffin mourned that "our laborers are falling rapidly in the field."[39] Conditions (and especially the intense racism among many of the white aid workers) were such that many teachers—especially African American teachers— could become deeply discouraged. Black teachers were also paid notably less than their white counterparts; fellow institute graduate Frances Rollin, for example, resigned because of the pay differential (Morris 466). "For a salary of $15 per month," the historian Robert Morris writes of Daffin, "she taught day, evening, and Sunday schools; visited black families; aided the sick and wounded; and assisted the teacher at the hospital across from the mission house" (462). Like many of her compatriots, she had growing choices both within and beyond the movement to aid the newly freed; she chose again and again to stay in the South, asserting that "I verily believe that I shall never again be satisfied to teach in Northern schools, but my highest ambition in life is to devote what talent God has given me in this great cause hoping that I may be the humble instrument through God in enlightening many."[40] In short, Daffin seems to have seen—and then began representing—Norfolk's fascinating mix of the newly freed who were flocking to the city, the former slaves and free blacks who had lived there before the war, and the small cadre of northern free black teachers as a kind of community.[41] Were these changes in Daffin's sense of the newly freed simply the reflections of a teacher who finds that her class is teaching *her,* they would be valuable enough. But Daffin begins to hint that she can conceive of both the literate and the literary coming out of this most unexpected place—a place where slavery still cast long shadows. Perhaps just as important given the parameters of this study, she chose to use the textual to represent this place to readers in more expected locations (like the urban Northeast). In so doing, she revised both the "outpost letter" genre common in the black press (a genre that Cole's letters to the *Elevator,* for example, also revise) and the itinerant's narrative by making the speaker female, by suggesting the margins' importance to any "center," and by emphasizing that the textual offered a way of binding and improving a new and wider black national presence.

Daffin's struggle—one not seen in her *Recorder* letters—became how to continue to be a part of the communities of the newly freed in the face of increasing difficulties with the American Missionary Association. After completing a year in Norfolk and three months in Wilmington, North Carolina, she took an extended break in Philadelphia during which she requested a formal reappointment to Wilmington. That request seems to have been denied.[42] She was sent instead to Mount Pleasant, Maryland, and then, after a brief sojourn in Washington, D.C., to the "Freedmen's Village" in Arlington. There, Daffin was essentially demoted in favor of a less-qualified white teacher and faced with "false accusations."[43] On 14 May 1867, she sent a terse note to the A.M.A.'s Reverend E. P. Smith that read, "Dear Friend, Circumstances compel me to tender to the American Missionary Association my resignation to take effect on the first of June, 1867." Though, in Daffin's words in a 31 May 1867 letter to Smith, "much has transpired to cause unpleasantness," the A.M.A. attempted to convince her to stay with them, and Daffin initially accepted an appointment to Carsonville, Virginia. Her time there, though, was short, and she finally severed her relationship with the A.M.A. However, she did not leave the work or the place(s) that she had become committed to, and that led to her perhaps most stunning piece to appear in the *Recorder.*

By early 1868, Daffin was in eastern Tennessee teaching both adults and children at a newly founded school in Clinton.[44] A "Citizen" who wrote a "Letter from East Tennessee" published in the 25 April 1868 *Recorder* noted that "the effect of Miss Daffin's able and assiduous labors were visible in the bright, attentive faces, and the perfect order manifested in the school." Later in the year, a meeting of community members passed a series of resolutions—printed in the 3 October 1868 *Recorder*—praising her "untiring efforts as a teacher, as well as her own example," in "a time when an unjust and most disheartening prejudice against the education and improvement of the colored race existed in the minds of a large portion of our community."

Months before that praise was published, though, another black citizen's meeting created the "Anderson County Immigration Society" and elected Daffin "permanent Corresponding Secretary of the Society." Given Daffin's early hopes to become a missionary in Africa, as well as her frustration with the A.M.A.'s handling of black education (and educators), one might initially suspect that this was a colonizationist effort. It was most definitely not.

Rather, the stated purpose of the group was to invite "our brethren in the North . . . to come and settle permanently among us"; that is, to encourage African Americans in the North—and especially, given the *Recorder's* large base in Philadelphia, the urban North—to move to the rural South. The letter that shared this information with *Recorder* readers, a letter cosigned by Daffin (and probably written by her, as the organization's secretary) and published in the 1 February 1868 issue, argued that this would "be the only true method by which the permanent happiness and liberty of the colored citizens of the South can be secured." Daffin and her fellow officers claimed that

> it is in the interest of our people, both North and South, to have men of their own color, competent to transact business of all kinds. We have in East Tennessee a healthy, beautiful, and well watered country, well adapted for the raising of stock or the growth of grain of all kinds[;] corn, wheat, oats, rye, grass, potatoes of both kinds, and all vegetables flourish in our valleys and hill slopes. Our mountains abound in the most valuable and useful minerals, copper, iron, zinc, and stone coal. Our forests furnish an exhaustless supply of excellent lumber, for which the demand is great and constantly increasing. Our streams furnish water power probably superior to that of New England, while we are not subject to the vicissitudes of the harsh climate and the scanty soil of the Eastern States.

To this verdant language so reminiscent of the calls west of Meachum, Weaver, and Carter, Daffin and her Tennessee compatriots added the assertions that "East Tennessee is destined to become one of the greatest manufacturing districts of the Union," that it "offers rare inducements for the employment of capital in any branch of milling or manufacturing," and that, perhaps most important to pre–Fifteenth Amendment African Americans, "we have, also, here political privileges which are not, as yet, enjoyed by our brethren at the North."

Foretelling the calls of the later Exoduster movement, this letter, probably largely written by a Philadelphian sent out as a missionary to the hinter-
lands, argued, in short, that "if men of our own color, possessed of capital,
intelligence, and education will come and settle among us the result will be
most beneficial both to us and to them." It further asked that the A.M.E.
Zion newspaper, *Zion's Standard and Weekly Review,* copy the letter.

Daffin followed this call and letters recounting her initial work in Tennessee with a letter published in the 13 March 1869 which assured *Recorder*
readers that "the colored people of this section are making good progress
in political and educational matters," were loyal to their race even when
former Confederates attempted to buy or influence their votes, included
many "professors of religion," and, in short, held great potential.

What led Daffin to leave Tennessee is not clear. She reported, in a letter
published in the 27 March 1869 *Recorder,* that the combination church/
school in which she had been working had been burned to "a smolder-
ing heap of ashes" by an arsonist (or arsonists) who "probably applied
the flame to the Bibles and other books," recognizing that the fire would
quickly spread in the all-pine building. Daffin, though, seemed committed
to staying there. She said that "through the kindness of our white friends,
we obtained possession of one of their churches in which to teach, until ours shall have been rebuilt" and that she was already actively raising
money to help with that rebuilding. She asserted that, in addition to the
$175 she had collected, "offers of assistance in doing the work and teams for
hauling purposes have also been generously made, and we hope in a short
time to have a much more comfortable house than the one . . . which has
been destroyed." She bravely concluded that "the day school has not been
stopped for a single hour; and we verily believe, that what seemed so great
a misfortune at first, has been productive of good results." Certainly, her
depiction of Bible- and book-burning racists was designed to anger readers into contributing additional funds to her efforts. However, nothing else
appeared in the *Recorder* on these efforts. Daffin came to Philadelphia for
a "visit," as reported in the 31 July 1869 *Recorder,* and I have not been able
to locate her definitively in the 1870 federal census.[45] Her name would not
appear again in the *Recorder* until she was firmly ensconced in the Washington, D.C., school system in 1873.

Daffin may well have begun under the missionary umbrella that allowed
female free black teachers from the North amazing mobility—and that by

extension, for example, helped support Frances Harper's postbellum lecturing and writing careers—and she may well have returned to that sense
when she moved to Washington, D.C., especially given the small and select
black community with Philadelphia ties that she joined there. Still, for a
moment in Clinton, Tennessee, she demonstrated that Philadelphia's—and
specifically the *Recorder's*—reach might also lead to much more challenging efforts like those in the unexpected place of Clinton, a place in which
a small group of blacks essentially hoped to found a new nation, one connected to, but both far from and ultimately (they hoped) far richer in potential than the urban centers of the Northeast.

"FIGHT WITH YOUR WHOLE SOUL"
Recovering Lizzie Hart

If Sallie Daffin was initially emblematic of the missionary spirit of the *Recorder*—reporting on minds and souls enlightened by a northern urbanite's
travels to far outposts—then Jane Elizabeth Hart embodied another trend
common in the *Recorder*: the resident of the (seeming) "outpost" writing
not simply to report on the local events that caused James Lynch so much
consternation but also to make—and essentially demand that—her voice
be heard on national issues. Roughly Daffin's contemporary, Hart published
four poems and a dozen letters in the *Recorder* under the names "Lizzie,"
"Lizzie H.," and "Lizzie Hart." While much of her story—and the focus of
this section—centers on the small towns of Morrow and Roachester, Ohio,
I want to begin my consideration of Hart in a very different place: Fort
Duane, near Beaufort, South Carolina, in late 1864.

Among the African American troops at Fort Duane were those in the
Twenty-sixth Regiment of the U.S. Colored Infantry. Organized in February 1864 at Riker's Island in New York, these 1,600-plus men came from
all over the New York area and beyond. They had arrived at Beaufort on
13 April 1864 and already seen action at Johns Island, James Island, and
Burden's Causeway, and would go on to fight at the Battle of Honey Hill in
November. By the time they were mustered out at the end of August 1865,
30 of them would die as a result of battle wounds, and 115 would die of
disease and other causes.[46]

Initially a private in the Twentieth Colored Troops, Theodore Ro(d)
gers would rise to the rank of sergeant in the Twenty-sixth and would aid

regimental surgeons.[47] Like a number of the literate men in the Twenty-sixth—including Chaplain Benjamin Franklin Randolph, who would later become active in Reconstruction-era South Carolina before being assassinated[48]—Rogers was a reader of the *Christian Recorder*. Two of Rogers's letters were even published in the *Recorder*: a brief note offering to write letters from and read letters to his colleagues in Company C was published in the 10 December 1864 issue, and a slightly longer piece addressing the war effort had been published in the 10 September 1864 issue.

Rogers's longer letter read, in part, "Mr. Editor: - By chance, your journal happened to come within my sight. I read in it a letter from Miss Lizzie Hart. I also read your editorial in relation to the colored people and the colored soldiers, and I must concur with you. All we want is that those at home should take care of our families, and speak cheerful words to us, do their duty as Christians, and we will do ours as soldiers."

"Those at home" seem to have consistently been on the minds of many in the Twenty-sixth; William Waters, a soldier in Company K, wrote a letter published in the 15 April 1865 *Recorder* that spoke of how "we left our homes, our firesides, and our families, to fight for our country's cause, which we have done nobly."[49] Waters—and Rogers, Hart, and the staff of the *Recorder*—saw such as deeply necessary: "we have often heard it said, that the negro would not fight, would not stand fire, was only intended to stand behind the white man's chair. . . . Has not the negro proved to be a true soldier?"

Rogers could have been speaking of either Hart's letter published in the 28 May 1864 issue or her letter published in the 30 July 1864 issue. Her 28 May letter focused on "the late massacre at Fort Pillow" and had been written two weeks earlier, when reports of the 12 April battle near Henning, Tennessee, were still coming in. With a much larger force, Confederate major general Nathan Bedford Forrest pummeled the Union garrison of six hundred men, split almost evenly between black and white troops. While there is still some controversy over exactly what happened, northern newspapers and especially the black press reported widely (and probably correctly) that race became the central factor as the victorious Confederates finished the battle: of the two hundred Union troops still alive and taken prisoner at the end of the day, only fifty-eight were African Americans. That most reports asserted that much of the killing of black troops took place *after* they had surrendered, that many of the dead African Americans had been former slaves, and that there were many reports of

Confederates committing atrocities against black soldiers only stoked the fires of what quickly became a rallying point for the North and especially for black troops.[50]

Hart wrote that "if the atrocious crimes that were perpetrated there be not enough to convince the North that the South is in earnest, we might as well surrender to-day." She thus urged the "friendly soldiers"—almost certainly an assumed audience of black troops reading the *Recorder*—that "when and wherever hereafter you may be attacked by the enemy" they should "remember Fort Pillow, and at the same time remember that you are fighting men who are enemies to you—those who are trying to destroy your manhood, and rob you of your God-given rights.—Then fight with your whole soul, mind and strength, and die rather than surrender—for I would rather die the death of the brave than . . . live the life of a coward." After telling "the many who have lost friends in the massacre" that—as one who has also been "separated from loved ones, by the hand of death"— Hart sympathizes with them deeply, she concludes nonetheless that to "put down this wicked rebellion . . . some of the best blood of the nation must be spilt."

If Hart's location of the blood of Fort Pillow's black troops as some of the country's "best" is fully in line with (black) nationalist rhetoric, her letter of 30 July recognized that the Union was far from morally perfect in its treatment of its own black soldiers. "Shame to this boasted Republic," she wrote, for "refusing to pay men what is just and right, for no other reason than that they are colored men." Speaking to a broad black audience, Hart said, "When I think of our poor soldiers, who have sacrificed all the comforts of life, and given the parting hand to loved ones, and even offered their lives, if need be . . . without receiving equal pay with the white man, I feel sorry, indeed for them. Just think of the Paymaster offering men, who are soldiers in every sense of the word, the pitiful sum of seven dollars per month." But then she narrowed her address: "Soldiers, let me beseech you, by all the ties that bind you to your country, never take seven dollars per month . . . you can well afford to fight awhile longer for nothing." Like many black activists—both in and out of the military and both in and beyond the pages of the *Recorder*—Hart thus argued for the power of moral suasion: a long line of black troops in blue stoically reminding those in power of their true worth.[51] "Soldiers," she wrote, "remember, you are not fighting to restore the Government to what it was; but you are fighting to make it what it should be." She signed herself "yours, for the cause of freedom and the elevation of my race, Lizzie Hart."

Hart's rhetorical skill, deep sense of current events, and gender make her fascinating enough to demand consideration by scholars of nineteenth-century African Americans, but her physical location makes her of especial interest to this study. The vast majority of her columns were headed with datelines like "Morrowtown, Ohio, May 14th, 1864" or titles like "From Marrawtown [*sic*]." Each of her *Recorder* pieces thus became not only a reminder that free black America had grown far and wide—certainly far wider that the urban centers of the Northeast—but also that even in the tiniest and seemingly most unlikely places, black voices were fully cognizant of and participating in national events.

Morrow, Ohio, sometimes called Morrowtown, is located in Warren County, deep in southern Ohio and a bit southeast of the county seat, Lebanon. In 1860, the federal census counted only 638 residents in Morrow—compared with about 2,500 in Lebanon; only a handful were African Americans. Nonetheless, the relatively small black community of Warren County teemed with activity: Lebanon's African Methodist Episcopal Church, formally founded in 1858, built a "neat little brick meeting house" in the fall of 1861 (Beers 500); a Baptist church was also active (28 March 1878 *Recorder*); and a school for black children was founded in the 1850s and had ties to, former pupils enrolled in, and teachers who were graduates of Wilberforce and Oberlin. The black community in Warren County certainly did not live on an ideal island, though: even as late as 1878, Reverend W. H. Yeocum wrote to the *Recorder* that the Normal School at Lebanon "will not admit colored students, simply because they are colored" (28 March 1878). Still, the African Americans of Warren County clearly saw themselves as contributors to a larger black American identity: the Strange family, for example, sent several members into combat for the Union cause, including patriarch Reuben Strange, who, though at least thirty-nine when he enlisted, served as a seaman on the USS *Petrel*.[52] Black ministers like William Hunter (a Wilberforce grad and Union soldier) as well as Edward D. Davis of Wilberforce sent news and subscriptions from Warren County and the surrounding area to the *Recorder* with some regularity.

Lizzie Hart is listed in three of those subscription lists. The 4 April 1863 *Recorder* notes that she paid $2.25 via Reverend Hunter, and the 26 August 1865 *Recorder* notes that she paid $2.50. Most fascinating—especially given the dates of her letters—is the note in the 3 September 1864 *Recorder* that tallied $1.15 from "Miss Lizzie Hart, to send *Recorder* to a soldier." Hart, then, not only saw what she could say from Morrow, Ohio, as of value to the national readership of the *Recorder,* but also saw the paper's combination of national and regional voices as important enough to send—itinerant-like— into the battlefield.

How Hart came to these conclusions, like much of her biography, sadly remains ground for speculation. Still, we can begin to sketch the basic details of her life to inform such theorizing. Born in late 1837 in Kentucky, she was the daughter of Cupid and Judith Hart, free African American residents of Logan County; her first entry into official records was a hash mark in the "Free Colored Females under 10 Years of Age" column of the 1840 federal census of Logan County (219). The 1850 census offers more detail: it locates the Hart family specifically in Russellville, a small city on the southern edge of Kentucky perhaps best known as the seat of the Crittenden family. It lists Cupid Hart as a forty-five-year-old "mulatto" whose occupation was noted as "House Carpenter" and who had been born in North Carolina and could not read or write. His wife "Judy" was also a forty-five-year-old "mulatto," though her birthplace is listed as Virginia. The couple had four children— Able (age fourteen), Jane E. (age twelve), James M. (age eleven), and Judy H. (age seven)—all born in Kentucky (133). These details and the fifty dollars of personal property Hart owned mark the family as of the class of free African Americans who migrated west in the early 1830s, hoping that the possession of an in-demand trade by the head of the household might allow them to carve a new life. Of their time pre-Kentucky, we, as yet, know nothing beyond three brief but fascinating notes tied to Cupid Hart's 1889 death: a pair of Warren County death records that claim that his father's name was Edward and that his mother's maiden name was "Winsor," and a brief obituary in the 8 August 1889 *Lebanon Gazette* that says that his "freedom" had "been given him by a benevolent friend."

While I have not been able to determine when the Hart family moved to Ohio or to find them in the 1860 federal census, it seems likely that the move happened in the early 1850s—perhaps even as late as 1856, as Cupid Hart's *Lebanon Gazette* obituary claims.[53] In addition to the kind of promise families like William Jay Greenly's and Elisha Weaver's would have found from living on the "free" side of the border and close to population centers born of both the river trade and westward expansion, the Harts would likely have been well aware of increasing sectional tensions—and of the powers in Kentucky that would, at the outbreak of the war, lead that state to flirt with secession. (Notably, the center of Kentucky's flirtation was Russellville.)[54]

Cupid and Judith Hart would live the rest of their lives in Warren County. Working as a day laborer, Cupid Hart was able to put together an impressive economic base: the 1870 census of Roachester (Warren County) lists the family with $1,200 in real estate and another $100 in personal property.[55] When Cupid Hart died, on 2 August 1889, he was well known enough for the *Gazette* to run the item mentioned above—which noted that "another resident of this place quietly passed away," that he was "a colored man, and formerly a slave," and that "he was a man respected by all who knew him and was a firm believer in Chrisitianity." He was buried in Roachester's "Old Quaker Cemetery" next to his wife, Judith, who predeceased him on 13 January 1879. The Harts' careful striving allowed opportunities for their children that they themselves never knew. While Cupid Hart would continue to be listed as illiterate until 1880, and Judith Hart's listing in the 1870 census carries a hash mark under "cannot write" (but *not* under "cannot read"), all of their children are listed as literate from 1850 on. As noted above, Jane Elizabeth—"Lizzie"—became a subscriber to the *Recorder* in early 1863, via her minister. That she paid $2.25, the price of a full-year's subscription, suggests that she had both some disposable income and a real thirst for the textual. She began contributing her own texts less than a year later, when, in the 13 February 1864 *Recorder*, readers were introduced to "Lizzie" from "Morrowtown," who hoped that the Civil War would lead to having "freedom . . . proclaimed on every Northern hill-top and every Southern vale."

A family tragedy occasioned her second *Recorder* contribution, and her response to that tragedy not only confirmed her sense of A.M.E.-centered domesticity but also linked such with the public sharing of the domestic through textual means. On 12 May 1864, her younger sister—whom census and cemetery records list as Judy or Judith (their mother's name) and whom the 28 May 1864 *Recorder* (which was typeset from a handwritten letter put through the interstate mails) listed as "Julia"—died "of neuralgia, after two weeks of painful illness, which she bore without a murmur." The 28 May 1864 letter that describes the younger Hart's death in the sentimental and religious language common to *Recorder* obituaries (and the period generally) was followed by a short poem, "Lines Written on the Death of Julia Hart / By Her Sister Lizzie."[56] The poem concludes "when twilight cometh, / There is none we miss like you" and conveys Lizzie Hart's great love for her sister, who would be buried in the same "Old Quaker Cemetery" plot in which her parents would later find rest.

That young Judith Hart's death was a deeply felt family and local event is clear, but just as clear is the fact that Lizzie Hart wanted it nationalized. Hart's letter and poem about her sister appear in the *same* issue as her letter about the Fort Pillow massacre—and Judith Hart's death is undoubtedly what "Lizzie H." referred to when she said, "To the many who have lost friends in this late massacre, I pity you much. I know what it is to be separated from loved ones, by the hand of death."

Hart's sense that the national was the local—and vice versa—would shape all of her contributions to the *Recorder,* although those contributions would sadly and abruptly end with the 30 December 1865 issue.[57] Still, the reader of Lizzie Hart's *Recorder* work is immediately struck by how little most of her contributions say about her physical location in a small town in Ohio. Her very first letter boldly opened, "Mr. Editor: —When I look around and mark the progress of our people and the many changes that have taken place in the last twelve months, it is no wonder that many are exclaiming, 'Truly God is a shroud of mysteries!' This is but the dawn of a brighter day" and thus set a national focus—far from the innumerable local items James Lynch despaired of. Rather than offering the "sights and sounds" of an outpost in far Ohio, Hart's letter assumes that she is worthy of a place in a national dialogue. In this vein (and in a recognition of northern racism reminiscent of Harriet Wilson's *Our Nig*), that first letter asserted that "there was never a people more oppressed than ours. Hatred and oppression have met us on the right and on the left, in the North and in the South." But, Hart continued, "to-day we have men and women who have no superiors. Look at our land, so well dotted with churches and schoolhouses, and yet we are building more." Where Hart found most hope was in the move among black men to join the Union army: "It was a motive higher than greenbacks that prompted you to go, and that caused the old man in Baltimore to thrown down his hoe and at once become a soldier and a man. It was the freedom and elevation of your race." She closed, "There is a glorious future just before us. God speed the happy day! Yours, for the cause, Lizzie."

While Hart's letter and poem on her sister's death certainly place Morrow and its environs as sentimental, similar tone, content, and lack of discussion of the physical place certainly mark her next two letters—those mentioned above regarding Fort Pillow and black soldiers' pay. By her 1 October 1864 *Recorder* letter, her goals were clear: she was seeking to define the moral location of America rather than simply a physical space in Ohio. In that "Letter from Morrowtown," Hart asked readers, "What must be done with the negro? is the daily topic of discussion." After quickly exploding colonizationist arguments (in part by arguing that "America welcomes the potato-eaters to come from Ireland" as well as "the French, Welch, Dutch, German, and Scotch" and, erroneously of course, "the red men"), Hart asserted simply, "If America could hold four and a half million of slaves, can she not hold them when they become four and a half million of freemen?" Hart concluded that any end to the Civil War and any peace must, presaging Martin Luther King Jr., "recognize men—not by their color—but by their integrity." Only then, she asserted, could "the colored man . . . find a home in America, and a grave in American soil."

Uncompromisingly asserting that the physical place of America must embody its supposed philosophical place as a nation founded on liberty, Hart again told soldiers in her 7 January 1865 *Recorder* letter that they should not allow themselves "to forget Fort Pillow," and, in an 8 April 1865 letter that "we desire peace—but not a peace like that of 1776—not like that of 1812—not a peace which holds four and a half million human beings in worse than Egyptian bondage—but a peace such as the world never saw." And while, in a 27 May 1865 letter, she asserted that "there was never a time since the birth of the country, when such universal sadness prevailed, as on the day the sad news was received of the death of President Lincoln," she also argued that "the foundation of universal freedom, which he so firmly laid, can never be torn down." Hart argued that "it still stands, and will continue to stand, till time shall be no more." While Hart's participation in the *Recorder's* (and the black press's larger) mythmaking surrounding Lincoln here is notable, what is more striking is that she turns to the doubly domestic metaphor of Lincoln as a house- and nation-builder—as, in Hart's words, "the master mind who planned and built it"—a metaphor that neatly dovetails with the sense of Lincoln as a rail-splitting, log-cabin-building pioneer, that takes location as its implicit subject, and that has a vehicle (and perhaps tenor, too) that embodies the sense of expansionist settlement and germinal mobility so key to the writers in this study.

This sense of the nation also imbued its inhabitants with both rights and responsibilities—rights and responsibilities Hart was quick to claim as her own specifically because of her place: "Some have sneeringly inquired why I meddle about the rights and wrongs of the braves [*sic*] who have defended the country," Hart wrote in her final 30 December 1865 *Recorder* letter. She then asked rhetorically, "Have I not a right to do so? Is not this a free country? Am I not an American woman, born and reared on American soil? Have I not been subject to the oppressive laws of the land? Have I not a right to complain? I earnestly hope, that the day is not far distant, when we as American men and women, long and wrongfully oppressed, both in the North and South, shall enjoy all the rights of a free and happy land."

Had she continued to write for the *Recorder,* Hart might have done more pieces that were explicitly local within this nationalist ethos—more work that studied the place of Morrow within and as the place of a larger America. (As discussed in chapter 3, Jennie Carter certainly experienced a similar broadening.) Nonetheless, the single letter from Hart that focuses on such—published in the 9 December 1865 *Recorder*—is worth close examination. Headed "A Flying Visit to Wilberforce," the letter summarizes her journey with the bridal party of Anne Strange of Roachester just after Strange's Cincinnati marriage to a "Mr. N. L. Childs."[58] On 17 November, the group "started for Wilberforce," and, after a brief stop in Xenia, on "a perfect day," they traveled to the site of the A.M.E.'s black college, Wilberforce University. Hart's discussion of the "lofty hills and deep ravines," of "the grounds and many facilities afforded for an education," and the "grand spot, one calculated to imbue the young mind with lofty aspirations" were certainly in line with the rhetoric Daniel Payne used to place his still relatively new school at the center of A.M.E. higher education efforts. It was also consonant with the rhetoric of the *Recorder* and the General Conference, both of whom consistently praised Wilberforce and advocated for donations both large and small to aid the college.

But Hart's letter participated in this nationalizing of Wilberforce in other ways, too. In addition to talking of the Shorter family—scion James Alexander Shorter would be the ninth bishop of the A.M.E. Church and son Joseph was one of Wilberforce's teachers—Hart noted "the extreme pleasure of shaking hands with Elder Davis," Edward D. Davis, who regularly contributed to the *Recorder* and was recognized as a leader in the region.[59] Perhaps most striking, though, is Hart's noting "the pleasure of seeing Major Delaney's [*sic*] son." The use of the title "Major" to identify Martin Robinson Delany meshes neatly with Hart's consistent concern for black troops; one of the leading recruiters for black soldiers, Delany's commissioning as an officer was a key event in the ongoing struggles for civil rights in and beyond the military. I have not yet been able to determine which of Delany's sons Hart met at Wilberforce, but some readers of the *Recorder* would have known not only of Delany's commitment to the Union, but also of his family's, as his eldest son Toussaint L'Overture Delany enlisted in the famed Massachusetts Fifty-fourth in late 1863.[60] Through noting this brush with the famous, Hart demonstrated both that Wilberforce was a centerpiece of black education, black literature, and the new black nation—*and* that her tiny home in Morrow was only a few miles' journey from that center.

The logistics of gender and an approaching marriage among the small middle-class African American community in Warren County may well have silenced Hart's national voice; they certainly limited her mobility. Still, for a time, she joined a set of voices that would continually remind *Recorder* readers that their nation was large and contained multitudes—and that the textual might someday (indeed, might already be beginning to) both reach those multitudes *and* spring from them.

A "WHITEWASHER'S SON" IN PARIS
William Steward's *John Blye*

Writing from Springfield, Illinois—on a midwestern tour reminiscent of Elisha Weaver's earlier journeys—Reverend Henry McNeal Turner claimed, in a letter published in the 19 September 1878 *Recorder,* that "I have never known a story to attract more attention than 'John Blye, the Whitewasher's Son'. . . . I am asked on all sides if it is fiction or a true story. I have to answer, 'I don't know,' but nearly all say it is true. . . . A certain minister has preached two sermons from it."

The serialized *Recorder* novel that Turner praised so highly had begun running in the *Recorder's* 11 July 1878 issue, was then in its eleventh installment, and was signed simply, "By Will, Author of 'The Gem of the Alley,' &c." While most of its original separate installments are available in the online *Christian Recorder* subscription database run by Accessible Archives, and all of the separate installments can be found in the massive (and unfortunately expensive) Black Periodical Literature Project microform collection, even these landmark efforts offer only severely limited access to a fascinating text and fail to identify *John Blye's* author. And while the novel was fondly remembered in the *Recorder* at least as late as 1884,[61] to my knowledge, *John Blye* is not mentioned in any history, bibliography, or critical study of African American literature published to date.

While as both a friend of *John Blye*'s author and the *Recorder*'s business manager, Turner certainly had some self-interest in promoting the story, his praise—like the prepublication accolades of editor Benjamin Tucker Tanner—should be figured in dialogue with the *Recorder*'s willingness to create space for all *twenty* of the novel's installments, as well as Tanner's 8 August 1878 claim that "word comes that 'John Blye,' is already becoming quite a hero in the eyes of RECORDER readers."[62] In short, the *Recorder* recognized *John Blye* as an important literary event. As such, and as a very early serialized novel by an African American that considers the Civil War (among other topics) and that appeared in one of the leading black periodicals of the time, *John Blye* and its author are worthy of broad consideration. In beginning to reintroduce *John Blye*, this section shares information on the identity and biography of "Will," places his authorship in the context of the Tanner-era of the *Recorder*, and closely considers the novel's treatment of (and roots in) a set of unexpected places as well as its representation of a domestic black mobility that is not just national but international.

Poems by "Will" began appearing in the *Recorder* in December 1876; a half dozen poems followed in 1877. By the time the serialized short story "The Gem of the Alley"—briefly discussed below—began appearing in the 25 April 1878 issue, most regular *Recorder* readers probably knew that "Will" was A.M.E. Book Concern clerk William Steward. Steward's better-known brother, Reverend Theophilus Steward, published a tribute volume to their mother, *Memoirs of Mrs. Rebecca Steward*, in late 1877, which includes a four-page poem "In Memoriam" that is bylined "William Steward ('Will.')" In addition to being repeatedly praised in the *Recorder*, the volume was advertised there regularly—as in the 3 January 1878 *Recorder*, which noted that the book included "a beautiful original poem by Wm. Steward ('Will')."[63]

Born in May of 1840, Steward was the eldest son of James and Rebecca Gould Steward of Cumberland County, New Jersey. The Stewards were part of a small community of free African Americans who were pushing into the middling classes. James Steward, already thirty-three years old when he married Rebecca Gould in December 1838, had become a "bound boy" after his parents joined one of the ill-fated colonization ventures encouraged by Haitian president Jean Pierre Boyer in 1824.[64] He ran away, ended up living with Elijah Gould (a relative of Rebecca's), grew into a skilled tradesman, and spent over fifty years working as a mechanic at the Cumberland Nail and Iron Factory. Rebecca Gould was tied to mixed-race families with the surnames Gould, Bowen, Pierce, and Cuff, who built the Gouldtown settlement in Cumberland County; she traced her specific ancestry to a (white) granddaughter of Englishman and property-holder John Fenwick named Elizabeth and an unnamed African American man, whose relationship led the elder Fenwick to disown his granddaughter.[65]

While neither James Steward nor Rebecca Gould Steward was associated directly with any church when they married, both formally joined the African Methodist Episcopal Church in 1846. Rebecca became especially known for her piety, her local activism, and her intellect, and she taught both Sunday School classes and adult Bible classes. While her own writing later in life—some of which is reproduced in *Memoirs*—was quite didactic and while Theophilus would write in *Memoirs* that "my whole recollection of my mother is of a Christian," Theophilus also remembered her as challenging easy notions of theology and as being as familiar with Milton, Shakespeare, and classical philosophers as she was with the Bible.[66]

The Steward family emphasized faith, literacy, and activism and grew together in what Albert G. Miller refers to as "a triangle consisting of home, Sunday School, and church" (2). As the eldest son, William Steward exemplified these values: by 11 May 1861, he was already listed as a subscriber to the *Recorder*, and he sent his first letter to the *Recorder* only two years later, in the 7 March 1863 issue. He published additional letters in the *Recorder*— generally in his role as a "recording secretary" for the New Jersey Colored Conventions and the New Jersey Equal Rights League—in 1865 and 1866.[67] His ties with the church and the paper suggest that he was not only growing familiar with national issues but also with black literature—and that he read authors like Collins, Daffin, and Hart.[68]

William Steward's younger brother Theophilus—who had entered the ministry early and eventually received much more national notice—had been chosen to accompany Bishop Daniel Payne on a tour of the South just after the end of the Civil War.[69] Working primarily in South Carolina and Georgia, Theophilus Steward not only served as a pastor at a number of A.M.E. churches but also became active in local politics and secured an appointment with the Freedmen's Bank. Probably in part because of his brother's growing clout, William Steward also spent some of the first years of Reconstruction among the newly freed people of the South. In addition to clerking for the Freedmen's Bank, he taught for a time in Americus,

Georgia, where he argued—as he would in *John Blye*—that the traditional subjects tied to basic literacy, mathematics, and civics needed to be supplemented by French, German, music, and algebra. Like Sallie Daffin, he found his students both young and old hungry for the educational opportunities that they had been so long denied (Seraile, *Voice*, 17–19).

Still, William Steward's heart was in New Jersey. He had married in 1862, and his wife Sarah gave birth to the couple's first child, a daughter named Ellen, in 1863. By 1870, Steward's growing family—now including daughters Grace and Clara (born in 1865 and January 1867, respectively) and son William (born in November 1869)—had settled among Goulds and Pierces in Fairfield, Cumberland County, New Jersey. There, probably on the strength of his experience with the Freedmen's Bank and his local reputation, Steward secured a position as a bank cashier. In 1870, the federal census taker recorded his real estate holdings as worth three thousand dollars and his personal property as worth one thousand dollars.[70] He continued to work with the New Jersey Equal Rights League and various state-level African American groups, but he had clearly not forgotten the A.M.E. Church or the *Recorder*, either—as he continued to send occasional correspondence and even made a donation to the A.M.E. Book Concern.[71]

At some point in 1876, Steward was invited to work in the A.M.E. Church offices in Philadelphia. His move certainly wasn't the kind of massive shift that "Western boy" Elisha Weaver experienced when he came to Philadelphia from the unexpected black literary location in Indianapolis. Still, Steward was leaving a relatively small community that is still often left off of maps of African American literary history and that was even then little considered by his brethren in the urban centers of the North. He was also coming with, if not Weaver's itinerant background, a version of the postwar mobility that so shaped Sallie Daffin's work. The man Steward would work for at the A.M.E. Book Concern was another powerful example of the changes the war brought about in terms of black mobility— especially in comparison to a figure like John Berry Meachum: Steward was listed in the 30 September 1876 *Recorder* as the "corresponding clerk" of Henry McNeal Turner. The son of free blacks in South Carolina, Turner was making a meteoric rise within the church, spurred in part by his evangelical talents and in part by his role as chaplain to the First U.S. Colored Troops in the Civil War. He had already served a term in the Georgia State Legislature, written a new hymnbook, and recently been appointed as the A.M.E. publications manager. On his way to being named a bishop in 1880,

Turner traveled throughout the nation, and this meant that he came to depend greatly on the "able gentleman" William Steward, whom he referred to as "my deputy" and "my deputy and chief clerk."[72]

Steward's duties quickly expanded beyond handling Turner's correspondence: he became the main clerk for the A.M.E. Publications Department and Book Room, doing everything from filling orders to taking inventory to even sometimes speaking for the department in the pages of the *Recorder*. This work undoubtedly brought him into close contact with Tanner, who was always looking for ways to enliven the *Recorder* and who probably suggested that Steward begin submitting work. Tanner may even have encouraged him to experiment with more extended fiction—given the success of Frances Harper's serialized *Recorder* novels *Minnie's Sacrifice* (1869) and *Sowing and Reaping* (1876–1877).

Steward's six-part "The Gem of the Alley" certainly fit with the kind of uplift literature Tanner was publishing. A moral tale of urban poverty set in Philadelphia, "The Gem" focuses on the conversion of African American "bad girl" Sallie Martin, brought about in large part by the growing faith of a black street child, Nannie Spikes (the title character), and shaped by a cast that includes a young black doctor, a dying A.M.E. clergyman, and the clergyman's self-sacrificing wife.[73]

However, *John Blye*, whose first installment began less than two months after the conclusion of "The Gem," was more ambitious. It was also more deeply tied to both Steward's own home and to the questions of black mobility considered in this study. While, like "The Gem," it focuses on a moral message and on black characters, *John Blye* is much more sprawling in scope and much more specific about postbellum racial elevation efforts building from both antebellum and Civil War accomplishments. The novel opens in circa 1850 Cumberland County, New Jersey, with a series of domestic tableaux showing the nine-year-old title character with his free black parents and emphasizing the value of hard work, domestic ideals, and faith. The novel initially follows the Blyes' struggles to enroll John in the town's all-white school—including assertions by the principal that he should instead go to the school in the all-black settlement several miles away, an assault on John by the principal, a successful court battle, and a growing friendship with the progressive white Holloway family.

After chronicling John's school years—during which John demonstrates an unusual aptitude for understanding machinery—the novel briefly treats his apprenticeship and first position as a machinist at the local ironworks.

Much of the novel then focuses on John's efforts as the newly chosen engineer at a mill being built by young Tom Holloway, a physician-turned-businessman and now fast-friend of the Blye family. Beginning circa 1857, this sequence mainly takes place in the nearby town of Edgefield and features John's growing battles with racism, including sabotage (by the evil white machinist Absalom Wheeler, who weasels his way into young John's confidence) and white mob violence. This section also depicts John's initial courtship with Eteline Voulons, the daughter of a wealthy black Philadelphian. Key to John's continuing rise are his deep faith, his father's acquisition of real estate, and his continuing education (including learning various European languages from his father's friendly immigrant tenants).

When the Civil War begins, John helps fill Union contracts, and when the Union begins accepting black troops, John attempts to raise a New Jersey regiment, only to be told that New Jersey blacks can only join the generalized U.S. Colored Troops and not the state regulars. Frustrated, he instead joins the famed Massachusetts Fifty-fourth and serves nobly. His greatest contribution, though, comes after being wounded and transferred: his mechanical prowess saves U. S. Grant's Petersburg campaign by ensuring that the supply trains run, and he is recognized by Grant himself. The novel's conclusion firmly places the now-married John and Eteline among a growing group of influential African Americans on the broader national and international stage: through his intelligence, skill, and persistence, as well as the intervention of now-president Grant, John Blye secures a diplomatic appointment to the U.S. consulate in Paris.

John Blye is, in some ways, a study in the postbellum shifts in the *Recorder*'s sense of black mobility. While the novel says comparatively little about its setting, it is clear that John was born in, as the opening 11 July 1878 installment says, "one of our Northern towns"; references like the 22 August 1878 chapter 7 comments on "Northern villages . . . where the population is small and where both foreigners and colored people are few" confirm a location in the North and place such outside of urban centers even though they tell little more. Even chapter 7's assertion that "The town that Mr. Blye lived in, though small, contained several manufactories, among which, were those of woolen goods, nails, glass, agricultural implements, &c, as well as several machine shops" offers little sense of geography. In some ways embracing the lack of specificity that marked many of Lizzie Hart's letters, Steward was both simultaneously building an "anytown" and asserting that this "anytown" was most definitely not an "any*city*." John's father's struggles to enroll John in the town school are emblematic of the steps settlers (like those noted in Carter's work) had to take as their "frontier" became more tied to the larger and white-dominated world. The moves to make John's hometown into any "anytown" thus give national importance to the family's settler-style educational struggles, in part because such are struggles for the exercise of citizenship: in chapter 4 (1 August 1878), John's father says he wishes "to avail myself of the State's provisions to give him an education," because he can give an affirmative answer to Mr. Holloway's query, "Do you live within the proper school limits?" Like Lizzie Hart, John Blye is marked as being "born and reared on American soil," and so as holding "all the rights of a free and happy land."

The elder Blye also terms Spring Bottom—the nearest all-black settlement, which is "several miles distant"—as too far away for young John to travel to in order to attend school. For area whites, Spring Bottom has other connotations. We learn in chapter 2 (18 July 1878) that it is not simply "a settlement of industrious colored people"; it is a location of antebellum freedom and agency because those "industrious" people are "mostly escaped slaves." While Spring Bottom is obviously too far to walk on a daily basis, it is, as the narrator reports in chapter 5 (8 August 1878), all too close for some of the white parents and school administrators; they fear that "there'll be a hull swarm of 'em up here from Spring Bottom an' they'll rule the hull school. Better put a stop to it before it begins."

The scenes surrounding John Blye's entry into the town school also establish the novel's integrationist ethos. When saying such, it is important to note that the novel focuses on integration in public settings—schools, work, the military, and so forth—rather than Philip Bell's "bugbear" of social integration (though even here, the novel bounces between the Blyes' ties to Spring Bottom residents, nearby black Philadelphia, and the white Holloways). In short, John Blye's physical location should, the novel argues, place him in a specific school; law and fairness, rather than race or social connections, should govern such. The elder Blye thus physically places himself in a school board meeting and then, with attorney Holloway, in a courtroom, where he is victorious.[74] Throughout, much is also made of the fact that John is religiously brought to school everyday—placed, as it were, in the location the bigoted whites in the community attempt to deny him, and that his specific residency and birth "on American soil" should grant him.

John's next entry into an "unexpected place" centers on similar conflicts and strategies. When John has completed his schooling, apprenticeship, and first years as a machinist, Tom Holloway takes him to the nearby town of Edgefield to build the engine for his new mill. In chapter 10 (12 September 1878), Holloway warns John—now a teenager—that "you will likely be reminded that you are in Edgefield where they are not accustomed to see black men in your occupation." The warning is prophetic: the town laborers refer to him as "Pompey Caesar" and "Julius Alexander Cicero," assume that he is there to fetch and carry for them, and—when they find he is an engineer—threaten John's place in the mill by refusing to work, again citing not only his race but the possibility that, if John works, "all the negroes from Spring Bottom'll be down here and there'll be no such things as managin' them." They also promise physical violence.

The scenes that follow, however, offer a fascinating revision of the school sequence: black folks from Spring Bottom *do* come. In the next installment, published in the 19 September 1878 issue, the white Holloway says that "I'll go up to Spring Bottom and bring down a gang of laborers." When they arrive, while the threats to John continue, because some of "the Spring Bottom laborers . . . 'could fight,'" the whites of Edgefield become "a little shy of committing any outrage upon him." One could certainly argue that the mobility—or the agency behind the mobility—here is mostly Holloway's, but the Spring Bottom workers quickly show that they are capable workers and strong defenders of their place. Though it takes several more chapters, John also demonstrates that his proper "place" is indeed in the mill as its engineer: he withstands further verbal abuse and a physical attack by a white mob and then, when he figures out that the mill's works are being sabotaged, he saves the mill. By chapter 16 (24 October 1878), the narrator tells us that "anyone in the village . . . having anything to say against John Blye—the engineer, was advised to 'sing it small' as his friends soon numbered the entire population of the place." Coming so soon after Hayes's deal to pull out federal troops and essentially end Reconstruction, this sequence seems designed to argue that public sphere integration could still take place if blacks could demonstrate that they were as skilled and capable as John Blye and the Spring Bottom workers—and were *present* for opportunities for integrated spaces. That these scenes are punctuated by moments of more interaction between the Blye family and the larger Spring Bottom community suggests a kind of growing coalition among blacks spread across "Northern towns" to ensure that such happens.

This coalition also, though, reaches more and more into *expected* places, too. Late in the mill sequence, in chapter 11 (19 September 1878), "a wealthy colored gentleman in the city of Philadelphia" who knows the Blye family's reputation asks them to board his wife and daughter in their "quiet country town for a few weeks where they could rusticate while he should be absent in Boston." Even before they arrive, the beautiful, cultured, intelligent, and pious Eteline Voulons is marked as a "Philadelphia girl"—as when John's father asserts "with a mischievous look" that "I reckon we'll lose our boy" because during the visit, "this Philadelphia girl will capture him, sure as gun." As described in chapter 12 (26 September 1878)—appropriately titled "A New Sociality"—John expresses skepticism that he can compete with "the brilliant and polished gentlemen" of Philadelphia for the attentions of "the rich city lady," and the Blyes' Spring Bottom friends similarly wonder, in the next chapter, about the "Phidelfy people." However, Eteline quickly proves herself to readers by telling her mother that "John Blye is much more worthy of being idolized than your worthless daughter," to which her mother replies: "It is a very high mark of excellence that" the Blye family has "worked their way from modest beginnings up to" a "position of respect and comparative wealth."

The extended courtship is interrupted by Blye's Civil War service, which, in itself offers a second coalition with more "expected" places as well as a key reconsideration of black mobility in the novel. In chapter 16 (24 October 1878), John attempts to assert his location—as his family did with his schooling and as he did in the Edgefield mill—by going "to war as a State volunteer," as "he felt that to go any other way would be an acknowledgement . . . that he was not a citizen of a State." When New Jersey rejects his service—and that of other blacks, John instead founds "a pretty strong club of stay-at-homes . . . declaring they would not go to war unless they could be accredited as volunteers to the State to which they belonged"; they even, in correspondence presented in the novel, write a letter to Secretary of War Edwin Stanton offering to serve as New Jersey troops—with black officers and with the same pay and rations as white troops. At once a very specific and real event and another fictional "anytown" moment, this brief sequence again argues that the myriad locations of blackness across the North were attempting and must attempt to be part of the national life.[75] In this, Blye seems to almost consciously echo the dramatic calls for equal pay and participation made by figures like Lizzie Hart.

Frustrated by the government's denial, Blye joins what is probably the most "expected" and overdetermined group of African American soldiers in the war, the Massachusets Fifty-fourth. Unfortunately, Steward offers few details of Blye's wartime experiences—though Blye fights nobly and is even wounded—and depends heavily on his readers' knowledge: in chapter 17 (31 October 1878), for example, the narrator relates that "the course of the 54th Massachusetts Regiment is too well known to be gone over. Its conduct on the field of battle soon enlisted the sympathy and won the plaudit of every Union heart." Only a few pages later, Steward similarly asserts that "all know the story of the assault upon Fort Wagner and the death and glorious burial of the brave Col. Shaw . . . in glory's bed 'with his Negroes'—the brave dead of the Fifty-Fourth Massachusetts Regiment." Blye's military time—via a transfer from the Fifty-fourth to a unit stationed with Grant at Petersburg—does, though, allow Steward to mark Blye's amazing mobility, and, just as certainly as that mobility springs from Blye's desire to serve his "native State," so, too, does it serve the domestic purpose of—through Blye's amazing technical skill—both figuratively (by helping win the battle of Petersburg) and literally (by ensuring lines of transportation) knit the nation together again.[76]

That deeply domestic task accomplished and, later, the domestic war, won, Blye can "return to his native town" in chapter 18 (7 November 1878), complete his courtship, and travel briefly to wed Eteline in "the beautiful home of the Voulons in Philadelphia" under the celebratory blessings of "a brilliant assemblage of Philadelphia's most polished colored society" led by an unnamed A.M.E. bishop as well as "a number of their friends from Spring Bottom." Soon after, in chapter 19 (14 November 1878), though, "John Blye and his beautiful bride . . . departed for their new home in John's native town," where, conveniently, his father has amassed significant real estate and wealth.

Were this a tale from the early years of the Reconstruction, *John Blye* might well end here—with the eminently mobile hero's marriage resulting in a clear linkage between blacks in an "expected" urban place and in a representative "Northern town." It might alternately end with John Blye and his wife taking the missionary journey south—as, for example, John Mifflin Brown and his wife did (to say nothing of Sallie Daffin) and as Harper's *Minnie's Sacrifice* depicts. Indeed, the absence of discussion of the newly freed southern blacks in *John Blye* is in some ways baffling, especially given Steward's own experience as a teacher in the South. That said, *John Blye* is largely a novel about "Northern towns," and Steward seems to find documenting—however briefly—the increasing racism in the postwar North (even against heroic soldiers like John Blye) and depicting an international mobility more important. Signaling the first, Blye says to Eteline in their "nice comfortable parlor"—albeit also in a conversation that was arguably happening across the black nation, often in much more painful circumstances—that it "is a little mortifying to note the change that is coming over the people of my native town. Once I was considered a good enough workman to be at the head of my trade, and nothing was thought about my color; but now, because I have been a black soldier, it seems that there is a strong feeling against even having me work in the shops." Almost on a lark, Eteline suggests that they go abroad, but her comment quickly becomes the base for serious discussion, for contact with the now-congressman Tom Holloway, for a trip to Washington, and, ultimately, for Blye's application for a diplomatic posting.[77] Certainly Blye's success at obtaining an appointment—getting beyond the Dickensian appointment clerk through the intervention of President Grant himself—is a marker of a relatively new kind of international mobility, but even in this Steward is quick to point out the potential limits imposed by racism. Blye, who has become fluent in French, Spanish, and German through learning from his father's immigrant tenants and through reading and study, is initially offered an appointment on Turks Island in the British West Indies.[78] Steward thus shows his abilities as a close reader of the early diplomatic appointments offered to African Americans—appointments mainly in areas perceived to have "black" issues (for example, the West Indies and Africa). Blye instead argues that he is well suited for a position at the French consulate, and the novel actually leaves the Blyes in Paris where "the gay, happy and polite French" receive them "as polished representatives of the mightiest Republic on the face of the globe."

Still, these are not the final words of the novel, and *John Blye*'s conclusion only serves to reemphasize Steward's argument about blacks in unexpected places: the ending reads, "On the Western shores of one of our great lakes, stands a large Machine Works, owned and managed by a colored man, whose inventive genius, whose early trials, whose mechanical skill, persevering energy, and final triumph . . . have been not altogether unlike those of the hero of our story." That "colored man" was Steward's cousin Hezekiah Gould, who, Steward claimed in his 1913 *Gouldtown*, was the basis for most of John Blye's early life.[79] Certainly the invocation of a man like John Blye busily shaping the West is consonant with both the *Recorder*'s sense of nation-building and, more broadly, with many of the other works in this study. Pairing such with John Blye's fictional appointment to Paris suggests a real place for African Americans in not only America's (western) future, but in the world's future. The novel's split ending—between Paris and Michigan—and, more generally, *John Blye*'s rich sense of growing up free and black in New Jersey reminds readers that national (even international) accomplishments can begin *anywhere* (and *everywhere*) in black America. And while Gould did not serve in the Civil War, he did continue to build a life from his love of technology; while Gould did not enter the State Department, he did turn pioneer and move to rural Michigan, where he continued the kind of engineering work described in *John Blye*.[80]

That *John Blye* was never published in book form, that William Steward returned to New Jersey soon after its serialization (where he worked as a journalist and advertising manager for Bridgeton newspapers for several years), and that his nationally distributed fiction seems to have been limited to his time with the *Recorder* (though he may well have written for other papers) is, in some ways, emblematic of the Nadir—a period in which Sallie Daffin and Lizzie Hart also fell silent and in which the presence of the *Recorder* on the national literary scene, in part because of Tanner's loss, lessened considerably. The rise of writers like Paul Laurence Dunbar and Charles Chesnutt, the growth of dialect literature in mainstream magazines, the continuing difficulty of establishing long-term and economically stable black periodicals and other publication efforts, and the chilling effects of post-Reconstruction Jim Crow both South and North all may have contributed to the comparative absence of these voices in our sense of African American literary history.

Still, these circumstances did not stop African Americans from continuing to create literature in unexpected places. Indianapolis became the home of the long-running newspaper the *Freeman* in 1884. It joined Detroit's *Plaindealer,* which was founded in 1883 as an important black midwestern voice; two of the *Plaindealer*'s editors, Walter H. Stowers and William H. Anderson, even pseudonymously authored a fascinating and massive novel under the byline "Sanda" titled *Appointed: An American Novel* in 1894. San Francisco's black community—and specifically a writer named James L. Young, about whom little is yet known—produced a novel in 1891, *Helen Duval, a French Romance.* These texts and groups remain little studied, and there may well be countless other examples—examples that demonstrate that the African American literary in the nineteenth century (and beyond) goes far beyond the handful of sites on our current map, examples suggesting that our relocation of black literature is just beginning.

Epilogue

(Re)Locating "Hannah Crafts"

I initially conceived of this study's conclusion as a series of short and provocative close and contextualized readings of texts not considered in the previous chapters—both samples of other "unexpected places" and reconsiderations of better-known texts' relationships to the frameworks offered here. Among those better-known texts, I've been most fascinated with *The Bondwoman's Narrative,* a manuscript novel published for the first time in 2002 that may (or may not) be semiautobiographical. Signed with what most critics assume to be a pseudonym, "Hannah Crafts," *The Bondwoman's Narrative* tells a rich first-person story of a young woman's experiences in slavery and eventual escape. Initially discovered in manuscript by pioneering black librarian and bibliophile Dorothy Porter Wesley,[1] *The Bondwoman's Narrative* was rediscovered and eventually edited by Henry Louis Gates Jr., the preeminent scholar of our generation in terms of the recovery of nineteenth-century African American literature and culture.[2]

Several features of *The Bondwoman's Narrative* connect to the questions in this study in complex ways: the main character's increasing sense of agency is represented through her growing control over her own mobility; her escape essentially allows her to become a settler in a simultaneously expected *and* unexpected place (expected in that her final freedom is found in a sentimental home as a minister's wife, unexpected in that this home is in rural New Jersey); the narrator is both implicitly and explicitly concerned with textual communities (from depictions of the main character's learning to read to the inclusion of passages lifted from and arguably signifying on the work of Charles Dickens);[3] the author is deeply conscious of not simply the act of writing but also the act of *sharing* writing[4]; while certainly a novel in a general sense, *The Bondwoman's Narrative* plays with expected notions of genre in complex ways.[5] The list could continue. As a scholar deeply interested in composition, publication, distribution, and circulation history, I am particularly drawn to the fact that the protagonist-narrator's final home looks very much like the New Jersey black homes in William Steward's *John Blye*—and that the protagonist-narrator looks a bit like Sallie Daffin, Lizzie Hart, and perhaps even Jennie Carter, because she, too, is a strong woman advocating the use of the textual to aid both nascent black nationalism and domestic values.

But this, of course, is where things get messy. Gates has marshaled impressive evidence of the book's composition date and context, and he argues persuasively for seeing the author as an African American woman. Subsequent scholars have deeply enriched the possibilities for close reading that he has suggested. But, as Gates and Hollis Robbins assert in introducing the essays on the novel they collected in *In Search of Hannah Crafts*, "Questions of Hannah Crafts's actual identity are put aside in most of the essays that follow. These scholars take it as a more or less settled matter that the author was a woman of African descent who wrote this text after attaining freedom in the North" (xi). More simply put, we still do not know who Hannah Crafts was—even though some are already beginning to take her identity as a given.

I want to emphasize that I am *almost* persuaded by the arguments of Gates and the other scholars in *In Search of Hannah Crafts* that center on, to use Nina Baym's summary, the sense that "many aspects of the narrative confirm that the author was female and African American. That she was a woman is deducible from the overwhelming preponderance of female characters and the female-centered domesticity of most events in the novel. . . . That [the author] was African American is inferable from the social nuancing and frankness with which she criticizes other black people, characteristics Gates elegantly analyzes in his introduction" (317). As a reader familiar with a wide range of texts by nineteenth-century black women, I found myself identifying with Baym's descriptions: "When I read the text for the first time I felt—it was an intuition, but I haven't changed my mind about it—that [the author] was not a fugitive slave" as Gates and others have argued "but a free woman" of African descent (323). Nonetheless, while I find the case for "placing" Hannah Crafts as a (free) black woman rich with possibility, the specter of Emma Dunham Kelley-Hawkins, the now-white "black" writer of the late nineteenth century (discussed in more depth below) gives me great pause—as does my own recognition of just how *many* authors, texts, and whole locations remain unknown to many of us.[6]

Because I share with several scholars in *In Search of Hannah Crafts* the sense that, in Gates and Robbins's introductory words, *The Bondwoman's Narrative* is "a serious and important piece of writing that has dramatically changed how we view the antebellum literary landscape," I am especially concerned that we have, in addition to passing by the looming gap of the author's biography, also missed some steps in placing the text (xi). I applaud the sense that the black literary can include a text left only in manuscript (and *never* published within the lifetime of its author). But placing a never-published manuscript within a framework of bound books and asserting that it changes the literary landscape—before talking in great depth about a much larger number of black stories in all sorts of other *published* forms (like those in periodicals)—seems premature.[7] We are only now—thanks in large part to massive efforts like Gates and Robbins's work with the Black Periodical Literature Project and Gates and Higginbotham's with the *African American National Biography*—beginning to even have the materials to draw more detailed guides to the "antebellum literary landscape."

Because we do not definitively know who Hannah Crafts was and we do not yet have a real map, I do not think we can fully place her within African American letters, and I suggest that our inability to locate Hannah Crafts—in all of the senses of that word—is emblematic of a set of issues that complicate any sweeping conclusions about early African American literature. If *The Bondwoman's Narrative* becomes—or, as its *New York Times* bestseller status and subsequent significant course adoption suggests, is already—a key text in nineteenth-century African American literature, then we put ourselves at some risk, especially if we uncritically assume the placement of "Hannah Crafts" in a specific community we are still defining. We also run the risk of—once again—setting aside a historical sense of what many black literary figures of the nineteenth century saw *as* literature and saw literature *doing,* and we lean again toward (over)favoring specific genres—the novel, the slave narrative, rich though both are—instead of considering the much larger range of extant and verified African American literature.

In short, because it is a wonderfully fascinating text, I want very much to write a chapter in this study about *The Bondwoman's Narrative.* I cannot. We have too much other work to do first.

In making this claim, I'm reminded of a dinner conversation I had with a friend as I was conceptualizing *Unexpected Places*. We were, of all places, in Philadelphia—actually only a few blocks from William Still's home, where Frances Ellen Watkins Harper, Mary Harper, Charlotte Forten Grimke, Francis Grimke, and Sallie Daffin gathered in 1884, as briefly noted in chapter 4. One of us—I'm not sure who, though to give due credit, I think it was my friend—joked that there was a time when literary historians could receive tenure by documenting what Herman Melville had for breakfast while writing *Moby Dick*. We shared a good laugh about eggs over easy and "the whiteness of the whale."

In retrospect, I must admit that my continuing fascination with our laughter is not simply tied to an interest in minutiae or in the ways institutional structures shape what scholarly work gets done.[8] It also came from some real jealousy. I have yet to determine birth and/or death dates for some of the authors in this study; some have parents, spouses, and children about whom I know little or nothing. While I have photographs of Frederick Douglass and Sojourner Truth staring at me as I write (and have seen dozens of Emerson, Melville, Stowe, and Whitman), I have no idea what Jennie Carter or Lizzie Hart looked like. Manuscripts by almost all of the authors in this study seem to be long lost. Many wrote more texts that we have not yet found. Readers still have to turn to microfilm to find the known *Elevator* letters of Peter Cole and Thomas Detter—and to film or online databases for the known publications of Sallie Daffin, Lizzie Hart, and "Will." Doing the kinds of "literary geoscapes" for nineteenth-century African American literature and culture that are described in the introduction of this work is, as yet, a dream. Breakfast, indeed! We need the texts, the authors.

As noted in this volume's introduction, the recent publication of several new resources—the wondrous *African American National Biography* perhaps highest among them—offers great promise in these struggles; such works allow us to come closer to practicing the kinds of polycentric approaches to early black literature and culture that Hogue has articulated for twentieth-century studies. I should also note that, given a host of factors—some tied to individual and institutionalized racism and some to the ways in which texts were produced, circulated, valorized, neglected, repressed, and/or even destroyed[9]—my definition of that fuller sense of nineteenth-century African American literature and culture is no easy totality. Finally, I generally agree with Janet Gray's comments in "Passing as Fact": "It would be impractical for everyone involved in recuperative scholarship to be skilled at all trades, able to cross borders between specialized tasks and subdisciplines; indeed, it would divert from the broader ethical project of learning and telling stories that need to be told" (69). However, I note that Gray ends her provocative essay by suggesting that her research on the black writer her essay considers—Detroit's Mollie E. Lambert—"illustrates that much remains lost and much work remains to be done" (71). While recent efforts offer great hope—especially, I think, those examples of literary and cultural history that address nineteenth-century African American experiences through a "new regionalism" and other formations that emphasize a fuller range of texts and authors—we are still not "there" yet.

It seems to me, then, that the field of nineteenth-century African American literary and cultural study is in the fascinating position of being simultaneously both exceedingly mature and almost completely nascent. To explain this, to further consider the various locations of Hannah Crafts, to begin to theorize the timing and placement of conclusions and mistakes in our criticism, and to speculate on the future of "unexpected places" in African American literary study, I want to close with discussion of two recent "relocations" that have, in ways complexly intertwined with my discussion of *The Bondwoman's Narrative* above, reshaped early black literary study: the stories of Emma Dunham Kelley-Hawkins and Mollie E. Lambert / Mary Tucker Lambert.

Kelley-Hawkins wrote two novels in the 1890s—*Megda* (1891) and *Four Girls at Cottage City* (1898)—which center on characters who are, as Molly Hite asserted in her 1988 introduction to the Schomburg reissue of *Megda*, "not only white, but very white" (xxix). Critics in the last two decades who considered the novels generally placed them within the (very real) phenomena of black authors experimenting with white characters and "white" stories and genres.[10] Her central fame, though, initially came less from the quality of her novels than from Gates's assertion, in his foreword to the forty-volume Schomburg Library, that his discovery of *Four Girls* led him to decide "to attempt to edit a collection of reprints" of works by early black women "and to publish them as a 'library' of black women's writings" (xx). That library, of course, became the Schomburg series, easily one of the most germinal republication efforts in the field.

However, as Holly Jackson detailed in her *Boston Globe* piece and a later *PMLA* article, as Katherine Flynn documented in her "A Case of Mistaken Racial Identity: Finding Emma Dunham (nee Kelley) Hawkins" (which was in galleys at the *National Genealogical Society Quarterly* when Jackson's *Globe* article appeared), and as has been retold now in countless forums, Kelley-Hawkins was white, and was of a family who was—as Flynn's painstaking research demonstrates—all white for several generations.

Assessment of the import of these findings has varied widely. Gates was simply quoted with a terse assertion that Kelley-Hawkins's novels would be pulled from the series if the Schomburg was reissued—though no one offered much speculation on when (or if) any publisher would have serious interest in republishing a forty-volume series in the near future. On the other hand, Charles Johnson's recent assertions that "fifty years of scholarship based on these mistakes—articles, dissertations, courses in African American women's writing that include the work of Kelley-Hawkins—turns out to be an illusion created by the blinding intentionality of those who wrote about this white author based on a tangled knot of beliefs and prejudices" are almost silly in ascribing to the discoveries of Kelley-Hawkins's whiteness an almost apocalyptic power (41). Kelley-Hawkins was never writ large in African American literary scholarship. Her novels have only been discussed in a handful of monographs, articles, and dissertations since their 1988 republication. I have found no evidence that they have been taught widely. What Jackson's *Globe* piece calls an "enormous historical misconception"—a quote Johnson seizes on without also picking up Jackson's contextualization—might be enormous in the tiny field of Kelly-Hawkins scholarship and certainly has ramifications within nineteenth-century studies, but reads differently in the much larger discussion of African American literature, where Kelley-Hawkins has never been more than a (very) minor presence.

Johnson also seems to miss the fact that if Gates's mistaken acceptance of the racial identification of Kelley-Hawkins as black is responsible for the Schomburg series, then we should be exceedingly glad of the temporary perpetuation of that mistake.

What Johnson refers to as an "intellectual scandal" is actually much more important in our study of methodology than of content (42). What we should gain is not simply the knowledge that Kelley-Hawkins was white—or that scholars and bibliographers followed a mistake that seems to trace to bibliographic efforts in the 1950s[11]—but that, for each author we study, for each text we consider, we need to dig into the archive as Flynn and Jackson did. We need to locate—in all senses of that word—authors and texts before we articulate the kinds of definitive conclusions that a handful of scholars made about Kelley-Hawkins.

The initial discussion about method that has followed the revelations about Kelley-Hawkins—especially in the pages of a special 2007 issue of *Legacy* titled "Racial Identity, Indeterminism, and Identification in the Nineteenth Century" and edited by Gabrielle Foreman and Cherene Sherrard-Johnson—may cause real shifts that reorient the field to the archive in useful ways. It may simultaneously teach us more about the field's presence in the wider public sphere. Kelley-Hawkins was not, of course, the first author included in the Schomburg series to be (re)identified as white; as discussed below, Mary Eliza Tucker Lambert was actually revealed as white before, in, and after the publication of the Schomburg series. Contrasting the significant silence over discoveries about Lambert's misidentification with the much wider interest in that of Kelley-Hawkins is beyond the scope of this volume, though we should begin to ask why the Kelley-Hawkins "scandal" gained so much traction in more popular venues—and whether such was tied to Gates's location of one of Kelley-Hawkins's texts as the seed for the radical Schomburg project.

Rather than engage fully in studying the new—and perhaps still raw—Kelley-Hawkins discussion here, though, I want to turn to Janet Gray's essay on the earlier revelation about the misidentification noted above, "Passing as Fact: Mollie E. Lambert and Mary Eliza (Perine) Tucker Lambert Meet as Racial Modernity Dawns," to help frame my placement of Kelley-Hawkins and especially Hannah Crafts. Gray's article includes the following summary of the errors that "conflated" the Alabama-born white poet Mary Eliza Tucker Lambert and the Detroit-based black writer Mollie E. Lambert:

> Others discovered the error before I did, yet their efforts to correct it remained invisible to the producers of important new resources. Ann Allen Shockley noted the error in the introduction to *Afro-American Women Writers, 1746–1933*, in 1988. That same year, Oxford University Press perpetuated the error by reprinting Tucker Lambert's two books of poetry [*Poems* and *Loew's Bridge*, both published in 1867] in the Schomburg Library of Nineteenth Century Black Women Writers. In the introduction to the bibliography on African American women's writing published in the Schomburg series

in 1991, Jean Fagan Yellin referred to Shockley's discovery of the error. Yet a poetry anthology published in 1992, part of Rutgers University Press's American Women Writers series, includes selections from Tucker Lambert's poetry headed with the conflated biography. *The Database of African American Poetry* on CD-ROM, published in 1995, reproduces Tucker Lambert's two books. The first published occurrence of the error in 1974 tentatively presented Lambert as an African American poet, inviting future researchers to explore a scanty list of sources. Today the error has become protocanonical and self-proliferating, resistant to correction. (12)

Gray adds in a footnote that "Oxford University Press staff pondered how to correct misidentification of authors for a paperback edition" but "decided against publishing the paperbacks" of the Schomburg's four-volume subset of black women's poetry "because they anticipated low sales" (72n7).[12]

Given the life of the misidentification, Gray considers *three* versions of "Mrs. M. E. Lambert": the black Mollie E. Lambert, the white Mary Tucker Lambert, and the "Imaginary Lambert," who has grown from the conflation. In dealing with the first two figures, she offers the most detailed biographies of both (especially Mollie Lambert) to date.[13] However, woven throughout these discussions and especially prominent in her consideration of the "Imaginary Lambert" is a pointed reflection on the "fable about the crossroads between history and theory in the recuperation of marginalized writing," a story that recognizes that the "Imaginary Lambert" is "not just an artifact of the existing material conditions of research but a suitable figure for a desire materialized in recuperative scholarship . . . to move . . . within and among categories of identity" because "in the landscape of recuperative scholarship, categories of identity are all-important (and thus provisionally essentialized) because the object of such study is to decenter the overall body of knowledge by loading onto it materials and experiences that have been edged out by virtue of their pertaining to oppressed and suppressed identity categories" (42, 60).

Thus, Gray argues that a reading of the white Tucker Lambert's *Loew's Bridge* "against the possibility of its having been a passing text" supposedly written by a black writer and actually written by a white author "extends the fable of the crossroads by showing that a text concerned with the adaptability of whiteness—its reconstruction and re-empowerment amid ideological change—may adeptly mimic a text about the elusiveness of race" (68).

Gray recognizes this conclusion as a clear cautionary to the question she was repeatedly asked when she told colleagues of the errors surrounding Tucker Lambert's books: "Couldn't someone who read the poems carefully tell from their content that the author was white?" (44).

But beyond offering a new reading of Tucker Lambert's poetry, Gray credits her (re)discovery of the misidentification with leading her to interrogate critical practices she might not have questioned—and to conclude usefully that "I wonder if critical acts that resemble passing" like those tied to the history of the "Imaginary Lambert" can "tend for a time . . . to eclipse other, more difficult kinds of critical acts. That greater difficulty seems to me related to the continuing collective historical trauma surrounding identity categories, the difference identity makes in how one experiences such trauma and its sequels, the continuing vulnerability of marginalized pasts to disappearance, and the almost necessary turning away from past injury that accompanies a search for upward-moving joy, tranquility, commerce, and light" (70).

In both the case of Kelley-Hawkins and the case of Tucker Lambert, after the errors were corrected, the misidentification of supposedly Black authors allowed valuable reflection and created some valuable critical and historical work. Certainly, then, in Gray's words, "errors can be productive, perhaps above all because they provide opportunities to refresh our awareness of what is at stake in keeping active the tensions between historical research and skeptical theory" (69). And I think that several of the insights offered by critics writing on *The Bondwoman's Narrative* will be valuable to the study of nineteenth-century black literature *regardless* of the identity of its author—Katherine Flynn's fascinating recovery of information surrounding fugitive slave Jane Johnson, Baym's discussion of the texts that teachers wrote for their students, and William Gleason's consideration of antebellum architecture and race, for example. And if the author of *The Bondwoman's Narrative* could be identified as a specific free African American woman from/of a specific place. . . .

However, much as I agree with many of Gray's arguments, much as I value the postcorrection dialogues on Lambert and Kelley-Hawkins, and much as I'm intrigued by *The Bondwoman's Narrative* and the critical work that has followed its publication, I cannot yet "place" that novel. I think Gray's dismissal of Ann Allen Shockley's concerns is too quick: "Explaining the error, Shockley is doubly emphatic about the irrelevance of Tucker [Lambert]'s work to African American recuperative projects; not only was the author white and a 'rebel,' 'her writings do not speak to or of blackness'" (64, quoting Shockley 118). Gray then asserts that "*Loew's Bridge* particularly, however, does speak to and of whiteness, and it has this in common with passing texts" and so is important to a mutually constitutive sense of race (64).

Yes. But this misses the root of Shockley's race-d recovery-centered project. Shockley's comments actually seem to me quite akin to Gates's seemingly flip but perhaps actually quite wise response to the discovery of Emma Dunham Kelley-Hawkins's race. Both seem to say, "O.K., let's move on. We have more work to do on *black* literature." Gray's attention to whiteness—and to the fact that there are *some* mutually constitutive qualities between definitions of blackness and whiteness—is certainly valuable, as are her metacritical comments on the practice of recuperative scholarship. But, in themselves, they do not *do* recuperative work in black studies (even though Gray's biography of Mollie Lambert within the body of her essay *does* do such work). The findings on Kelley-Hawkins similarly offer valuable opportunities to continue discussions of whiteness and of the broader theoretical questions involved in recovery work (as well as some of the gaps in black studies), but they do not *recover* black literature and culture. Most of what has resulted from these two misidentifications will help us better practice the literary history and criticism of nineteenth-century black literature, but, valuable as such is, it tells us mainly—explicitly and implicitly—about what is *not* part of nineteenth-century black literature and culture.

Unexpected Places is concerned first and foremost with broadening the list of authors, texts, and places we consider in discussing nineteenth-century African American literature. For both better and worse, Emma Dunham Kelley-Hawkins and Mary Tucker Lambert simply aren't on that list. Hannah Crafts may be there someday—but I *must* use the word "may." And I must assert that before we re-center nineteenth-century African American literature based on *The Bondwoman's Narrative,* we need a much, much fuller discussion of just what that literature consisted of—of the authors, texts, influences, and contexts like those studied here. Mine is a project like what Gray describes as designed to "decenter the overall body of knowledge by loading onto it materials and experiences that have been edged out by virtue of their pertaining to oppressed and suppressed identity categories" (60). While I must point out that our "loading" would be better understood as a careful, slow process (one that depends on fully locating authors and texts before adding to the collected oeuvre), I assert that specifically *because* of the conditions surrounding the "continuing vulnerability of marginalized pasts to disappearance" that Gray observes, it seems both right and necessary that, at least at this point in our field, "in the landscape of recuperative scholarship, categories of identity are all-important" (60).

When Gates recovered Harriet Wilson's *Our Nig*—in what must be seen as a key germinal moment in thinking about black literature in unexpected places and in the practice of the "new regionalism" in nineteenth-century black studies—he was careful to establish that she had, indeed, authored the book, that she represented and identified herself as black, and that others participating in the historical recording process (from census takers to compilers of city directories) represented and identified her as black. Because Gates so carefully placed Harriet Wilson in the category that defines our work, she could—and can—not be pulled from the field in the ways that Tucker Lambert and Kelley-Hawkins have had to be removed. (Thus, while the stunning recent discoveries about Wilson—especially those by Gabrielle Foreman, Reginald Pitts, and Katherine Flynn—have deeply complicated reading *Our Nig,* those discoveries have focused on black literature, not on what is *not* part of black literature.)[14]

"Hannah Crafts" needs—deserves—that kind of placement before we (re)locate her to the landscape of nineteenth-century African American literature, a landscape she would share with the authors in this study. Because Gates and subsequent critics have worked so diligently to "place" Harriet Wilson, for example, readers of *Our Nig* and visitors to Milford, New Hampshire's Bicentennial Park will be constantly reminded that the nineteenth-century black literary reached into the most unexpected places. Perhaps because of that careful public work, they will come to think of Wilson—and hopefully also, one day, the writers studied in *Unexpected Places*—as being from and of places that might not need to be conceived of as "unexpected." Perhaps they will even be driven to document the black presences in their own histories, their own places—and to realize that, ultimately, we cannot let our expectations limit us.

Notes

1. Other literary-minded activists at the 1856 California Convention included educator Jeremiah Sanderson, abolitionist Frederick G. Barbadoes, and ministers James Hubbard and John Jamison Moore. Poet James Monroe Whitfield would join with remnants of this group when he moved to California a few years later. Most of the figures above are considered later in the volume; however, for more on Townsend, see my "Jonas Holland Townsend."
2. Hughes's reduction of the West to "the cowboys" is, of course, problematic in itself.
3. Our full sense of the black presence in Indiana, for example, relied almost completely on Emma Lou Thornbrough's 1957 *The Negro in Indiana before 1900* until recent work like Stephen Vincent's 1999 *Southern Seed, Northern Soil*. There are also corollaries in twentieth-century black studies; Kenneth Jolly's 2006 *Black Liberation in the Midwest*, for example, offers a St. Louis-based corrective to scholarship on the locations privileged in studies of the modern civil rights struggle.
4. These absences have become almost self-replicating. Thus, early African American writers are left out of collections like Edward Watts and David Rachels's 2002 *The First West* and are considered in only a handful of critical studies, including Johnson, *Black Masculinity*; Moos, *Other Americans*; Allmendinger, *Imaging the African American West*; Lape, *West of the Border*. Even these studies treat few nineteenth-century works.
5. While certainly an oversimplification of the historiography of African American literary criticism, the broad strokes above are, I think, still generally accurate. For a more in-depth discussion of midcentury critical practices (building from Baker's thoughtful "Generational Shifts and the Recent Criticism of Afro-American Literature"), see Hogue, *Discourse and the Other*, 7–17. Hogue also begins to consider the ways in which black women—a central force in later twentieth-century criticism—shifted the terms of the field; see *Discourse*, 17–21. For primers on the development of black literary criticism, see Mitchell, ed., *Within the Circle*, and Napier, ed., *African American Literary Theory*.

6. The words are John Stauffer's, from his otherwise rich foreword to McCarthy and Doughton, *From Bondage to Belonging: The Worcester Slave Narratives*—a volume that, for the first time, collects several narratives published by former slaves connected to Worcester, Massachusetts. I choose the quote from Stauffer because it encapsulates several of the issues common in the field of nineteenth-century African American studies—and because, given his revolutionary 2001 *Black Hearts of Men,* his landmark recovery of the writings of James McCune Smith in his 2006 *The Works of James McCune Smith,* and his groundbreaking 2006 coedited collection *Prophets of Protest: Reconsidering the History of American Abolitionism,* the quote illustrates that even some of the most innovative thinkers in the field, even some of those scholars most dedicated to broadening our sense of African American literature, can fall into a generalized and narrow sense of nineteenth-century black literature.

7. Covering periodicals, dissertations, and select books published after 1925, the MLA electronic index contains over two million records, with over sixty thousand added each year. It is widely recognized as the standard database for literary study.

8. While I have heard editors at several major conferences pray for articles on someone other than Toni Morrison, even her "score" needs to be figured in context. White canonical figures from the nineteenth century like Nathaniel Hawthorne and Herman Melville are listed as subjects of over four thousand entries each. While some of this accumulation comes from the years before African American literature fully entered the academy, the disparity is still striking. It is also worth pointing out that the MLA Index has traditionally been much weaker in terms of fully surveying the contents of monographs—which have been, especially in the last two decades, a key site for critical work on lesser-known black texts and authors. Still, given that many monographs are built in part from dissertations and scholarly articles, the numbers above do offer a representative sketch of publications in the field.

9. In similar ways, a handful of twentieth-century black writers—Morrison high among them—have been appropriated as representative. In addition to some similar tokenism, this has led to the assertion of curiously simplified versions of the trajectories noted above: Jacobs to Morrison, with perhaps Hurston as the pivot, or Delany to Wright. Such direct lines ignore complex and conflicting genealogies of influence, place, sociopolitical networks, and context generally. While I disagree with—and, indeed, am troubled by—much of Charles Johnson's recent "The End of the Black American Narrative," I think that the approaches I outline above create allowances for rhetorical moves like Johnson's criticism of "the pre-21st century black American narrative," with its heavy emphasis on the singular. Fully responding to Johnson's piece is beyond the scope of this study; that said, even more troubling than Johnson's reduction to *the* "pre-21st century black American narrative" is his assertion that this one "master" story centers on victimization.

10. One assumes that he would place slave narratives among the "better" kinds of biography (and so within historical literature)—though he was quick to note that biography and history generally could be "either sacred, profane, or ecclesiastic" (109).

11. Martin Delany, for example, would become one of Payne's "closest friends" (Levine 3). Payne also interacted with Douglass, Brown, Harper, and scores of other black powerhouses of the nineteenth century.

12. Even among better-known black writers of the nineteenth century—including writers who published a book or books—the periodical press (and the short forms often demanded by such) was the bedrock of publishing prospects. Per McHenry, "rather than bound books, newspapers were the primary sites of publication and sources of literary reading for African Americans in the nineteenth century" (12). Thus, two of the earliest black novels were serialized in periodicals, and three of Frances Harper's four novels were serialized. Frederick Douglass, William Wells Brown, and Daniel Payne all wrote books, but also wrote scores of texts for the black press. And while two of these writers began their careers with slave narratives, all three—and, as John Ernest has skillfully shown, many other black writers—turned to Payne's first category of the "historical" as a key mode in books and other formats. Many writers like Elisha Weaver, Jennie Carter, and Philip Bell "failed" to publish books not because of the quality of their writing, but because they seem to have consciously decided that the black press, in the end, offered better opportunities for circulation and community elevation.

13. We may also have to reconsider the ways in which our judgments of "quality" have been shaped by modern principles that often are represented as being context-free. Sven Birkets's negative *New York Times* review of Julia C. Collins's *The Curse of Caste* offers a key example of this problem; exactly what he judges to be the book's greatest sins are those qualities that make it fit (in fascinating ways) with the traditions of sentimental fiction, serialized novels, and the literature of elevation so prominent in the *Christian Recorder* (the periodical in which *Curse* was originally serialized).

14. In addition to the works discussed above, I would call attention to the *Norton Anthology of African American Literature,* the small set of Oxford and Cambridge *Companion* volumes, and the forthcoming *Cambridge History of African American Literature* as among the handful of such works.

15. On both of these projects, see Howard, "Literary Geoscapes."

16. On this, see my "'Face to Face.'"

17. I see, for example, Nwankwo's rich *Black Cosmopolitanism* as a landmark text in that its formulation of black cosmopolitanism challenges much of the overtheorized and undertextualized previous work in this subfield and grounds its analysis in the "dynamic interaction" between trans-Atlantic impulses and "national affinity" (13). However, even this fine work has slippages similar to the Stauffer quote above—as when Nwankwo (rightly) says that a twentieth-

century focus "has allowed us to miss the pivotal importance of nineteenth-century texts in the development and public articulation not just of Black or African Diasporan identity" but then, in the very next sentence, reduces *all* of these potential "texts" to "slave narratives" (18–19). In this vein, I am also appreciative of Sandra Gunning's recognition that "the most recent privileging of diaspora identification almost to the point of romanticizing the revolutionary and subversive power of this identification threatens to elide the very real impact of color, status, region, and gendered experience as sites of intra-racial difference within the context of the black diaspora" (33). I would add that it similarly threatens to reduce African American literatures of the nineteenth century to a small handful of texts with clear trans-Atlantic thematic emphases.

18. Hogue's definition of polycentrism builds from work by Walter Laquer and Samir Amin that has strong roots in Marxist thought; Hogue's *The African American Male, Writing, and Difference* weaves together such discussion with a sense, per Raymond Williams and John Guillory, of the ways in which previous approaches to African American literature have too often centered on building (and so tacitly accepting some definitions of) cultural capital through articulating and even replicating specific senses of literature.

19. This project, in turn, was partially made possible by the carefully constructed—if still somewhat difficult to access—*Black Biographical Dictionaries* microform project, which was also led in part by Gates.

20. The project's index—but only the index—is available online through ProQuest/Chadwyck-Healey's "Black Studies Center," an expensive but nonetheless more readily available product that is at least moving into larger "Research 1" institutions.

21. While I disagree with some of their assertions, I am especially in conversation with Amy Kaplan's sense of "manifest domesticity" and Lora Romero's work in *Home Fronts.*

22. Frances Smith Foster's comments on the black press are similarly instructive here; she argues that the black press was "undeniably pragmatic" in considering its audience, function, and production and worked from "the desire to create a positive and purposeful self-identified African America" as much "as to any defensive" attempts "responding to racist attacks or libel" ("A Narrative" 717–18).

23. In many ways, slave narratives are very much about trying to obtain enough agency to exercise the specific form of mobility embodied in escape—and thus to gain freedom. Such texts are thus often about the ways in which slavery either removes agency from movement (as in the forced journeys from master to master, or on a master's business) or/and immobilizes—one thinks of Harriet Jacobs's assertion that "I lived in that dismal little hole, almost deprived of light and air, and with no space to move my limbs, for nearly seven years" (224).

24. Unfortunately, some of the recent multicultural approaches to travel literature seem especially prone to the generalizations and limitations noted above—and

especially to removing black writers from their contexts in order to lump them in with other notably different authors. Slave narratives, I assert, are *not* travel literature, for example, even though they are very much about the politics and exercise of mobility. That said, there are some important exceptions that have actively advanced a context-sensitive sense of black writers vis-à-vis travel *and* mobility. Farah Jasmine Griffin and Cheryl Fish's 1998 anthology *Stranger in the Village: Two Centuries of African American Travel Writing* begins to offer a range of texts to a broader readership, even though it places some emphasis on twentieth-century texts. Fish's 2005 *Black and White Women's Travel Narratives* places work by Nancy Prince, Mary Seacole, and Margaret Fuller in a fascinating dialogue that is often aware not only of race, class, and place, but also of the links between the physical and metaphysical manifestations of such. Sandra Gunning's "Nancy Prince and the Politics of Mobility, Home, and Diasporic (Mis)Identification" is similarly rich and thoughtful.

25. For more on Gilliard, see my "James E. M. Gilliard." It is notable, in considering the arguments about what we have forgotten and ignored above, that this *African American National Biography* entry is the first modern study of Gilliard.

26. Lewis's life story has proven much more difficult to track, in part because of the commonness of his name. He had been a delegate to the 1855 convention, but is not listed among those who participated in the 1857 San Francisco Convention or the 1865 California Convention—the first well-documented large California meeting of the 1860s. I have not yet been able to determine his relationship (if any) to the John Lewis who was also active in the California Convention movement. It is likely that he was the David Lewis who was listed in the 1850 Federal Census of Nevada City (then—prior to the founding of Nevada County—located in Yuba County) as a thirty-five-year-old "Mulatto" cook at Jones's Tavern and as a native of Ohio (313). He does not seem to have written for the paper(s) he supported, and the gaps in his biography paired with his passion for the textual remind of how much work still needs to be done to find not just black writers, but black *readers* of the nineteenth century. My work on the original owners of Harriet Wilson's *Our Nig* represents one set of directions such might take; Elizabeth McHenry's fascinating *Forgotten Readers* offers several others. Both use strands of the book and reader-centered history—seen in the work of scholars like James Machor, Ronald Zboray, and Mary Saracino Zboray—and attempt to adapt those strands to the specific contexts that shaped African American reading in the nineteenth century.

CHAPTER 1

1. On McIntosh and Lovejoy, see especially Gerteis, *Civil War St. Louis,* 7–17. See also 5 May 1836 and 26 May 1836 *Missouri Republican;* Herman, "The McIntosh Affair"; Dillon, *Elijah P. Lovejoy;* Tabscott, "Elijah Parish Lovejoy."

2. In addition to a close reading of St. Louis city directories and census records, information in this paragraph draws on Primm, *Lion of the Valley: St. Louis, 1764–1980*. Echoing Primm, Thomas C. Buchanan says that "by the 1840s, the city was clearly the most important port in the upper South" (40).

3. In addition to material in Primm and work with primary sources noted above, this paragraph relies in part on Greene, *Missouri's Black Heritage,* and Bellamy, "Free Blacks in Antebellum Missouri, 1820–1860." Perhaps the most exciting study touching on nineteenth-century black St. Louis to come out in recent years, Thomas C. Buchanan's *Black Life on the Mississippi* also adds richly to our sense of the lives of blacks in St. Louis tied to the river trade.

4. Primm—who at times maintains that "slavery was an encumbrance" to St. Louis, that the city "was getting rid of it," and that "the local tradition was that slavery was comparatively mild in St. Louis" (186–87)—and Buchanan's more recent study offer an interesting contrast on the place of slavery in the city, though both agree with scholars like Walter Johnson (in *Soul by Soul*) that St. Louis was a center of the trade.

5. Brown's notable success—his 1847 *Narrative* was quickly reissued in an expanded second edition the next year—was also, of course, tied to his skills as an orator, marketer, and politician. While the reading of Brown's *Narrative* that follows diverges significantly from other critics—many of whom limit their consideration of Brown's St. Louis contexts—I am especially indebted to discussions of the *Narrative* in William Andrews's introduction to Brown's autobiographies, *From Fugitive Slave to Free Man,* and in Andrews's *To Tell a Free Story.* Buchanan's brief comments on the *Narrative* (which he juxtaposes with the writings of Mark Twain) have certainly also shaped my reading, as he asserts that "for Brown, mobility was filled with remorse and sadness even as it created possibilities for freedom and independence" (5).

6. On St. Louis's representation as a gateway, see Primm, *Lion of the Valley;* Buchanan, *Black Life;* McCandless, *A History of Missouri.*

7. Walker and powerfully mobile slave traders like him appear repeatedly in Brown's later work, including a very similar slave trader in his 1856 play *The Escape.* On *The Escape,* see especially Ernest, "The Reconstruction of Whiteness," and Gilmore, "'De Genewine Artekil.'"

8. Almost all of the white- and black-authored press accounts that offered sympathetic treatment of Lovejoy's martyrdom were published outside of St. Louis—mainly in the Northeast; the most important book-length treatments— Edward Beecher's *Narrative of the Riots at Alton* (1838) and Joseph Lovejoy's *Memoir of the Rev. Elijah P. Lovejoy* (1838)—were published in Alton and New York, respectively.

9. Not all of Meachum's slaves found him to be a good master. Judy, aka Julia Logan, filed a suit for her freedom against Meachum in December 1834. Later, in April 1836, as Polly Wash would do for her daughter Lucy Delaney, Judy had

herself named as the "next friend" of her five-year-old son Green Berry Logan and filed a suit for his freedom on his behalf, too. Judy's suit went to the Missouri Supreme Court, which ruled against Meachum, in part because he relied on another African American's testimony to stand against one of Judy's white former owners. Other freedom suits were occasionally filed against Meachum, including a set by Peter Charleville, a free African American who filed suits as the next friend of Brunetta Barnes and Archibald Barnes. Meachum fared badly in all of these cases. See, *Judy (aka Julia Logan) v. John Berry Meachum*; *Green Berry Logan, an infant of color v. John Berry Meachum*; *Judy v. John Berry Meachum*; *Brunetta Barnes v. John Berry Meachum*; *Archibald Barnes v. John Berry Meachum*—all in the St. Louis Circuit Court Historical Records Project. It should also be noted that St. Louis Circuit Court records of emancipations do not list as many emancipations by Meachum as his *Address* claims.

10. For the *Colored American*'s later discussion of St. Louis abuses, see the issues of 26 September 1840, 4 September 1841, and 11 September 1841. On free black life in this period more generally, see, e.g., Buchanan, *Black Life*, and Bellamy, "Free Blacks in Antebellum Missouri."

11. Meachum occasionally hired whites to be present at meetings, given Missouri's hesitation about and eventual banning of black assemblages. On these issues, see Durst, "The Reverend John Berry Meachum."

12. The convention movement in the Northeast (which spread West and led to, among other meetings, those in California discussed in the introduction) was one of the key modes through which free African Americans agitated not only for freedom for the enslaved in the South but also for broader civil rights for all blacks. Philip S. Foner's work has been most valuable in recognizing their importance; see his edited *Proceedings of the Black National and State Conventions, 1840–1865*. See also Patrick Rael's fine *Black Identity and Black Protest in the Antebellum North*.

13. In a similarly complex rhetorical move, Meachum also says—of the Spanish move to replace Native American slaves with African slaves—"Thus you perceive he enslaves one nation to liberate the other. Strange benevolence this" (8).

14. Israel became a key trope within several black traditions. For discussions that begin to consider such—as well as the broader theological issues above—see especially Glaude, *Exodus!*; Durst; Rael, "Black Theodicy"; Moses, *Black Messiahs and Uncle Toms*.

15. In one of the few direct mentions of whites in the *Address*, Meachum says that "if God had given our white friends grace to establish Sunday schools for your children, I should think that you ought to have grace enough to send them" (54). Certainly this comment spoke to the ongoing debate over the creation of trade schools for African Americans that would take much space in, for example, Frederick Douglass's newspapers later in the century.

16. One of the few times Meachum notes slavery in the *Address*, this final quote continues, "and you say you do not like slavery" (45–46).

17. Winch's edition, with extensive and carefully researched apparatus, has done more to bring Clamorgan into contemporary discussion than any other work. Still, while the volume was lauded by select historians—Lloyd Hunter's review in the *Journal of Southern History,* for example, praised it as "a wellspring of information" (453)—literary scholars have essentially ignored it. The MLA Index turns up no hits for the keyword "Clamorgan."

18. Clamorgan's was not the first book to take this general approach. See Winch's edition of Joseph Willson's 1841 *Sketches of the Higher Classes of Colored Society in Philadelphia by "A Southerner"* for an earlier and somewhat more staid text.

19. Probably correctly, Winch says Clamorgan "grossly overestimates the value of various estates" (18); however, in an uncharacteristically easy assumption, she uses census-taker's estimates as her evidence, even though modes of fooling government officials about assets and miscounting by census-takers (especially of ethnic minorities) were commonplace.

20. Clamorgan is careful to note that the moral Smith demanded that when "a man has had as much as he can stand," he drink no more (61). Gambler Samuel Mordecai, for another example, was "strictly honest" and, were he in Paris, "would be received into the first circles" (51).

21. In these prefatory remarks, Clamorgan does pay lip service to the sense that a book by a "colored aristocrat" should demonstrate that his fellows "have been placed in the path of comparative respectability" and could exercise some "manner" of "political influence" (45, 47). He speaks briefly but hopefully of how some positive political change in the city was tied to "the unwearied and combined action of the wealthy free colored men of St. Louis," though he says that they "know that the abolition of slavery in Missouri would remove a stigma from their race, and elevate them in the scale of society" (47). He also, with a touch of impudence, notes that "many" of the "free colored people of St. Louis . . . are separated from the white race by a line of division so faint that it can be traced only by the keen eye of prejudice—a line so dim indeed that, in many instances that might be named, the stream of African blood has been so diluted by mixture with Caucasian, that the most critical observer cannot detect it" (45). Indeed, Clamorgan asserts, "We, who know the history of all the old families of St. Louis, might readily point to the scions of some of our 'first families,' and trace their genealogy back to the swarthy tribes of Congo or Guinea" (45–46). Most of these claims, however, remain underdeveloped—and often ignored—by the rest of the pamphlet.

22. Clamorgan even comments (in his discussion of McGee and his wife) that "to those who have been in the habit of regarding even the most intelligent of the colored race as destitute of proper sensibility in matters pertaining to the domestic virtues, it may appear strange that a bare suspicion of former disregard of the proprieties of life should exclude a family from familiar intercourse with an aristocratic circle; but, in this respect, there is reason to believe that the colored people are more strict than the whites; for it is a notorious fact that

among the latter a full purse covers a multitude of sins, and ladies who have forfeited all claims to virtuous respect are admitted as ladies of the *ton*. It was only the other day that one of the white aristocracy flogged his wife for deviating from the path of virtue, and yet the lady is still received into what is called 'good society.' If she had been tinctured with the blood of Ham, the door would have been closed against her" (57–58).

23. This meant, not inconsequentially, that many who fit Clamorgan's definitions had been, like Mrs. Nancy Lyons, brought up "among the French inhabitants" where they "learned their language" and were "educated in the tenets of the Catholic Church"; it also meant that many, again like Lyons—who Clamorgan says "resembles an Indian, and may possibly have the blood of Pontiac in her veins"—were light skinned (54).

24. Winch's introduction and notes, as well as her subsequent work (like her entry on Clamorgan for the *African American National Biography*), chronicle Clamorgan's lifelong back-and-forth over the color line.

25. Beyond the partial survey offered by Winch, scholars have not yet attended to the various suits over the Clamorgan estate—suits that continued into the twentieth century and in which litigants occasionally even tried for congressional action to aid their cases. These suits, in many ways, offer yet another complex set of St. Louis black stories.

26. Clamorgan continued much the same pattern after writing his pamphlet— traveling widely, returning regularly to St. Louis even though his family relationships continued to be stormy, pursuing his claims on his grandfather's estate, and so on. Winch was the first scholar to uncover the details of his final years and of his death in a St. Louis poor house on 13 November 1902.

27. In this, Clamorgan was a bit like David F. Dorr; Malini Johar Schueller asserts, in introducing the 1999 edition of his 1858 *A Colored Man Round the World,* that "Dorr uses travel writing to project a leisurely, gentlemanly self and to fashion an aristocratic selfhood through the display of inherited 'cultural capital'" (xi).

28. For specific discussions of freedom suits in Missouri, see Foley, "Slave Freedom Suits before Dred Scott," and Moore, "A Ray of Hope Extinguished." The general concept is discussed in several histories of slave law. Information on the St. Louis Circuit Court Records Project's efforts to find, preserve, and offer access to the St. Louis Freedom Suits can be found at http://www.stlcourtrecords.wustl.edu/index.php. On the Scott case, see especially Ehrlich, *They Have No Rights,* and Vandervelde, "Mrs. Dred Scott." Until 2007, several key details about Delaney's case remained shrouded; see my "'You have no business to whip me'" and "'Face to Face.'"

29. Similarly, proving matrilineal descent from a free woman or a Native American (who could not technically be enslaved) would make an enslaved plaintiff "once free" and so "always free." A few suits focus on other reasons—willed

emancipations, for example—but the vast majority focus on extended residence or lineage.

30. While the crackdowns mentioned earlier in this chapter defined many aspects of free black life after Lovejoy, some in the legal system worried about St. Louis's larger national reputation vis-à-vis vigilante justice. Thus, when the nationally followed trial of free African American Madison Henderson and his "gang" came in 1841, they attempted to represent this trial as an ideal of balance. See Seematter, "Trials and Confessions." See Buchanan, *Black Life,* for an alternate reading that argues that "the Missouri justice system gave the men little chance to mount a defense" (143).

31. On questions of comity and slave law generally, see Finkelman, *An Imperfect Union* and *Slavery and the Courtroom.* Some of the best recent work on the nexus of race, slavery, law, and rhetoric has been done by Ariela J. Gross.

32. My examination of all extant St. Louis freedom suit case files, conducted in consultation with archivists and other scholars working with the collection, shows a relatively small number of attorneys who represented enslaved plaintiffs and an even smaller number who did so on a regular basis. (Francis Murdoch, for example, represented slaves in perhaps a third of the freedom suits filed in the early 1840s.)

33. When the enslaved Mary Robertson heard that her case was dismissed (because her attorney missed a court date) and sought out another attorney, her objections included an assertion that she had paid the original attorney by working for him as a washerwoman. See *Mary Robertson v. Ringrose D. Watson.*

34. See Delaney, 33–35. For additional discussion of these events, see my "'You have no business to whip me.'"

35. Few were finished within a year, many took two to four years, and Foley has documented the fact that the cases surrounding the Scypion family took decades. Two developments in 1845 made filing and winning freedom suits even more difficult. During its January 1845 term, the Missouri Supreme Court found—in *Gabrielle S. Choteau v. Pierre (of color)* reversing a previous win by the enslaved plaintiff Pierre—that "in a suit for freedom, it is a good objection to a juror, that he would feel bound by his conscience to find a verdict in favor of the plaintiff, notwithstanding the law should hold him in slavery." See January Term, 1845, *Reports of Cases Argued and Decided in the Supreme Court of the State of Missouri,* 3–10, for the full decision. This physically narrowed an already sometimes narrow-minded jury pool: there had never, for example, been any provision to challenge potential jurors because they were slaveholders, and some jurors in the 1840s had even been *defendants* in other freedom suits. Most of the freedom suits of the 1840s had at least one slaveholder—and usually more than one—on their juries. Beyond this chilling development, the general assembly removed the requirement that the court absorb *any* costs of suits of slaves suing as poor persons—and so forced enslaved plaintiffs to find a white attorney

or friend willing to bond themselves for *all* costs incurred in the prosecution of their freedom suits. (Kristin Zapalac was the first to discover this later development and to speculate on its implications.) The numbers of freedom suits filed dropped precipitously after these shifts.

36. In addition to Andrews, *To Tell a Free Story,* my sense of the capital-S, capital-N genre of Slave Narratives—far different than simple narratives of slaves—owes a great deal to Braxton, *Black Women Writing Autobiography;* Davis and Gates, eds., *The Slave's Narrative;* Foster, *Witnessing Slavery;* Sekora and Turner, eds., *The Art of the Slave Narrative;* Stepto, *From Behind the Veil.*

37. Such an approach begins to explain the predominance of judicial rhetoric in many movement-sponsored slave narratives—including the language of "witnessing" and "testimony" in William Wells Brown's *Narrative;* it also articulates a basis for why, as DeLombard notes, "it is not surprising to find abolitionists injecting antijudicialism into their print propaganda" and so feeding into both "the ancient tradition of popular constitutionalism" and "Jacksonian concerns about the judiciary as a potential threat to popular sovereignty" (21, 19, 18). In addition to DeLombard, my reading of the transition of judicial rhetoric into the abolitionist public sphere and into slave narratives is influenced by the work of Gabrielle Foreman and Lindon Barrett.

38. Schueller's language aptly summarizes what many scholars have observed: "The movement of slaves . . . was simply the movement of a slaveowner's property, a right protected by the Constitution"; slaves were thus always already "part of an entourage" of a white master with agency (ix).

39. The St. Louis press's rare mention of freedom suits similarly removed black agency. A story written in 1837 by "Topaz" and discovered by the historian Bob Moore ascribed the agency behind freedom suits to greedy white lawyers (8).

40. That is, at least, not by the black plaintiffs; I have suggested elsewhere that high-powered white attorneys like Bates sometimes involved themselves in freedom suits for practice in competitive oratory.

41. In addition to Andrews's work on Douglass, see Giles, "Narrative Reversals and Power Exchanges"; Levine, *Martin Delany, Frederick Douglass, and the Politics of Representative Identity;* Sekora, "'Mr. Editor, If You Please'"; Leverenz, "Frederick Douglass's Self-Refashioning." On Box Brown, see Ernest's apparatus to the *Narrative of Henry "Box" Brown.*

42. There has, of course, been useful discussion by Andrews and others on how such statements can impinge on the narrative proper; one thinks of Douglass's move to the 1855 preface by African American activist James McCune Smith as a kind of declaration of independence. There has been, however, less discussion of how the black authors of the slave narratives shaped white prefatory statements, which strikes me as a way to gain certain types of agency by sacrificing others.

43. All quotations noted as being from the Wash case file are from the unpaginated *Polly Wash v. Joseph M. Magehan.*

44. See Delaney 9; this claim disagrees with all other records I have found.

45. Wash claimed that Robert Wash had hired her out "to one Capt. Wayne of the steamboat Banner as a chambermaid and in that capacity . . . made several trips up the Illinois River as far as Peoria" and "at one time within the jurisdiction of the State of Illinois was detained for at least five weeks." The reason her suit instead focused on her youth was likely because St. Louis courts and juries would be deeply hesitant to limit slaves' hiring in the river trade.

46. Creek and Cherokee attacked the Crockett family in 1777, and Joseph was shot in the arm, leading to a later amputation. Family legend tells that he wore a prosthesis with a silver end affixed to help him carve food and eat; the relative poverty of the Crockett family, though, suggests that such stories may be apocryphal. See Shackford, *David Crockett*, 4–5; Crockett, *A Narrative of the Life of David Crockett of the State of Tennessee, passim;* Crockett descendant to the author, 10 June 2004; Hauck, *Crockett: A Bio-Bibliography.*

47. Wash was sold to Missourian Thomas Botts, who soon sold her to Taylor Berry, a firebrand Missouri land speculator, War of 1812 veteran, sometime-attorney, sometime-gentleman with powerful connections. (Both Berry and his wife, Fanny Christy Berry, were distant but still friendly cousins of President Zachary Taylor.) See Brewer, *From Log Cabins to the White House: A History of the Taylor Family;* Zachary Taylor to Major Taylor Berry, 25 April 1816, Presidents Collection, Missouri Historical Society Library. Though Berry supposedly agreed to free Wash (as well as the man Wash married while owned by him and the two children Wash and her unnamed enslaved husband had), when Berry was killed in one of Missouri's most famous duels in September 1824, his will remained silent on the issue other than to convey all of his property—including but not specifically naming Polly's young family—to his wife and children. See Will of Taylor Berry, *Howard County Probate Court—Will Book,* 1: 202–5. Robert Wash, through marrying Berry's widow, came into possession of Polly Wash before eventually selling her to Joseph Magehan, the named defendant in the freedom suit.

48. Magehan's loses may even have been limited. I am currently investigating a fascinating set of warranty cases in which William Randolph sued, of all people, Robert Wash (Polly Wash and Lucy Delaney's former owner), alleging that, because he lost ownership of a slave Judge Wash had sold him through a freedom suit (*Alsey, a woman of color v. William Randolph*), Wash breached an implied warranty—in essence, fraudulently representing as enslaved an African American who had been "once free" and so was "always free."

49. The first document showed that she had received the wages she earned while hired out by the court, and that document is part of the case file. The second document was a form of registration required of all free African Americans in St. Louis, and it is part of the Tiffany Collection at the Missouri Historical Society.

50. I have not been able to determine if Haydon could or did issue Polly Wash a pass. No extant court record gives Wash permission for her trip to Illinois; no

extant court document outside of the depositions even mentions such. Either way, Wash's trip across into a free state to talk with the deponents represents clear black agency and mobility.

51. Neither the justice of the peace who took the depositions nor the attorneys who were present noted her attendance. However, Mary Moore referred to "the plaintiff who is now present" and Samuel Wood referred to "the negro girl now called Polly & now present."

52. Later in *From the Darkness,* Delaney echoes this story, saying that her mother "had ample testimony to prove that she was kidnapped, and it was so fully verified that the jury decided that she was a free woman" (24).

53. I have not been able to find any proof of her escape, but this, along with Delaney's report of Wash's hand-picking of future attorney general Edward Bates to represent her daughter in her freedom suit suggest an amazingly active and mobile enslaved woman; see Delaney 35–36.

54. This promise does bear a striking resemblance to the promise Delaney describes as being made by Taylor Berry to his slaves—that they would serve until he and his wife died and would then be set free; see Delaney 11.

55. According to *Circuit Court Record Book (CCRB)* 14: 67, the jurors were Reuben B. Austin, Gibson Corthion, William Bailey, Henry G. Soulard, Ally Williams, William Wiseman, Thomas Wiseman, Robert G. Coleman, Thomas Sappington, Green Park, Enoch Price, and Ralph Peters Jr. I have found most in contemporary city directories and/or censuses. Austin worked for a sawmill, and Bailey was a lumber merchant, so it is quite plausible that they knew lumberman/carpenter Magehan.

56. Far too little work has been done on the freedom suits generally or on Murdoch specifically. In the surprisingly sparse commentary on Murdoch vis-à-vis the Scott case, Walter Ehrlich asserts that he was "not a slave lawyer," and Lea Vandervelde and Sandhya Subramanian claim that Murdoch's "precipitous departure" after the Scotts' filing "left the Scotts with a lawsuit but without a lawyer" (37, 1088). As part of a forthcoming study on race, rhetoric, and St. Louis, I have gathered information demonstrating that Murdoch *did* actually devote a significant portion of his practice to "slave law" and specifically to freedom suits, that he did not leave St. Louis precipitously, that the Scotts may well have chosen to move their action to a different attorney (as, in essence, Polly Wash did) after the initial filing, and that Murdoch would later become a staunch antislavery, pro-Lincoln Republican as editor of the *San Jose Patriot* in California.

57. See especially Peter P. Hinks, *To Awaken My Afflicted Brethren,* as well as Hinks's edition of Walker's *Appeal.* Garnet (1815–1882) had a long and distinguished career as an abolitionist and a Baptist minister. Though that career included several flirtations with colonization and, later, Pan-Africanism—ending in his receiving an appointment to Liberia at the end of his life—he also helped lead Union recruiting efforts among African Americans and helped set up both the

American Missionary Association and a series of relief efforts aimed at the newly freed. He wrote throughout his life—probably beginning with letters to the *Colored American* under the penname "Sidney" (see the 13 February 1841 and 6 March 1841 issues)—and was president of Avery College in Pittsburgh in 1868. On Garnet, see Foster, "Henry Highland Garnet"; Ofari, *Let Your Motto Be Resistance;* Schor, *Henry Highland Garnet.*

58. Clamorgan refers to Robinson as Roberson, calls him "one of the talking barbers who can rattle out more nonsense in ten minutes than any sensible man would believe in a week," and says that "he is not in the best standing, and he is too great a gossip and meddler to let the affairs of others alone" (59); see Winch 95 for biographical material on Robinson.

<h3 style="text-align:center">CHAPTER 2</h3>

1. See Edwin S. Redkey's fascinating 1992 collection *A Grand Army of Black Men* for sample letters written by black troops.

2. See chapter 4 of this volume for a fuller discussion of the later *Recorder.*

3. The only scholarly treatments of the *Repository* are found in Bullock, *Afro-American Periodicals;* Foster, "A Narrative"; McHenry, *Forgotten Readers;* Zboray and Zboray, *Literary Dollars,* and my *PMLA* edition of two *Repository* texts by Maria Stewart.

4. Excerpts from Greenly's title play, along with my introduction and notes, are forthcoming in *African American Review.* William Wells Brown's 1858 *The Escape* is generally recognized as the first full-length play published by an African American; however, African Americans were writing plays well before *The Escape*—including Brown himself, whose 1856 *Experience* was discussed in the abolitionist press but has not yet been found. See also White, *Stories of Freedom in Black New York,* and McAllister, *White People Do Not Know How to Behave,* for information on New York City black resident William Brown's African Grove company and playwriting. No plays by this earlier Brown have yet been found, though, again, such were reported in the press.

5. As in Missouri, free blacks in Indiana were technically required to register and post a bond in their county of residence. However, I have yet to locate Elisha Weaver's bond or those of his parents among the severely incomplete handful of extant rosters of Indiana's free African Americans.

6. In brief discussion of "B. C. Hobbs" in the November 1858 *Repository,* Weaver refers to Hobbs as "my old school-master" (131). This Hobbs is almost certainly Barnabas Coffin Hobbs (1815–1892), who would later become Earlham College's first president and who had moved from Ohio to Richmond, Indiana, in 1844 to begin a long career of working not only with Quaker schools but also with Indiana's public education system. On Hobbs, see 1850 Federal Census of Wayne Township, Wayne County, Indiana, 150; 1860 Federal Census of Penn, Parke County, Indiana, 603; Hamm, *Earlham College.*

7. In addition to Thornbrough, see Vincent, *Southern Seed, Northern Soil,* and Coy Robbins, *Forgotten Hoosiers.* Thornbrough, *The Negro in Indiana before 1900,* 33–37, specifically discusses Quakers who moved from the upper South to Indiana.

8. One thinks especially of the family of Grace Bustill Douglass, whose Quaker commitments remained deep even as they sometimes complicated familial relations. See my "Grace Bustill Douglass." DeBlasio and Haefeli, "Society of Friends and African Americans," provides a useful overview on this topic.

9. Among the number of sources on Oberlin and African Americans, see Brandt, *The Town That Started the Civil War;* Bigglestone, "Oberlin College and the Negro Student"; Horton, "Black Education at Oberlin"; Larson and Mitchell, "The Antebellum 'Talented Thousandth,'" as well as Fletcher's more general 1943 *A History of Oberlin College.*

10. On Quinn, also see Handy, *Scraps of African Methodist Episcopal History,* 113, 138, 163–65, as well as LaRoche and Palmer, "William Paul Quinn."

11. On Payne, see my "Daniel Alexander Payne"; Vicary, "Daniel Alexander Payne"; Coan, *Daniel Alexander Payne;* Smith, *The Life of Daniel Alexander Payne;* and Payne's own work. On Wilberforce, see McGinnis, *A History.*

12. Payne's struggles on this issue can be seen in the various extant A.M.E. Conference proceedings and are discussed in both Payne's *History* and his *Recollections.*

13. On this, see Handy, *Scraps of African Methodist Episcopal History,* 202, 205, 214, as well as Payne's *History,* 295, 313; Weaver was one of the ministers chosen to sort out the first round of controversy surrounding A.M.E. bishop Willis Nazrey's move to Canada (to become the first bishop of the newly founded British Methodist Episcopal Church in 1856). On Nazrey, see Handy, *Scraps of African Methodist Episcopal History,* 193, 197, 210–17, as well as Wright, *Centennial Encyclopedia,* 280 and 295.

14. Payne essentially credits Weaver with foregrounding the debate over the place of music in the Church and says that "at the Annual Conference of that year an animated discussion followed" (*Recollections* 234–35). Writing several years later, Payne summarized the eventual result: "But now it is the aim of every Church in the Connection to have a good choir" (235). See also Southern, *Music of Black Americans,* 129.

15. While beyond the scope of this study, the ways in which black letters on transit questions constitute a fascinating counter-discourse to white travel writing are worth in-depth consideration.

16. Shadd (1823–1893), a Delaware-born free African American woman, moved to Windsor, Ontario, after the passage of the Fugitive Slave Law, published two important pamphlets that encouraged black emigration to Canada, helped Samuel Ringgold Ward found the *Freeman* in 1853, and, by her 1856 marriage to Thomas Cary, was the leading force behind much of the paper. See Rhodes, *Mary Ann Shadd Cary.* Weaver also probably wrote this letter in Detroit; because

the nearby *Freeman* had a foothold there, it would thus have been the most logical venue for the letter's publication.

17. In addition to the biographical sources on Payne cited in note 11 above, see the October 1858 *Repository,* 131.

18. Willis R. Revels has been much less studied than his better-known brother Hiram R. Revels. Still, a leading A.M.E. minister in the West since 1840, he is mentioned in most church histories, including Tanner, *Apology,* 338–43, and Wayman, *Cyclopedia,* 134. On Hiram Revels, see Thompson's *Hiram R. Revels, 1827–1901* and "Hiram R. Revels, 1827–1901: A Reappraisal."

19. A staunch early defender of Payne, Brown (1817–1893) pastored in both the Ohio and Indiana Conferences before being assigned to a multiyear "mission" in New Orleans by Payne in the early 1850s. Brown and Weaver may have met prior to 1850—as Weaver talked in mid-1858 of not having seen Brown's family in close to a decade (65)—and Brown likely interacted further with Weaver when he was called to Asbury Chapel in Louisville, Kentucky, in 1857. He was firmly ensconced in the *Repository* leadership by May 1858, when he accepted charge of Baltimore's Bethel A.M.E. See Glazier, "John Mifflin Brown."

20. This is also the first issue of the *Repository* to advertise the Indianapolis day-school that was run by Weaver and attached to his church.

21. Weaver had asked, in the third issue of 1858, for aid in his hope "to swell the number" of *Repository* subscribers "to 5000 subscribers by the first of January, 1859"—a hugely overoptimistic goal given church membership (144).

22. See especially, for example, Weaver's three-part "Advice from the Editor of this Paper to the Many Freedmen throughout the South," published in the 9 December, 16 December, and 23 December 1865 issues of the *Recorder.*

23. A brief reading of the appointment lists given in Payne's works, Wayman, and the especially the *Christian Recorder* illustrate the A.M.E. Church's emphasis on itinerancy.

24. It should be noted that, for Weaver, gathering new subscriptions was a key embodiment of this expansion; he often specifically lauded ministers who were successful in securing subscriptions as they traveled and preached.

25. Schueller's introduction to David F. Dorr's 1858 *A Colored Man Round the World* offers a useful primer on white travel writing. More detailed studies on whites visiting Europe can be found in Stowe, *Going Abroad,* and Mulvey, *Transatlantic Manners.*

26. On Clark (c. 1794–1874), who attended Jefferson College (outside of Pittsburgh), became close friends with Martin Delany, edited the *Recorder* between 1852 and 1854, and was active in the A.M.E. Church throughout his life, see Wood, *The Moral of Molliston Madison Clark;* Tanner, *Apology,* 394–97; Wayman, *Cyclopedia,* 36–37. I have not yet been able to determine if Weaver was familiar with other (and now better-known) early black travel writing like Nancy Prince's narrative or Dorr's travel narrative. Certainly the international sense that shaped Dorr's work would have been of interest, given the *Repository*'s discussions of

Africa, colonization, and so forth, and given Dorr's Ohio location. However, the *Repository* does not seem to have noticed this text. Weaver's "sights and sounds" travelogue also has notable similarities to white travel writing that appeared in a range of newspapers, although with the marked revision that Weaver depicts a free black man (himself) as the agent visiting the national landmarks.

27. He recounts—with some specificity—church conditions, attendance, and character, noting, for example, in what might have been an inside joke, how he gave an evening sermon at Baltimore's Big Bethel after an afternoon sermon by the more formal Payne and "received a succession of old fashion amens, which reminded me of my boyhood in old North Carolina" (167).

28. Much of Greenly's early biography is based on his preface to *The Three Drunkards;* see my "William Jay Greenly's Antebellum Temperance Drama."

29. Vashon's son George, as noted above, took an A.B. at Oberlin and embarked on a lifelong literary career as a poet and especially as a teacher. Woodson, because of his important letters in the *Colored American* under the name "Augustine" as well as his activism in both the A.M.E. Church and battles for black civil rights, is now seen as a key early black nationalist. Delany's large oeuvre is becoming recognized as crucial to antebellum black literature, and his early newspaper *The Mystery*—after both purchase and relocation—eventually became the base for the original *Christian Recorder.* On the Vashons, see Thornell, "The Absent Ones and the Providers" as well as Levstik, "George Boyer Vashon." On Woodson, see Tate, "Prophecy and Transformation" and "The Black Nationalist–Christian Nexus" as well as Miller, *The Search for Black Nationality.* On Delany, see Levine, *Martin R. Delany;* Ullman, *Martin R. Delany;* Sterling, *Making of an Afro-American.*

30. Early black Pittsburgh remains understudied, though Trotter, *River Jordan* and *African Americans in Pennsylvania,* as well as Blockson, *African Americans in Pennsylvania,* offer useful beginnings.

31. The discussion of New Albany that follows is based on the sources listed in note 7 but also owes much to Hudson, *Fugitive Slaves and the Underground Railroad in the Kentucky Borderland,* and Peters, *The Underground Railroad in Floyd County, Indiana.*

32. "William J. Greenlee," forty-eight years old, "Dark Brown, height 5 feet 6 inches," and born in Pennsylvania, is listed in the Floyd County registry on an undated bond cosigned by I. N. Akin; his "Dark Brown" wife and two daughters are also listed on separate bonds. See Coy D. Robbins, *Indiana Negro Registers,* 12. Isaac N. Akin (c. 1822–?), clerk of the County Court of Common Pleas, is mentioned as being antislavery in Peters, *The Underground Railroad in Floyd County, Indiana,* 121; see also the listing for Isaac and his wife, Rebecca (McCoy) Akin, in the 1850 Federal Census of New Albany, Floyd County, Indiana, 333.

33. I have not been able to determine what, if any, relationship Greenly had with A.M.E. clergyman George Greenly, who was admitted to the Philadelphia Conference on trial in 1842, ordained as a deacon in 1843, and placed in charge

of the Bucks County, Pennsylvania, circuit in 1847—though William Jay Greenly did have a son named George, who was born circa 1839. On the Reverend George Greenly, see Payne, *Recollections,* 20 and 30; Wayman, *Cyclopedia,* 70; Payne, *History,* 133, 158, 198.

34. For Greenly's playlet, see *Repository,* 92–95. Sarah Mapps Douglass also chose this genre for her work for the *Repository.* Her short "Dialogue Between a Mother and Her Children on the Precious Stones" appeared in the October 1859 issue of the *Repository* (156–59) and is reprinted in Foster, *Love and Marriage in Early African America.* On Douglass, see Winch, "Sarah Mapps Douglass."

35. On early black temperance activism and writing, see, e.g., Yacovone, "The Transformation of the Black Temperance Movement, 1827–1854"; Crowley, "Slaves to the Bottle"; Levine, "Whiskey, Blacking, and All"; Rosenthal, "Deracialized Discourse."

36. Though Brown's play was designed to be read/recited as a one-man show— and, indeed, perhaps because of such—*The Escape* can be read aloud quite easily and plays actively with voice and sound. For more on *The Escape* see Ernest's introduction to the 2001 reissue; Gardner, *Major Voices;* Ernest, "The Reconstruction of Whiteness"; and Gilmore, "De Genewine Artekil."

37. It seems doubtful—although still possible—that Greenly knew of Brown's earlier foray into drama, the no-longer-extant one-man play *Experience.* It is more likely, though, that he heard about the dramatic readings of Mary Webb, "the Colored Siddons" and wife of (later) novelist Frank J. Webb, as such were widely reported in the abolitionist press at about the same time Greenly began writing (in large part because of Webb's connection to Harriet Beecher Stowe and recitation of Stowe's 1855 dramatization of *Uncle Tom's Cabin, The Christian Slave*). Webb's reading tour of late 1855 and early 1856 took her at least as far west as Cleveland. On Webb, see my "Mary Webb."

38. For primers on minstrelsy, see Lott, *Love and Theft,* and Toll, *Blacking Up.*

39. The sermon preached when Tim and Zack join the church takes as its text "Except ye repent, ye shall all likewise perish" (22). On the theological issues noted here, see, for example, Miller, *Elevating the Race,* and Bailey, *Around the Family Altar.*

40. See, e.g., Rosenthal, "Deracialized Discourse." It is also worth noting that many white temperance overtures to African Americans often embodied troubling racial stereotypes.

41. Zack's opening tirade about "the papers . . . talking loudly of the Presidency—the Governor—the Prohibitory Liquor Law—Free Whiskey—democracy—Know-Nothingism—Americanism—Republicanism—Abolitionism—Fusionism—Peopleism—Perkinsism, and a thousand other isms, cisms, and tisms" seems exceedingly a- and even anti-political (3). However, the play marks these as a drunkard's words, and Zack inclines much more deeply toward community activism after he gains sobriety. Later in the play, he sees temperance as the key to becoming a good citizen.

42. Yacovone, "The Transformation of the Black Temperance Movement, 1827–1854," and Crowley, "Slaves to the Bottle," are especially articulate about these connections.

43. The jealousy against Stiles is also part of a larger and long-standing discourse of suspicion surrounding itinerant peddlers; see Jaffee, "Peddlers of Progress."

44. On Greenly's Terre Haute activities, see the 7 May 1862, 14 May 1862, 2 August 1862, and 18 October 1862 issues of the *Recorder*. Strother (c. 1810–c. 1872) was a leader in the Midwest A.M.E. Church, but remains little studied.

45. McHenry misreads this as a positive gesture of expansion (133); in the context of the *Recorder / Repository* debate and Brown's consistent losses to the "official" A.M.E. organ, it seems more like a move based on desperation and on a Baltimore-centric sense of the magazine.

46. The Mt. Pleasant Library—founded by area African Americans in 1842 and active into the 1860s—represents one of these fascinating pockets. See Vincent, *Southern Seed*, and especially O'Bryan, "Mount Pleasant Library," on this subject.

47. On Campbell (1815–1891), see Tanner, *Apology*, 158–73 and Wright, *Centennial*, 58–59. On Hammond (1814–?), see Tanner, *Apology*, 215–18. The debate flared not only in the *Recorder* but also—albeit in less-pronounced terms, because of its publication schedule—the *Repository*, as well as the New York *Anglo-African*. See, for further discussion, the 23 March 1861 and 30 March 1861 issues of the *Recorder*.

48. Though there were anti-Nazrey letters published in the *Recorder*, editor Stanford was actually a Nazrey appointee. See, e.g., Stanford's "Inaugural and Prospectus" in the 13 July 1861 *Recorder*.

49. See the 28 December 1861 *Recorder*.

50. A 10 January 1863 *Recorder* letter from E. B. Joiner of Muscatine, Iowa, used almost the same language: "You will please inform me whether the *Repository* is dead or alive, as there are some of the sisters here who subscribed for it and received b[ut] one or two numbers."

51. See, e.g., the brief comment in the 21 March 1863 issue.

52. The one significant exception to the relative silence on the *Repository* was an extended diatribe in the 18 April 1863 issue from Thomas Strother, Greenly's pastor, against Brown's slighting of the Indiana Conference in an argument Brown seems to have had with Willis Revels and Indianapolis's Bethel A.M.E. Church. Among other attacks, Strother said that "just because every member of the Indiana District had not done as much as 'Massa' John Brown thought each one ought to have done, he arose, and stood on our Conference floor, and abused us indiscriminately. . . . I wrote Brown [saying that] I would have nothing more to do with the Repositories [*sic*]."

53. A 23 January 1864 *Recorder* letter from Henry McNeal Turner referred readers to "the article written by Rev. James Lynch, in the Repository, for Dec. 1863."

54. The letter said that "the first number of the new book will make its appearance Sept. 1ˢᵗ [1864]. It will, this time, hail from Norfolk, Va." Brown had moved there to work with the newly freed and with teachers like Sallie Daffin, who is considered in chapter 4 of this volume.

55. Given the rarity of the *Repository,* page citations are to my edited *PMLA* reprinting of Stewart's work rather than to the original.

56. Richardson, *Maria W. Stewart,* still remains the key authority on the biography of Stewart (1803–1879), though Peterson, *Doers,* and my introduction to Stewart's *Repository* pieces provide crucial additional details. It is worth noting that, while the contents of Stewart's 1835 *Productions* vary widely from the movement-driven slave narrative (which would soon become the dominant genre in the nascent national African American literature), the book's publication circumstances— down to the naming of the Garrisonian "Friends of Freedom and Virtue" as publisher—do not. Also see Moody, *Sentimental Confessions,* and Roberson, "Maria Stewart."

57. Stewart reports moving to Washington, D.C., in mid-1861, though she may have moved back and forth for up to a year before settling in D.C. She was almost certainly the "Mrs. Steward of New York" and the "Mrs. Stewart, formerly of New York (colored)" who is mentioned as a teacher, respectively, in Thomas H. C. Hinton's 16 April 1864 and 14 May 1864 *Recorder* letters on the newly freed in Washington; the 1870s saw her appointment as a matron of the Freedmen's Hospital in Washington.

58. Taylor and Moore, in *African American Women Confront the West, 1600–2000,* discuss African American women in the West and present the stories of some alternative paths Stewart might (or might not) have considered.

59. Black Episcopal priest and historian George Freeman Bragg, for example, who would later (in 1891) become the rector of the same St. James Protestant Episcopal Church where Stewart delivered her *Repository* lecture, drew fairly clear delineations between "the two colored congregations in Baltimore" in the 1840s: "St. James was one of these, while Bethel A. M. E. Church was the other. Bethel abounded in numbers and ignorance" (*History* 96). While Bragg tempered such statements by arguing that Daniel Payne's arrival in Baltimore in 1843—the arrival of a man "not only learned, but a man of God, absolutely bold and fearless" (96)—changed the character of Bethel, his *History* maintains a sense that black Episcopalians were clearly superior. Peterson rightly notes that "Episcopalianism was the religion of choice among upper-class African Americans, promoting an image of social exclusiveness" (58).

60. Several *Recorder* pieces of the early 1860s speak to the power and national importance of Baltimore A.M.E. clergy; of especial early interest is the 10 August 1861 report of their creation of a Baltimore pastoral association—which also hints at cross-denominational connections. Some of these ministers were important voices in the late-nineteenth century discussion of a never-to-happen

merger between various black denominations. On Wayman (1821–?), see Bragg, *Men of Maryland*, 111–13, as well as his own writings. On Turner, see Angell, "Henry McNeal Turner," as well as chapter 4 of this work. Watkins was running an A.M.E.-affiliated school in the early 1860s that was mentioned in the 20 July 1861 *Recorder*, and he was ordained an A.M.E. elder in 1864 (Handy, *Scraps of African Methodist Episcopal History*, 241). Only three years younger than his famous cousin, George Watkins shared space in William and Henrietta Watkins's home with Frances Watkins throughout the pair's formative years. Given George Watkins's prominence in both education and religion in Baltimore's black community, it is likely that Stewart met him during this period; it is even possible that, probably prior to Frances Watkins's November 1860 marriage to Ohioan Fenton Harper, Stewart saw or even met Frances Watkins on one of her visits to and/or lectures in her home city of Baltimore.

61. Black Episcopalians never mounted the kind of publication efforts that grew in the antebellum A.M.E. Church; even Stewart's later *Meditations* found no financial aid from her church (though it did carry a supportive letter from leading black Episcopalian Alexander Crummell).

62. Weaver's lecture "Woman—Her True Sphere," delivered in front of the "Ladies' Literary Society"—probably of Indianapolis—and published in the July 1858 *Repository*, for example, offers an exceedingly conservative view of gender and cites how Eve looked to Adam "for protection, and gently rested her head, clustering with curls, upon his broad, firm breast," asserts that "the gentle maiden" nurse was much more attractive to him than Joan of Arc, and even opens with an image of "the flower, which, with fragile stem, lifts its head to greet the light" (58, 59, 57). He seems to have grown somewhat more egalitarian in some of his later public statements.

63. Frances Smith Foster—agreeing with Hallie Brown's language—first places Harper in Ohio in "about 1850" (*Brighter Coming Day*, 9; Hallie Brown, 98). Other historians have asserted that Harper was at Union between 1850 and 1852. Payne's *Recollections* and the 1885 *Wilberforce Alumnal* seem to suggest that she may have been there a bit earlier—and so closer to Brown's initial engagement in 1847 (225, 4). All, however, agree that Brown and Harper worked closely together at Union. Both Brown and Harper were listed in the 1850 Census of Columbus—Brown as a thirty-one-year-old Delaware-born clergyman in Ward 1, and Watkins as a twenty-five-year-old Maryland-born resident without a listed occupation in Ward 2 (who is curiously marked as illiterate); see 1850 Federal Census of Columbus, Franklin County, Ohio, 385 and 335. Brown, who described Harper as "faithful" and praised her "zeal" and "sacrificing spirit" in his 1851 *Annual Report*, surely knew of Harper's poetry, as her not-yet-recovered *Forest Leaves* was reportedly published in 1845 or 1846; her poetry appeared in the *Christian Recorder*, the *Liberator*, *Frederick Douglass's Paper*, and the *Aliened American* as early as 1853 (Payne, *Recollections*, 302; Foster, *Brighter Coming*

Day, 56–60); and her book-length collection *Poems on Miscellaneous Subjects* appeared in 1854.

64. A representative example is Elizabeth Satchell's "Address" on Wilberforce published in the July 1859 *Repository.*

65. "The First Stage" opens with this deeply autobiographical statement: "The writer of this article has become so very obscure in life, these late years, so much immersed in care and anxiety of mind. . . . In order to become a writer the mind must be stored with useful knowledge[:] it requires study, deep thought, nay, more, it requires profound meditation, and fervent prayer. And how is this frame of mind to be acquired, this intellectual food obtained, amid the perplexing care of what shall I eat, and what shall I drink, and where withal shall I be clothed" (162).

66. The story's sense of setting is complicated by the hazy unknowing that marks all of Letitia's interactions with the world: after we learn of her mother's desire to go to the city, for example, we learn that Letitia "must have been in the country, but the word country, she had never heard, she knew not what it meant" (163).

67. See the 24 August 1861 and 14 September 1861 issues of the *Recorder.*

68. It was also a chance for the West to be showcased in the *Recorder*—something the members of the Indiana Conference knew well enough to ask that their invitation to Weaver be published in the 15 June 1861 *Recorder.* That invitation said, in part, "Our people in this city are in prosperous circumstances generally, and are very liberal in all charitable enterprises, as I trust you will be able to testify when you visit us in behalf of your excellent paper."

69. Nathaniel Lyon (1818–1861) was the first Union general to be killed in the Civil War. His abolitionist sympathies and his fight to keep Missouri from the secessionists would have endeared him to Weaver. Over fifteen thousand attended the funeral exercises Weaver described. See Downhour, "Nathaniel Lyon."

70. In some of these accounts, paragraphs begin with language like that in Weaver's 31 August 1861 *Recorder*: "Friday morning, 16ᵗʰ inst. Conference met per adjournment. Bishop Quinn in the chair."

71. Perhaps one of the most fascinating examples is his refinement of the naming of names seen in his 14 December 1861 "Our Eastern Tour," where he tells of how, in New Bedford, "at the conclusion of our remarks, a very sprightly-looking, intelligent boy, by the name of FREDERICK WAUGH, who resides with Rev. Henry J. Johnson, sprang to his feet, and moved that a vote of thanks be tendered by the school for the address we had delivered to them." Two weeks later, the *Recorder* printed a pair of letters noting that Weaver had gotten the name wrong—and that the "sprightly" young man was actually named Elijah Webb. But beyond simply reporting the name, this was an occasion for the New Bedford leaders—and the *Recorder*, by printing their letters—to tell the boy's story, and so to make a series of key political points about New Bedford and the

nation: Elijah was "a son of Mrs. Elizabeth Webb. . . . His father is a slave, who was sold from Portsmouth, Va., to some of the extreme Southern states, ten or twelve years ago; his mother, being free, was compelled to leave for the North with her four children. . . . She was reduced to poverty. But notwithstanding all this, she has kept her children in the week-day school, and, more particularly, in the Sabbath School. . . . [Now, Elijah] has to work at the interval of school hours for the sustenance of himself and his mother. [However] He now reads, writes, and ciphers tolerably well."

Chapter 3

1. The earliest extant *Elevator* letter from Cole, labeled "Letter from Japan, No. 2" and appearing in the 20 September 1867 *Elevator*, is continued in the 27 September 1867 issue; it mentions an earlier "May letter." Cole's third letter was published in the 29 November 1867 issue and continued in the 6 December 1867 issue; fourth, in the 10 January 1868 issue; fifth, in the 17 January 1868 issue; sixth, in the 21 February 1868 issue; seventh, in the 10 April 1868 issue; eighth, in the 22 May 1868 issue; ninth, in the 29 May 1868 issue; tenth, in the 24 July 1868 issue; eleventh, in the 28 August 1868 issue; twelfth, in the 1 January 1869 issue; fourteenth, in the 27 May 1870 issue; fifteenth, in the 17 June 1870 issue; and sixteenth, in the 24 June 1870 issue. The thirteenth letter is missing; it was probably published in one of the many now-lost issues of 1870. Given the dearth of extant issues from both 1870 and 1871, I do not, as yet, know if there were letters after the sixteenth. No contributions from Cole appear in the extant *Elevator* issues from 1872. In addition, Cole's "Notes by the Way"—not numbered and not in the form of a letter per se—appeared in the 31 July 1868 *Elevator,* apparently reprinted from the *Japan Times.*

2. This attitude can be seen, for example, in *Japan through American Eyes: The Journal of Francis Hall, Kanagawa and Yokohama, 1859–1866*, ed. F. G. Notehelfer.

3. Cole is mentioned briefly in Walker, *Encyclopedia of African American Business History,* 303, which offers the above information and says that Cole lectured on "Commercial Trade with Japan" in 1865. Parker and Abijian—in *Walking Tour of the Black Presence in San Francisco*—list the birth date, birth place, and Cole's teaching, and add a death date of 1900, as well as an assertion that "after his return from an 1865 trip to Japan, Egypt, and Palestine he advocated that blacks purchase a vessel to be used in trade with Japan. He wrote *Hints in regard to Commencing Commercial Trade with Japan*" (5). Neither work offers citation of primary sources to explain these assertions. I have located no copies of *Hints.*

4. Neither Walker nor Parker and Abijian note Cole's letters. They are studied in most detail in Shankman, *Ambivalent Friends;* however, while Shankman shares some of the biographical details above, his discussion of Cole and his work is

comparatively brief. Daniels, *Pioneer Urbanites*, notes an item from Cole in the 4 October 1862 *Pacific Appeal,* but says nothing about his *Elevator* letters (70).

5. For more Garnet, see chapter 1 of this work.

6. Reason (1818–1893), writer, abolitionist, and anticolonization activist, made a massive impact on black education—serving in New York schools for more than fifty years, working as the first black American college professor (appointed in 1849 by New York Central College), and engineering an important turn-around for Philadelphia's Institute of Colored Youth in the early 1850s. See Hodges, "Charles Lewis Reason," and Sherman, *Invisible Poets.*

7. A pioneering black journalist, Day (1825–1900) would later attend Oberlin, work for the (white) Cleveland *True Democrat*, edit the abolitionist *Aliened American* in the 1850s, later aid the *Zion Herald* and *Our National Progress,* and become active in both Pennsylvania politics and the A.M.E.Z. Church. On Day, see Blackett, *Beating against the Barriers* and "William Howard Day."

8. See Records, *New-York Society for Promoting the Manumission of Slaves,* 8: 78, and Harris, *In the Shadow of Slavery,* 142–44, on these events. Harris offers an excellent introduction to both the African Free Schools and the New York City black community in general.

9. On Lyons, who was not only active in abolitionist politics, but also aided several fugitive slaves, see Harris, *In the Shadow of Slavery,* 142, 238–39, and 286.

10. Jacqueline Bacon's *Freedom's Journal* offers the first detailed history of this newspaper and the community of activists who created it.

11. For discussions of the *Colored American's* treatment of the West, see chapter 2 of this volume as well as material below.

12. Cole's column eulogizes Cornish, but does not provide much information on his life. Cornish seems to be the Pennsylvania-born shoemaker listed in the 1850 Federal Census of Philadelphia as thirty-five years old and married with three children and in the 1860 Federal Census of San Francisco as being a merchant born in Pennsylvania, forty-five years old, living with two other African American men but no family, and holding personal property worth one thousand dollars (430, 30). See also Lapp, *Blacks,* 98, and Daniels, *Pioneer Urbanites,* 45.

13. Just who at the *Mirror* Cole was arguing with is obfuscated by the almost pastiche-style of the opening pages of *Cole's War*—though it was almost certainly not coeditor William H. Newby or key supporter Peter Anderson. Cole himself notes that he was the secretary at the 1857 San Francisco Colored Convention (held in early August), which named Anderson as its president and formally praised Newby.

14. This local convention was a precursor to the later statewide 1857 convention, which resembled its predecessors described in the introduction to this volume. On Moore (c. 1814–1893), who founded the short-lived periodical *The Lunar Visitor* and would later become an A.M.E.Z. bishop, see my "John Jamison Moore." Anderson, Newby, and Detter are discussed below.

15. On Ward (1823–1894), a key figure among California blacks throughout the antebellum period (after his move west in 1852) and later an A.M.E. bishop, see my "Thomas Myers Decatur Ward."

16. It should be noted that many of the issues of the *Elevator* from 1865 and all from 1866 are missing.

17. While Cole regularly talks of P.M.S.S. ships like the "Colorado," the "Great Republic," and the "China" arriving in Japan (with much-awaited correspondence from the United States) and also discusses the goods being shipped out of Japan (mainly silk and tea), he neglects to consider the handful of Japanese of the period who chose to immigrate to the United States via these steamers' return trips and who arguably represent one of the first—albeit small—groups of Japanese Americans. On the steamer line, see Kemble, *The Panama Route*; Kemble, *Hundred Years*; Niven, *The American Presidential Lines and Its Forebears*; P.M.S.S. company history at http://www.mysticseaport.org. On early Japanese Americans, see Daniels, *Asian America*.

18. Jun rightly points out that even those texts that questioned policies that excluded the Chinese "were careful to simultaneously narrate black Orientalist disidentification" (1061).

19. The great flaw in Jun's otherwise-rich and landmark article on this topic is that it equates black press representations of the Chinese with "Black Orientalism," ignoring a range of representations of other Asians including both Japanese and Japanese immigrants. Jun also does not separate general discussions of the Chinese from those specifically about Chinese *immigrants* to the United States. Shankman begins to differentiate between depictions of the Japanese and those of the generalized Chinese, but radically oversimplifies Cole's columns and concludes simply that, "on the whole, Cole's portrait was unflattering" (33).

20. Cole also cautioned, in that same 22 May 1868 letter, that American readers and (especially) politicians needed to "remember that it is but a few years that have elapsed since we first came in contact with this people, whose every teaching from birth has been to the effect that disobedience to the ruler of the land cannot escape the punishment of the severe laws" and that "the people of Japan have been taught, and grew up in the belief that[,] Japan was made for the Japanese alone."

21. On these events, see Akamatsu, *Meiji 1868*; Beasley, *The Rise of Modern Japan*; Jansen, *The Making of Modern Japan*.

22. Bell's praise would have been amplified if readers recognized—as many *Elevator* readers would have—that his use of "cosmopolitan" echoed his own favorite pseudonym, "Cosmopolite."

23. Cole told readers that "there are some ten or twelve colored persons here in all, and so sparse is intelligent correspondence among us that our friends Mr. Charles Benjamin and Mr. Plummer despair of finding any place to while away an evening, except it be the tonsorial establishment of Prof. W. Everson." "Mr.

Plummer" was John C. Plummer, a longtime black resident of Japan who worked as an agent of the *Elevator*. "Tonsorial establishment" here simply signifies a barbershop. In his 24 June 1870 letter, Cole noted that "the men among us that can in any way be said to represent a decent portion of our community rate as follows: Professor W. H. Everson; J. B. McCauly, Esq., retired merchant, and Messrs. G. Cornelius and G. Goodman, ditto; R. Clark, baker; J. P. Johnson Howard, (Duke of Homura), studying law under Francis W. Marks, Barrister at Law, Yokohama, Japan; J. Wickers, Veterinary Surgeon, etc., to Her B. M's 10th Regiment, and to the community in general of Yokohama; Chevalier J. C. Plummer, Major H. Barton, and Lieut. J. Brown of the P. M. S. S. Co. [the Pacific Mail Steamship Company], and your humble servant, the undersigned. There are still a few others of whom it will possibly be necessary to note in proper time." At this point, I have not yet been able to unearth information on the lives of these men.

24. In some ways, then, Cole constructed his sense of black mobility in ways similar to some aspects of Cyprian Clamorgan's: the United States would become a home base if, like Clamorgan's St. Louis, it would allow and even empower (select kinds of) black travel.

25. Lapp, *Blacks in Gold Rush California,* remains the definitive study of this phenomenon.

26. Francis (c. 1814–?), a New Jersey-born free black, was a successful merchant and community leader in Buffalo. In the late 1830s, he became active on a broader scale, and pieces by or about him appear in, for example, the 27 June 1838, 19 January 1839, and 31 July 1841 *Colored American*. In addition to reports detailing his travels to California, he wrote another series of letters to *Frederick Douglass's Paper* in the mid-1850s from Portland, Oregon, where he was harassed because of Oregon's black laws. See, for example, his letter in the 24 August 1855 *Frederick Douglass's Paper*. He amassed considerable wealth in the West: the 1860 Federal Census of San Francisco lists him holding $12,000 in real estate and $1,200 in personal property—with another $10,000 in real estate owned by his wife, who is listed as "Synda" (1248). His later life remains, as yet, largely uncharted. Francis's "Sketches" are certainly worth study, as, like James Williams's later 1873 narrative *The Life and Adventures of James Williams, a Fugitive Slave,* they shed light on African Americans' sense of Central America—a key stopping-point on the mainly sea-based route from New York to California. They thus also offer an interesting counterpoint to the international mobility of Peter Cole.

27. Francis mitigates his praise a bit—as Newby would later—by following the quote above with, "Although it must be expected, in a mixed community like this, that crime walks abroad, it is far from holding that universal sway that strangers abroad would anticipate."

28. On Newby, see Foner, *Black Abolitionist Papers,* 4: 240–41n10; [Bell], "Colored Men of California, No. II, William H. Newby"; my "William H. Newby."

29. Dillon died 12 October 1857 in Paris, and his successor was not interested in working with Newby. After stays in New York and Haiti, Newby returned to San Francisco, where he organized the Dillon Literary Association. However, his health was fast failing, and he died in San Francisco on 24 March 1859. In a piece written under his pseudonym C[osmopolite] for the 20 June 1863 *Pacific Appeal*, Philip Bell praised him as "well worthy" of "all the honor we can confer upon him."

30. Newby asserted that the full black nation should support *Frederick Douglass's Paper*. In his 24 August 1855 column, for example, he wrote, "If one-tenth of the entire free colored population subscribed for it, and paid their subscriptions, it would effect more for our amelioration than all other efforts combined."

31. The reasons for the hiatus between the *Mirror* and the *Pacific Appeal* remain fuzzy and are probably tied to a combination of financial factors and political events: it seems very likely that the *Appeal* was largely founded because of California blacks' hopes vis-à-vis the Civil War.

32. Bell not only gave lectures and speeches at public meetings during the 1830s, but also, for example, made a statewide tour to alert free blacks to their political rights in 1837. See Montesano, "Philip Alexander Bell."

33. On Cornish, see Hodges, "Samuel Cornish," as well as Bacon, *Freedom's Journal*. On Ray, see Swift, "Charles Bennett Ray." Bell's personal life during this period has remained somewhat of a mystery. Many published accounts incorrectly assert that he never married or had children. In fact, as reported in the 2 June 1832 *Liberator*, Bell married Rebecca Elizabeth Fenwick, a former resident of Charleston, South Carolina, on 31 May 1832; his former classmate New York political powerhouse Reverend Peter Williams Jr. performed the ceremony. Within two years, the young couple had a son, Zadock, but Rebecca had died by 1850.

34. For example, he lectured at the New York Philomathean Society in January 1841 and was nominated as a delegate to the upcoming Colored Convention in October 1841.

35. Lajos Kossuth (1802–1894), former leader of Hungary, toured extensively in Britain and the United States, where he was celebrated by radicals, initially including many abolitionists. When pressed, though, Kossuth refused to fully embrace an immediatist abolitionist agenda and was then condemned by several antislavery stalwarts, including Garrison. See Stauffer, *Black Hearts of Men*; Blackett, *Building an Anti-Slavery Wall*; Fox-Genovese, *The Mind of the Master Class*.

36. They included, for example, reports on black New York's social and artistic scenes.

37. Wattles's work—some copied from the *Philanthropist* and some specifically for the *Colored American*—appeared sporadically between 1837 and 1840 and may well have been the catalyst for Lewis Woodson's letters. (See the discussion of

such in chapter 2.) Wattles was born Quaker in 1807, and he studied briefly at Lane Seminary in the midst of its debates over antislavery. Though he was procolonizationist at the time, he was integral in helping set up the black settlement of Cathagena, Ohio, as well as a host of black schools in Ohio. He later became an antislavery activist in Kansas and sometime-friend of radical John Brown. See Getz, "Partners in Motion," and Morse, "Sketch of the Life and Work of Augustus Wattles."

38. Bell's 20 June 1863 *Pacific Appeal* sketch asserted that "with Dr. [James McCune] Smith and Mr. Bell," Newby "opened a correspondence which continued [un]til his death."

39. I have not yet determined whether these letters were from Abner Francis or his brother Jacob Francis—or another of Portland's early black settlers. Bell did know Abner Francis well enough to include him in his "Colored Men of California" series.

40. The letter of "Cosmopolite, Jr." suggests a close relationship—one marked by the wit that had made the elder Bell famous. It opens with, "You ask me what I do with my money?" and goes on to describe a California dinner at which "the first toast . . . was to P. A. B. of N. Y.," after which the "perfect chip . . . responded in a long eloquent, and thrilling speech of a minute and a quarter." Zadock Bell's own interest in writing seems to have been unfortunately limited, and few other texts by him have been found.

41. His job is listed as "Employment Office," and he was living with "Zeddock Bell," a twenty-eight-year-old New York-born steward, and "Jemima Bell," a thirty-six-year-old dressmaker whose birth place is listed as England. I have not yet positively determined Jemima Bell's identity. See 1860 Federal Census of San Francisco, California, 1255.

42. On Smith (1813–1865), famed abolitionist and doctor who wrote several key texts under his own name as well as under the penname "Communipaw," see Stauffer, "James McCune Smith"; Stauffer, ed., *The Works of James McCune Smith*. On Anderson (c. 1822–1879), see Bragg, "Peter Anderson."

43. Elisha Graves Otis began marketing and selling his "safety elevators" in 1853 and gave a widely reported series of demonstrations at the Crystal Palace. The Occidental Hotel in San Francisco was one of the first hotels to house an elevator, though by the time it was complete, Bell was already familiar with the elevators Otis had installed in New York City. Beyond this, Bell was clearly addressing the sense of "elevation" per *Frederick Douglass's Paper* of the early 1850s. Todd Vogel's commentary is useful in considering such: "I use elevation here to denote an antebellum form of 'uplift.' This 'uplift' is different from that defined by Kevin K. Gaines for postbellum blacks in *Uplifting the Race*. . . . Antebellum blacks used elevation to denote a variety of means, such as schools, reading societies, and jobs, that would give free blacks a stronger role in the shaping of the country.

Indeed . . . antebellum blacks carried a much broader definition of uplift—one that tied together the entire community—than did postbellum blacks" (50n2).

44. On Spellman, see Simmons, 928–32. Among key British Columbia correspondents, Mifflin Wistar Gibbs (17 April 1823–11 July 1915) was an occasional writer; on his life, see Schweninger, "Mifflin Wistar Gibbs." Robert and Thomas Hamilton, the leading forces behind the *Anglo-African Magazine* and the *Weekly Anglo-African* were the sons of abolitionist William T. Hamilton; see Hodges, "William T. Hamilton," and Harris, *In the Shadow of Slavery.* On Still, see Gara, "William Still."

45. On Harte and the *Overland Monthly*, see May, "Bret Harte and the *Overland Monthly*"; Missen, *Bret Harte;* Scharnhorst, *Bret Harte.*

46. These events are detailed in my introduction to *Jennie Carter.*

47. In her 28 February 1868 letter, using the names Mr. and Mrs. Trask to represent Dennis Carter and herself, Carter tells a series of temperance-centered jokes about alcohol users that end with punchlines related to how "cold water" is a better drink (25). One is particularly instructive vis-à-vis Carter, humor, and town walkways: "After entering the town we found our way impeded by two of Erin's sons, with outstretched arms and reeling forms, declaring that we should not pass, as no 'nagur' or Chinaman should pass them. Mr. Trask said he would push them off the sidewalk but I said, 'No, poor fellows, they have probably been drinking too much *cold water.*' Mr. Trask laughed, while I addressed them in this wise: 'Gentlemen, Fenians, illustrious sons of the dominant race of Anglo-Saxons, bold advocates of a white man's Government, supporters of Andy Johnson—will you tell me if a herring and a half cost a penny and a half, how much will eleven pence buy?' And while they were figuring out that difficult problem we passed on" (26). Here, then, Carter uses humor to tell about—and to diffuse—a potentially violent situation; her wits and her wit result in expanded mobility.

48. In a 29 November 1867 piece called "Preparing for Company," Carter spun an extended story about planning for a perfect and perfectionist guest who never actually came to visit her less-than-perfect home. In a later column, she also talked of losing "the second piece" to a column on "Rights of Wives" because she had "been house-cleaning, and . . . tearing things to pieces, changing them from one place to another, and setting them to rights again" (35).

49. California did not ratify the Fifteenth Amendment until 1962.

50. That Carter steadfastly maintained that she would "never vote" because of her sex—or, at least, that women should not "talk of their rights and press the matter" until black men were clearly and firmly enfranchised—certainly genders her conception of mobility, but also marks race as her key allegiance (85, 81). See my introduction to *Jennie Carter* for further discussion of these issues.

51. Ward and Moore's placement in California was, in itself, an act of faith in itinerant ministry, as both were easterners appointed to "missionary" work in California (and the broader West)—by, for Ward, the A.M.E. hierarchy, and, for

Moore, the A.M.E.Z. leaders. On Ward's sense of Carter and especially Carter's writing, see *Jennie Carter*, 133.

52. Carter contributed nothing to the *Elevator* between these two columns, on "account of illness" (106).

53. This child is mentioned in no other letter or record of Carter yet located; see my introduction to *Jennie Carter* as well as 105n2 on this.

54. The mother's name was Dextra Hogan; her child's name is not given in Carter's account.

55. The historian Elmer Rusco was the central figure in unearthing and preserving Detter's biography; see his *Good Time Coming* as well as his "Thomas Detter." See also Foster's introduction to *Nellie Brown* and my "Thomas Detter" for additional information.

56. This is, of course, a rewriting of a biblical passage central to nineteenth-century black theologies—one that John Berry Meachum relied upon heavily; see chapter 2.

57. See his 3 July 1868 *Elevator* letter and especially his 4 December 1868 *Elevator* column titled "A Sorrowing Democrat," which praises Wade Hampton, a former Confederate general and southern Democrat with whom Martin Delany worked. On Hampton and Delany, see Levine, *Martin Delany*, 452–55.

58. On these emigrants—often referred to in the California press as the "White Piners," based on one of the central strike locations—see Carter, 58–59. The poet James Monroe Whitfield was among the White Piners.

59. Moos rightly points out that Cuddy and Hughes were general jobbers, but seem to have had ties to the black community, as seen in their printing of texts like the Reverend James H. Hubbard's 1873 *Orations* (89).

60. Foster rightly points out that the moment when Sue (the slave of the book's title character) senses trouble and tells her mistress, "youd better gib me my *free papers*" is an exception to this general rule. She also recognizes that considering the black folktale / "other sketch" titled "Uncle Joe" in relation to Sue or to the first-person narrator of another sketch titled "My Trip to Baltimore" makes "Detter's use of literary techniques such as irony and insinuation more obvious" and enriches the characterization of blacks in the book somewhat (65, xviii).

61. If the novella stood alone, we might question Foster's parsing here—as there are moments when "Nellie Brown" is clearly anti-divorce. However, "The Octoroon Slave of Cuba," which immediately follows the novella, has Jane Gray say to her husband at the story's penultimate moment, "I have sworn this day, in the presence of high heaven, never to live with you again. I have decreed my own divorce" (100). In the world where a planter can enslave and rape one sister and marry the other through subterfuge, Detter asserts, divorce might have a place after all.

62. This is perhaps foreshadowed by his 26 February 1869 *Elevator* column, which ends with the assertion that his fundraising comes at a cost—because he also

has to keep "the babes from crying for bread, and the old hen from grumbling—which they are apt to do when times are tight and money is scarce."

CHAPTER 4

1. There is no definitive scholarly history of the *Recorder*. For important discussions of specific issues in the paper, see Williams, *The Christian Recorder*; Penn, *The Afro-American Press and Its Editors*; Bailey, *Around the Family Altar*.
2. Similarly, in his 12 May 1866 "At Work for the Christian Recorder," Weaver asserted that, "WE HOPE THAT IN EVERY CITY, TOWN AND village, influential persons will be found, who will come up nobly to the work of circulating the CHRISTIAN RECORDER."
3. Perhaps adding insult to injury, according to the 2 June 1866 *Recorder*, the Philadelphia Conference—now Weaver's home conference—extended membership to Lynch at their 1866 annual meeting specifically because of his role as editor.
4. Weaver died on 14 June 1873. He spent many of the years between his editorship and his death—a period I am now researching—pastoring in New York and New Jersey.
5. On Tanner, see Bowden, "Benjamin Tucker Tanner"; Seraile, *Fire*. On Harper's novels, see Foster's introduction to *Minnie's Sacrifice*.
6. The 25 January 1868 *Recorder*, for example, features an unsigned "Letter from Georgia" that advocates elevating Weaver to a bishopric.
7. On this, see the special issue of *African American Review* devoted to *Curse*.
8. While Melba Joyce Boyd's *Discarded Legacy* begins to present some biographical material, and while Foster's edition of Harper's work offers both a wealth of primary sources and rich apparatus, there is no definitive biography of Harper, much less one that closely examines the phenomena surrounding her mobility.
9. On Philadelphia in the nineteenth century, see, for example, Lane, *Roots of Violence in Black Philadelphia*; Lane, *William Dorsey's Philadelphia and Ours*; Nash, *Forging Freedom*; Winch, *Philadelphia's Black Elite*. Though its focus is earlier than the period discussed here, Dunbar, *A Fragile Freedom*, offers a useful discussion of free black women in Philadelphia.
10. Hopefully, future studies will examine New York and especially Boston in this light.
11. Generally, such works note Daffin when they consider the racism within the white American Missionary Association and related systems. Morris, for example, notes that "after a tense year in which Sallie Daffin lived in the mission home" in Wilmington, North Carolina, American Missionary Association administrator Samuel "Ashby agreed to rehire the veteran teacher only if she would board with a Black family" (467). Weisenfeld mentions the same incident as a comparative to the furor created when Edmonia Highgate, a black teacher from Syracuse, offered to temporarily share her quarters with a white teacher passing through

Norfolk (496–99). Daffin's work is also mentioned in Coppin, *Reminiscences*, 145, 147, 184. Linda Britton Cabral's dissertation "Letters from Four Antebellum Black Women Educators to the American Missionary Association, 1863–1870" offers the most detailed study to date of Daffin; she places Daffin in dialogue with Highgate, Blanche Victoria Harris, and Clara C. Duncan. Cabral unfortunately presents little biographical material on Daffin outside of her teaching in the 1860s and does not discuss Daffin's contributions to the *Recorder*, even though she performs the valuable service of collecting Daffin's manuscript letters and reports to the A.M.A.

12. Beyond Cabral's dissertation, Forbes comes closest to such consideration when she mentions Daffin in her entry on "Civil War and Women" in *Black Women in America*, which asserts that Daffin was one of the "official" newspaper correspondents of the period.

13. Various documents report birth dates ranging between 1838 and 1845. The year 1838 most closely matches both the 1850 Federal Census of Philadelphia (370) and the account of Daffin offered in Tanner's *Apology* (370, 446–51).

14. This local census has been digitized by Swarthmore and is available online at http://www.swarthmore.edu/library/friends/paac1847/main.html; the "Daffney" household is described in record 1216 of 4308.

15. Harriet was probably born circa 1832, though later sources place her birth as late as 1840—even though she is always marked as Sallie Daffin's elder sister. Her birthplace is occasionally listed as Pennsylvania, but more often as the District of Columbia.

16. The school's location is given as "6th and Lombard," probably the Sixth Street Colored School.

17. In addition to more general treatments of Philadelphia during this period listed in note 9, on the institute specifically, see Coppin, *Reminiscences*.

18. Disagreeing with Tanner, the 1850 federal census lists her at "attending school" (370).

19. On the library, see the "Librarian's Second Annual Report"—covering 1854—in the 27 April 1855 issue of *Frederick Douglass's Paper*, which shared, among the statistics, the "glorious spectacle . . . [of] children bringing parents who have long dealt in mental darkness, to behold this marvelous light illuminating the mists of prejudice and realizing the dawn of a promising day."

20. See Winch, "Sarah Mapps Douglass." In addition to running the "female department" until 1877, Douglass (9 September 1806–8 September 1882) was an early African American advocate for opening medical studies to blacks and especially black women. Her lecture on "the circulation of blood in creative beings, the circulation of fluid in plants," and so forth, was reported in the 30 March 1861 *Recorder* and undoubtedly drew in part on her fascination with science and in part on her studies at the Female Medical College of Pennsylvania and the Pennsylvania Medical University—all of which culminated in a second career as a public health advocate.

21. See "Interesting Meeting at the Institute for Colored Youth" in the 6 April 1861 *Recorder* for an account of Douglass's "address to parents" arguing that "unless they had parental co-operation in the great work of educating the young, their labors would fail."

22. On White, see Yacovone, "Jacob C. White, Jr." On Catto, see Scott, "Octavius Valentine Catto."

23. See Heinl, "Ebenezer Don Carlos Bassett."

24. Dated 27 August 1859 and marked as being from Philadelphia, this piece is simply signed "Sallie," so its authorship is likely but not completely certain.

25. On Norfolk during this period, see, for example, Jackson, *Free Negro Labor and Property Holding in Virginia*; Cabral, "Letters from Four Antebellum Black Women Educators to the American Missionary Association, 1863–1870"; Morris, *Reading, 'Riting, and Reconstruction.*

26. Curiously, "Example Better than Precept" was first published in the *Repository of Religion's* June 1861 issue (107–9). I have found few texts published in both venues.

27. Daffin's first *Recorder* poem similarly focused on the moral, though its title and purpose spoke more directly to her Philadelphia roots; her "Sacred to the Memory of Mrs. M. C. Weaver," published in the 2 April 1864 *Recorder*, joined several other elegies to the wife of *Recorder* editor Elisha Weaver, whose death in early 1864 stunned all who knew the Weavers. Like most of the other memorial poems, Daffin's asserted that "the hour of pain and anguish" would be overshadowed by the hope that "we meet on heaven's bright shore."

28. Given the A.M.A.'s sometimes high-handed approach, Daffin may well have conceived of her early letters to officials as private or at least as being offered to a limited audience in the organization's hierarchy—rather than as documents that would be published in a magazine of significant circulation like the *American Missionary.*

29. Daffin was in Washington by at least early 1873, as the *Recorder* included an item "clipped from the Washington Daily Republican" in its 17 July 1873 issue that praised Daffin's work in the D.C. schools. She is listed in the 1880 Federal Census of the District of Columbia as a thirty-five-year-old "Mulatto" teacher living with her sister Harriet (whose age is given as forty). A reminder of Daffin's position within the large black community of Washington can be seen by looking at her neighbors: she was two doors down from the Reverend Francis J. Grimke and his Philadelphia-born wife, writer/activist Charlotte Forten Grimke. (Daffin is unfortunately not mentioned, however, in Grimke's extant diaries.) Post-1880 references to Daffin are rare; however, an item in the 4 September 1884 *Recorder* notes that Daffin visited Philadelphia and attended an "entertainment" at the home of activist William Still along with the Grimkes, Frances Ellen Watkins Harper, and Harper's daughter Mary, who offered "interesting elocutionary renditions."

30. Others were short and centered on the business of soliciting aid: her letter published in the 17 September 1864 *Recorder*, for example, simply and briefly acknowledged the box of books and clothing sent by the "Ladies' Freedmen's Aid Society, (white,) of Oberlin, Ohio"; her letter published in the 18 March 1865 *Recorder* thanked the Sabbath School Association of Mother Bethel in Philadelphia for a similar package; her letter published in the 9 December 1865 *Recorder* listed donations made for the newly freed.

31. Daffin used very similar language in her 30 March 1864 letter to George Whipple of the A.M.A.

32. Arguably, a similar distancing can be seen in the gap between Claire and the Tracy family slaves in *The Curse of Caste*. Readers of Collins's fascinating and slightly later novel were called upon to identify with the heroine (or perhaps the free black Juno) rather than the Tracy slaves—in part to flatter their positions and in part to call on them to be agents for aiding the slaves of the South as the objects of sentiment.

33. Similarly, in a letter published in the 17 September 1864 *Recorder*, Daffin opened with, "I have so often attempted to write you lately, and been so often prevented by circumstances which I could not control . . . but I have again started, hoping nothing will interrupt me until I get through. The work here 'goes bravely on.'"

34. Again like the work of many sentimentalists—white and black—this essay recounts historic women from Eve on, marks "numerous examples of female heroism, decision of character, and profound mental worth," stretches but does not break with a separate spheres ideology, offers extended paragraphs on women as wives and mothers, and ultimately concludes that readers should "say not, then, the mission of woman is a trifling one; for all are, to a great extent, indebted to her, for her many acts of kindness, self-denial, and love." Nonetheless, that Daffin included Joan of Arc as one of her role models—the very historical figure Elisha Weaver had questioned in the *Repository* (cf. chapter 2)—demonstrates that even in staying within the gender boundaries favored by her editor, she may well have been subtly challenging them.

35. Daffin's spelling of Games's name—or the *Recorder*'s typesetting based on her handwriting—is a bit off. Morris Gaines, who was born in August 1845 and lived much of his life in Burlington County, New Jersey (including several years in and around Mount Holly), added a few years to his age when he enlisted on 4 December 1863. His military record lists him as a farmer, 5'8", and of "dark" complexion with "black" eyes and "black" hair. He joined Company C of the First Cavalry of the U.S. Colored Troops, and was "appointed as Sergeant" for his role in the "organization of the company." He was repeatedly bounced between the ranks of private and sergeant over the course of the war before being mustered out on 4 February 1866. After the war, he returned to New Jersey, where he worked as a day laborer and raised a family. See *Compiled Military Service Records;* 1870 Federal Census of Westampton, Burlington, New Jersey,

673; 1880 Federal Census of Northhampton, Burlington, New Jersey, 452C; 1900 Federal Census of Northampton, Burlington, New Jersey, 5B. It should also be noted that Gaines's name often looks like "Games" in some of the records cited and that at least one of the indexes of Civil War veterans misnames him "Morris, Murro Gaines."

36. A quick skimming of the *American Missionary* during these years emphasizes how often the newly freed were represented as objects for sentiment and sentimental efforts, especially by whites.

37. A September 1864 letter to Whipple that was published in the November 1864 *American Missionary* stated, simply, "Every day finds my love for the work among the freedmen increasing" (259).

38. Daffin generally signed her letters simply "Truly yours."

39. For introductions to the fascinating Highgate, see Sterling, *We Are Your Sisters*, 294–304, and Cabral, "Letters from Four Antebellum Black Women Educators to the American Missionary Association, 1863–1870."

40. In Daffin's 20 February 1865 letter to Whipple, which was written after a short "vacation" in and around Philadelphia, she asserted that "while at the North, I was urgently solicited to remain there and take a position, which was considered highly advantageous, but I felt that I could not conscientiously give up work among these people. How often while absent from here did my heart yearn to be once more among these loved ones to witness their smiling faces and hear their merry voices." See also Daffin to Whipple, 20 January 1865.

41. Her later letters to Whipple further evince some of the shift toward understanding her students more fully. In a 1 March 1865 letter, for example, she says that "the order [of her classroom] may not be as good as formerly, but this may be attributed to the frequent changes many of these children have experienced." In the same letter, she tells the story of a group of boys who were hesitant to join her class because, they said, "we are ragged and dirty" and so thought that Daffin's students would "laugh at us." Daffin reported asking her students if they would "like to have them come in and learn what you are learning?" Receiving a "yes marm," Daffin then asked, "Would you laugh at them if they are not dressed as neatly as some of you?" Daffin said that her students gave "a prolonged unanimous 'No!'" Similarly, in a 1 July 1865 letter from her new school in Wilmington, North Carolina, Daffin reported that "I can well remember when a school girl, how gladly my schoolmates and myself hailed the last session of our school term—but not so with these freed children. . . . [N]othing will be sufficient to destroy that thirst for knowledge, which they have imbibed."

42. See Daffin to Samuel Hunt, 23 September 1865; Cabral, "Letters from Four Antebellum Black Women Educators to the American Missionary Association, 1863–1870," xxii. All letters from Daffin to A.M.A. officials appear in Cabral; originals are in the A.M.A. Archives at the Amistad Research Center at Tulane University.

43. See Daffin to Whipple, 8 May 1867. Daffin's letters throughout these final months consistently allude to arguments over the promotion of the white "Mrs. Potter," Potter's incompetence, and Daffin's growing frustration with the A.M.A.'s unwillingness to listen to her, even though she had repeatedly proven herself.

44. See "Acknowledgments," 1 February 1868 *Christian Recorder,* for Daffin's work soliciting *Recorder* subscriptions in Clinton. Daffin's Clinton school was reportedly connected to the Garnet League of Harrisburg, Pennsylvania, an organization first noted in the 8 April 1867 *Recorder* that was Harrisburg's chapter of the Pennsylvania Equal Rights League. The league published the short-lived *Freedman's Appeal* and was led by T. Morris Chester and J. Henri Birch. See Blackett, "Thomas Morris Chester," and Ristich, "J. Henri Burch."

45. It is possible that the seamstress named "Sarah Daffin" listed in Philadelphia's Seventh Ward in the 1870 federal census (269) is Sallie Daffin, though her birth date is listed as 1830 and she is listed with a Delware-born sixty-eight-year-old "Leidia Daffin"—a name I have been unable to connect to Sallie Daffin or Cecilia Daffin, though the latter is close in age (but was born in the District of Columbia).

46. This summary relies on the regimental history available through the National Park Service's online Civil War Soldiers and Sailors System at http://www.itd. nps.gov/cwss/. Of note, the regimental colors of the Twenty-sixth carried the motto "God and Liberty."

47. Rogers, whose signature generally included the "d" but whose official records omit it, seems to have initially joined the Twentieth Colored Infantry, a regiment that was also raised on Riker's Island. A twenty-two-year-old barber who had been born in Columbia County, New York, he was listed as 5'5", "Blk" complexion, "Blk" eyes, and "Blk" hair. Unfortunately, his service record is incomplete, and I have not yet located a pension record, so tracing him is difficult. He may be the Theodore Rodgers listed in the 1870 and 1880 censuses of Somerset County, New Jersey—a man who is close in age and also listed as black—but is listed as being born in New Jersey. He does not seem to be listed in the 1890 Veterans' Census. In addition to *Compiled Military Service Records,* see 1870 Federal Census of Bridgewater, Somerset, New Jersey, 423, and 1880 Federal Census of Somerville, Somerset, New Jersey, 392C.

48. Randolph (c. 1820–1868) founded and edited both the *Charleston Journal* and the *Charleston Advocate.* An A.M.E. minister, he was active in Republican politics and rose to the position of state senator before he was killed—probably by Ku Klux Klan members. See Hamilton, "Benjamin Franklin Randolph."

49. Waters enlisted in the Twenty-sixth in March 1864. He was born in Venice, New York, circa 1846, but listed his age at recruitment as twenty. He likely looked closer to his real age, as his father John, a farmer, co-signed his enlistment papers. According to the records, Waters was 5'8½", with "Black" eyes, "Black" hair, and a "Col." Complexion. Waters spent significant time, on the orders of

his captain, William Silliman, as an adjutant's clerk—suggesting both significant skills in reading/writing and math. Waters later settled in Ithaca, New York, where he worked as a clerk and a gardener and raised a family. See *Compiled Military Service Records;* 1870 Federal Census of Ithaca, Tompkins, New York, 269; 1880 Federal Census of Ithaca, Tompkins, New York, 21B; 1890 Veterans' Schedule of Ithaca, Tompkins, New York, 5.

50. A primer on Fort Pillow is available on the National Park Service's website, http://www.nps.gov/history/hps/abpp/battles/tn030.htm. More detailed discussion can be found in Ward, *River Run Red,* as well as a host of articles on the varying depictions of the battle and of Forrest.

51. For an introduction to the dispute over equal pay, see McPherson, *Negro's Civil War,* 197–207.

52. See Mullen, "The African-American Strange Family in Virginia and Warren County, Ohio."

53. James, born circa 1839, is even occasionally, as in the 1870 Federal Census of Roachester, Warren, Ohio, 383, listed with an incorrect birthplace of Ohio. To complicate matters further, Cupid Hart sometimes used the first name Benjamin.

54. See Hutchinson, *The Civil War in Kentucky.* Russellville's "place" in the Civil War is also discussed in some of the biographical material on the Crittenden family, e.g., those noted in Coulter, "John Jordan Crittenden."

55. While I have been unable to find their son Able, their son James became a barber; in 1870, he was living with his parents and brought in another $150 in real estate and $100 in personal property to the family portfolio. One measure of the family's closeness is the fact that the 1930 Federal Census of Scioto, Ross, Ohio, lists James—then noted as being eighty-five years old and without occupation—as living with one of his sister Lizzie's married daughters, Mary J. Spears, and her husband William, who was also a barber (4A).

56. For initial comments on this poem and on the genre of memorial poems in the *Recorder,* see my "African American Women's Poetry in the *Christian Recorder,* 1855–1865."

57. Warren County marriage records show that "Lizzie Hart" married Joseph Brown on 28 December 1867, after filing for a license on 27 November. Brown, a Mississippi-born barber, was two years her senior, and was clearly a member of the small middling class. He was in Ohio by 1860, when he is listed in the Federal Census of Lebanon, Warren County, Ohio (225). The family's listing in the 1870 Federal Census of Lebanon, Warren County, Ohio, records twenty-five hundred dollars in real estate and another five hundred in personal property; it also lists their first son James and three boarders (446). By 1880, son James is not listed, but the federal census lists five other children—Nancy, Mary, Joseph, Julie, and Hattie—all born at roughly two-year intervals. Lizzie Hart died prematurely on 9 March 1887 of consumption, according to Warren County death records; her

death brought only a brief notice in Lebanon's 10 March 1887 *Western Star* stating that "Mrs. Joseph Brown, East Silver street, died on Wednesday morning, of consumption. Funeral A.M.E. church, Friday at 2 p.m." I have found no *Recorder* mention of her passing. Her husband lived until 30 April 1916—staying for the last fifteen months of his life at the home of daughter Mary and her husband, William Spears. He continued working as a barber for most of his life, kept in contact with the couple's four surviving children, and was briefly eulogized in the 11 May 1916 *Western Star*.

58. I have not yet been able to find biographical information on this specific Anne Strange or her husband.

59. James Shorter (14 February 1817–1 July 1887) was a leading force in the postbellum church; on his work, see Wayman, *Cyclopedia,* 7, and passim, as well as Smith, *History,* 159–61. His son Joseph Proctor Shorter is now perhaps best known as the spouse of Susie Lankford Shorter; on her, see Wright, "Susie Isabel Lankford Shorter." Davis served actively in Ohio—especially working with Wilberforce— in the 1860s before his death in October 1866. His long illness and the difficulties of his wife, Martha, are chronicled in the 18 August 1866, 15 September 1866, 13 October 1866, and 27 October 1866 issues of the *Recorder.* See also Wayman, *Cyclopedia,* 48, and Wayman, *Recollections,* 123.

60. Delany lectured widely during the period, and it was common knowledge that his son was in the Fifty-fourth. The Delanys settled near Wilberforce to allow their children access to its educational opportunities. While Delany would travel far during the war years and then essentially settle in Reconstruction-era South Carolina, the whole family (including Martin) is listed in the 1870 Federal Census of Xenia, Ohio (254), and Catherine A. Richards Delany, youngest son Rameses Placido, and daughter Halle Amelia are listed in the 1880 Federal Census of Xenia, Ohio (400C). The fullest discussion to date of Catherine Delany (10 October 1822–11 July 1894) is Hallie Brown's obituary in the 16 August 1894 *Recorder,* though she is briefly considered by Delany's biographers.

61. The 11 December 1884 *Recorder* advertised a Christmas story by "Will" and noted both his identity and his authorship of *John Blye.*

62. Tanner promised readers of the 4 July 1878 *Recorder* that he could only "anticipate the relish . . . for those . . . fortunate enough to read 'John Blye.'" He even asked—in the 21 November 1878 issue—"Cannot the Manager somehow or other put 'John Blye' in book form?" Tanner noted its "very great popularity" and argued that "it would pay." Unfortunately, *John Blye* never appeared in book form. While this volume was in press, *African American Review* agreed to publish excerpts from the novel along with my critical introduction.

63. *Memoirs* also included contributions from A.M.E. bishop Jabez P. Campbell and *Recorder* editor Benjamin Tucker Tanner and was heralded in the *Recorder* as "The Best Book ever published by the colored press"; see 17 January 1878 *Recorder.* The 11 December 1884 *Recorder* notice cited in note 61 above, of course,

referred to William Steward directly. Steward himself included—and claimed as his own—short excerpts from the novel in his 1913 local history/genealogy *Gouldtown: A Very Remarkable Settlement of Ancient Date.*

64. The information in this biographical summary is drawn primarily from Steward and Steward, *Gouldtown;* Steward, *Memoirs;* Seraile, *Voice of Dissent;* Miller, *Elevating the Race;* Luker, "Theophilus Gould Steward."

65. In addition to the above-noted sources, "The Goulds" discusses the Fenwick connection. See also Bailey, "Rebecca Gould Stewart."

66. See Steward, *Memoirs,* 19; Seraile, *Voice,* 3–4.

67. See the 12 August 1865, 26 August 1865, 30 August 1865, 2 December 1865, and 29 September 1866 issues of the *Recorder.*

68. One of the most fascinating moments in *John Blye* is the description of the Blye family library, which emphasizes black literature in the context of world classics: in chapter 11 (published in the 19 September 1878 *Recorder*), Steward notes that the Blyes owned not only Wesley's sermons, Milton, Shakespeare, and various works on history, politics, and astronomy, but also "Dumas, Douglass' *Bondage and Freedom,* and Wheatley's *Poems.*"

69. On Payne, see chapter 2 of this work, as well as Vickary, "Daniel Alexander Payne"; Coan, *Daniel Alexander Payne;* Smith, *Life of Daniel Alexander Payne.* On Theophilus Steward, see sources listed in Note 63 and 65 above. Theophilus penned several books—mainly history and theology—though he did also turn briefly to fiction; on his 1899 novel *A Charleston Love Story,* see Andrews, "Liberal Religion and Free Love."

70. William Steward is listed in the 1870 Federal Census of Fairfield, Cumberland County, New Jersey, 266; 1880 Federal Census of Bridgeton, Cumberland County, New Jersey, 166D; 1900 Federal Census of Bridgeton, Cumberland County, New Jersey, 17A; 1910 Federal Census of Bridgeton, Cumberland County, New Jersey, 19A; 1920 Federal Census of Bridgeton, Cumberland County, New Jersey, 17A.

71. See 26 September 1868 and 10 July 1869 issues of the *Recorder.* Steward also wrote a *Recorder* letter (at Tanner's request) on the Freedmen's Bank; see 9 September 1875 *Recorder.*

72. On Turner (1 February 1834–8 May 1915), see Angell, "Henry McNeal Turner"; Angell, *Bishop Henry McNeal Turner;* Redkey, *Respect Black.* For Turner's comments on Steward, see 9 November 1876, 11 January 1877, 2 August 1877, and 13 June 1878 issues of the *Recorder.*

73. "The Gem" appeared in the 25 April 1878, 2 May 1878, 9 May 1878, 16 May 1878, 23 May 1878, and 30 May 1878 issues of the *Recorder.*

74. The narrator says in chapter 5 (8 August 1878) that "the way to follow up an agitation is always to be there—always on hand. . . . A good deal is to be gained by being on hand."

75. The narrative is actually broken into by the assertion that this was "an actual occurrence, the remarks being made by the Hon. P. L., now dead, in the presence of 'Will.' Instead of the words 'black men,' however, the word that was used may

be guessed." The same installment shows Blye telling his mother that "this is a white man's country, they say, and so far as duty is concerned, it is a white man's war; but I think it is a little more creditable to volunteer in the service of a State that acknowledges me as a citizen and places me in her militia than to wait and be drafted and credited to a State which does not so acknowledge me." His mother simply replies, "This country has no right to my son."

76. Blye's military service also functions as both a fascinating answer to *Minnie's Sacrifice*, which also includes a major character who serves in the Union army, and continuing efforts to define a black masculinity through soldiering— building from Frederick Douglass and William Cooper Nell, among others. See, e.g., Nell's *Colored Patriots of the Revolution*, as well as discussions of *Colored Patriots* in Ernest, *Liberation Historiography*, and Kachun, *Festivals of Freedom*.

77. Eteline is especially pleased with going to Washington because "there are so many of my friends from Philadelphia down there now teaching in the schools and in other employments." *Recorder* readers might have assumed that those "many" friends included people like the very real Sallie Daffin (as one would think that a figure of Eteline's worth might well have attended the Institute for Colored Youth) and Charlotte Forten Grimke (as one would think that the Voulons family's wealth would have put them into the Forten family's social circles). While such offers another concrete Philadelphia connection, though, it might also remind *Recorder* readers that figures like Daffin and Grimke—who were once "in the field" deeper South working with the newly freed—had moved to the urban Washington and its middle class promise.

78. Southeast of the Bahamas, Turks Island is perhaps best known to readers of African American literature as one of the locations at which Mary Prince stopped on her journeys.

79. Hezekiah Gould, the son of Jesse and Hannah Pierce Gould, was perhaps six years older than Steward. He was already working as a carpenter and living just two houses away from Steward in 1850; he later became a machinist at the Moore Brothers Machine Shop in Bridgeton. See Steward and Steward, *Gouldtown*, 106–7 and 180; 1850 Federal Census of Bridgeton, Cumberland County, New Jersey, 217; 1860 Federal Census of Bridgeton, Cumberland County, New Jersey, 42.

80. On Gould's later years, see the 1870 Federal Census of Lexington, Sanilac County, Michigan, 76; the 1880 Federal Census of Lexington, Sanilac County, Michigan, 147B; Walther, np.

Epilogue

1. Although their names regularly enter our footnotes, there has been no comprehensive study of early and important black bibliophiles like Wesley, her predecessor Robert Adger, or, more recently, Charles Blockson. On Wesley (25 May 1905–17 December 1995), see Battle, "Dorothy Burnett Porter Wesley";

on Adger (1837–10 June 1910), see Spady, "Robert M. Adger"; on Blockson (16 December 1933–), see Chan, "Charles L. Blockson," and Blockson, *Damn Rare.*

2. In bringing this text to the public, Gates's massive skills as critical reader, cultural historian, and literary archeologist were aided greatly by having the power and funding of Time-Warner behind his work, allowing detailed analysis by some of the leading experts on book history in the world—especially Joe Nickell, whose work is appended to the first edition of *The Bondwoman's Narrative.*

3. See especially Hollis Robbins's fascinating "Blackening *Bleak House*: Hannah Crafts's *The Bondwoman's Narrative.*"

4. See Priscilla Wald's perceptive reading of the potential play on the book's byline—making Hannah Crafts as, per her essay title, "Hannah crafts," in which the lowercase "c" turns the last name into a verb.

5. See Gates's comments generally, as well as John Stauffer's intriguing "The Problem of Freedom in *The Bondwoman's Narrative.*"

6. The scholarly questioning of the authorship of *The Bondwoman's Narrative* has largely been limited to a pair of articles in the August 2005 *Journal of American Studies*: Bernier and Newman, "*The Bondwoman's Narrative*, Text, Paratext, Intertext, and Hypertext," and Ballinger, Lustig, and Townshend, "Missing Intertexts in Hannah Crafts's *The Bondwoman's Narrative* and African American Literary History."

7. My hesitation here is why I find Nina Baym's "The Case for Hannah Vincent" especially valuable: almost alone in the criticism of the novel, it begins to theorize the book's "form" of (non)publication. Specifically, it argues that the book may never have been published because it was created within the tradition of female schoolteachers composing stories that were designed specifically for oral reading to their students. This kind of (non)publication strikes me as an important variation of the kinds of literary circulation that Elizabeth McHenry considers among black reading groups and literary societies in *Forgotten Readers*—one worth considering regardless of what we learn or don't learn about Hannah Crafts's identity and text—and as a crucial missing piece in understanding nineteenth-century African American literature.

8. On the latter, see especially Janet Gray's provocative comments in "Passing as Fact" that "the professional rewards for theorizing about race and gender generally outstrip those for hunting for and making available facts, texts, and authors" and that "collegial networks are of tremendous value in extending knowledge across such borders, but differences in status among professional labors—primary research, index-making, interpretive reading, theoretical analysis, curriculum development—can tend to block communication of discoveries beyond the close circle of workers involved in each separate task" (69).

9. One thinks especially of the strong possibility that most of the only nineteenth-century edition of Lucy Delaney's *From the Darkness* was pulped; see my "'Face to Face.'"

10. In addition to the discussion of Detter in chapter 3 and Foster's consideration of Detter in her introduction to *Nellie Brown*, studies of Frank Webb's late novellas address these issues.

11. On this, see especially Flynn, "Emma Dunham Kelley-Hawkins."

12. Gray also discusses similar developments with other seemingly black women writers, including Todd Gernes fascinating discovery of a white "Ada" that severely complicates attribution to Sarah Forten of some of the poems signed with this pseudonym. See Gray, "Passing as Fact: Mollie E. Lambert and Mary Eliza (Perine) Tucker Lambert Meet as Racial Modernity Dawns," 72n7, as well as Gernes, "Poetic Justice: Sarah Forten, Eliza Earl, and the Paradox of Intellectual Property."

13. Most fascinatingly, Gray's biographical research on Mollie Lambert shares an item from the 6 February 1886 *Cleveland Gazette* that reads "Mrs. M. E. Lambert, the noted colored author and poet of Detroit, is writing another novel, founded on the vicissitudes of the colored people in the free States of the North." I have located an un-attributed word-for-word repetition of this claim in the 18 February 1886 *Christian Recorder*. Lambert's perhaps-lost, perhaps-never-written novels (at least two, given the word "another") thus join a set of texts I dream of finding in some magic attic—including the missing chapters of Martin Delany's *Blake* and Frances Harper's serialized novels, missing issues of the *Elevator* and the *Mirror of the Times*, Harper's *Forest Leaves*, the manuscript conclusion (if such exists) of Julia C. Collins's *The Curse of Caste*, Frank J. Webb's missing novel *Paul Sumner* (which he mentions in 1870 letters to Mary Wager Fisher; see my "Frank J. Webb"), and the novel that black educator Richard Greener (1844–1922) was contemplating writing, as reported in the 14 August 1884 *Recorder*, that "shall deal with the race problem." (On Greener, who wrote for, among other publications, the *New National Era*, see Hoogenboom, "Richard T. Greener.")

14. Especially prominent has been the ongoing debate between Gates's assertion that the book is an autobiographical novel and William Andrews's claim that it is a novelistic autobiography. This wrangling over genre was caused in part by Oxford University Press's choice to emblazon their edition of Julia C. Collins's *The Curse of Caste* with the phrase "The first novel by an African American woman." See Gates, "Foreword" to *Harriet Wilson's New England*, for an introduction to these questions.

Works Cited

Nineteenth-Century Periodicals

American Missionary (New York, NY)
Anglo-African Magazine (New York, NY)
Christian Recorder (Philadelphia, PA)
Cleveland Gazette (Cleveland, OH)
Colored American (New York, NY)
Daily Transcript (Nevada City, CA)
Elevator (San Francisco, CA)
Frederick Douglass's Paper (Rochester, NY)
Freedom's Journal (New York, NY)
Freeman (Indianapolis, IN)
Lebanon Gazette (Lebanon, OH)
Liberator (Boston, MA)
Mirror of the Times (San Francisco, CA)
Missouri Republican (St. Louis, MO)
National Era (Washington, DC)
North Star (Rochester, NY)
Pacific Appeal (San Francisco, CA)
Plaindealer (Detroit, MI)
Provincial Freeman (Toronto, ON)
Repository of Religion and Literature (Indianapolis, IN, and Baltimore, MD)
San Jose Patriot (San Jose, CA)
Stockton Daily Independent (Stockton, CA)
Weekly Anglo-African (New York, NY)
Western Star (Lebanon, OH)

Archives

Amistad Research Center at Tulane University (American Missionary Association Archives).
Missouri Historical Society (Dexter Tiffany Papers and Presidents Collection).

Missouri State Archives at St. Louis (Circuit Court records; see below for specific cases).
New-York Historical Society (Records of the New-York Society for Promoting the Manumission of Slaves).

ST. LOUIS CIRCUIT COURT CASES

Alsey, a woman of color v. William Randolph, March 1841, Case Number 305.
Archibald Barnes v. John Berry Meachum, November 1840 Term, Case Numbers 41 and 120.
Brunetta Barnes v. John Berry Meachum, November 1840 Term, Case Numbers 40, 121, and 123.
Green Berry Logan, an infant of color v. John Berry Meachum, July 1836 Term, Case Number 22.
Judy (aka Julia Logan) v. John Berry Meachum, March 1835 Term, Case Number 11.
Judy v. John Berry Meachum, March 1837 Term, Case Number 40.
Mary Robertson v. Ringrose D. Watson, November 1841 Term, Case Number 30.
Polly Wash v. Joseph M. Magehan, November Term 1839, Case Number 167.

GOVERNMENT RECORDS (CENSUS, MILITARY, AND VITAL RECORDS)

An Act to Enable Persons Held in Slavery to Sue for Their Freedom. *Laws of the State of Missouri*. Approved 30 December 1824.
Battle Summary of Fort Pillow, National Park Service, online at http://www.nps .gov/history/hps/abpp/battles/tn030.htm.
Civil War Soldiers and Sailors System, National Park Service, online at http://www .itd.nps.gov/cwss/.
Federal Censuses of 1840, 1850, 1860, 1870, 1880, 1900, 1910, and 1920.
Federal Veterans Census of 1890.
Howard County, Missouri, Wills.
Quaker Census of African Americans in Philadelphia, 1847, online at http://www .swarthmore.edu/library/friends/paac1847/main.html.
San Francisco (California) City Directories.
St. Louis (Missouri) City Directories.
U.S. Compiled Military Service Records.
Warren County, Ohio, Marriages.

BOOKS AND ARTICLES

Akamatsu, Paul. *Meiji 1868*. Trans. Miriam Kochan. London: Allen and Unwin, 1972.
Allmendinger, Blake. *Imaging the African American West*. Lincoln: University of Nebraska Press, 2004.

Andrews, William L. "Liberal Religion and Free Love: An Undiscovered Afro-American Novel of the 1890s." *MELUS* 9, no. 1 (Spring 1982): 23–36.

———. *To Tell a Free Story: The First Century of Afro-American Autobiography.* Urbana: University of Illinois Press, 1986.

———, ed. *North Carolina Roots of African American Literature.* Chapel Hill: University of North Carolina Press, 2006.

———, ed. *North Carolina Slave Narratives.* Chapel Hill: University of North Carolina Press, 2003.

Angell, Stephen W. *Bishop Henry McNeal Turner and African American Religion in the South.* Knoxville: University of Tennessee Press, 1992.

———. "Henry McNeal Turner." *African American National Biography.* Ed. Henry Louis Gates Jr. and Evelyn Brooks-Higginbotham. New York: Oxford University Press, 2008. 7: 658–59.

Bacon, Jacqueline. *Freedom's Journal: The First African American Newspaper.* Lanham, MD: Lexington Books, 2007.

Bailey, Julius. *Around the Family Altar.* Gainesville: University Press of Florida, 2005.

———. "Rebecca Gould Stewart." *African American National Biography.* Ed. Henry Louis Gates Jr. and Evelyn Brooks-Higginbotham. New York: Oxford University Press, 2008. 7: 397.

Baker, Houston. "Generational Shifts and the Recent Criticism of Afro-American Literature." *Black American Literature Forum* 15 (Spring 1981): 3–21.

———. *Long Black Song: Essays in Black American Literature and Culture.* Charlottesville: University of Virginia Press, 1972.

Ballinger, Gill, Tim Lustig, and Dale Townshend. "Missing Intertexts in Hannah Crafts's *The Bondwoman's Narrative* and African American Literary History." *Journal of American Studies* 39 (2005): 207–37.

Battle, Thomas. "Dorothy Burnett Porter Wesley." *African American National Biography.* Ed. Henry Louis Gates Jr. and Evelyn Brooks-Higginbotham. New York: Oxford University Press, 2008. 8: 212–14.

Baym, Nina. *American Women of Letters and the Nineteenth-Century Sciences: Styles of Affiliation.* New Brunswick, NJ: Rutgers University Press, 2002.

———. *American Women Writers and the Work of History, 1790–1860.* New Brunswick, NJ: Rutgers University Press, 1995.

———. "The Case for Hannah Vincent." *In Search of Hannah Crafts: Critical Essays on* The Bondwoman's Narrative. Ed. Henry Louis Gates Jr. and Hollis Robbins. New York: Basic Civitas, 2004. 315–31.

———. *Woman's Fiction: A Guide to Novels by and about Women in America, 1820–1870.* Ithaca, NY: Cornell University Press, 1978.

Beasley, W. G. *The Rise of Modern Japan.* New York: St. Martin's Press, 1990.

Beecher, Edward. *Narrative of the Riots at Alton.* 1838. New York: Haskell House, 1970.

Bellamy, Donnie D. "Free Blacks in Antebellum Missouri." *Missouri Historical Review* 67 (January 1973): 198–226.

Bernier, Celeste-Marie, and Judie Newman. "*The Bondwoman's Narrative*, Text, Paratext, Intertext, and Hypertext." *Journal of American Studies* 39 (2005): 147–65.

Berube, Michael. *Marginal Forces / Cultural Centers: Tolson, Pynchon, and the Politics of the Canon*. Ithaca, NY: Cornell University Press, 1992.

Bigglestone, William E. "Oberlin College and the Negro Student." *Journal of Negro History* 56 (1971): 199–209.

Birkets, Sven. "Emancipation Days." (Review of Julia C. Collins's *The Curse of Caste*.) *New York Times* 29 October 2006.

Blackett, R. J. M. *Beating against the Barriers: Biographical Essays in Nineteenth Century Afro-American History*. Baton Rouge: Louisiana State University Press, 1986.

———. *Building an Anti-Slavery Wall: Black Americans in the Atlantic Abolitionist Movement, 1830–1860*. Baton Rouge: Louisiana State University Press, 1983.

———. "Thomas Morris Chester." *African American National Biography*. Ed. Henry Louis Gates Jr. and Evelyn Brooks-Higginbotham. New York: Oxford University Press, 2008. 2: 272–73.

———. "William Howard Day." *African American National Biography*. Ed. Henry Louis Gates Jr. and Evelyn Brooks-Higginbotham. New York: Oxford University Press, 2008. 2: 603–5.

Blockson, Charles. *African Americans in Pennsylvania*. Harrisburg: R. B. Books, 2001.

———. *Damn Rare: The Memoirs of an African American Bibliophile*. Tracy, CA: Quantum Leap Publications, 1998.

Boggis, JerriAnne, Eve Allegra Raimon, and Barbara A. White, eds. *Harriet Wilson's New England: Race, Writing, and Region*. Durham, NH: University of New Hampshire Press, 2007.

Bowden, Henry Warner. "Benjamin Tucker Tanner." *African American National Biography*. Ed. Henry Louis Gates Jr. and Evelyn Brooks-Higginbotham. New York: Oxford University Press, 2008. 7: 484.

Boyd, Melba Joyce. *Discarded Legacy: Politics and Poetics in the Life of Frances E. W. Harper, 1825–1911*. Detroit: Wayne State University Press, 1994.

Bragg, George Freeman. *History of the Afro-American Group of the Episcopal Church*. Baltimore: Church Advocate Press, 1922.

———. *Men of Maryland*. Baltimore: Church Advocate Press, 1914.

Bragg, Susan. "Peter Anderson." *African American National Biography*. Ed. Henry Louis Gates Jr. and Evelyn Brooks-Higginbotham. New York: Oxford University Press, 2008. 1: 138–39.

Brandt, Nat. *The Town That Started the Civil War*. Syracuse, NY: Syracuse University Press, 1990.

Braxton, Joanne M. *Black Women Writing Autobiography: A Tradition within a Tradition.* Philadelphia: Temple University Press, 1989.

Brewer, Mary Taylor. *From Log Cabins to the White House: A History of the Taylor Family.* Wooton, KY: M. T. Brewer, 1985.

Brooks, Daphne A. *Bodies of Dissent: Spectacular Performances of Race and Freedom, 1850–1910.* Durham, NC: Duke University Press, 2006.

Brown, Hallie Quinn. *Homespun Heroines and Other Women of Distinction.* 1926. Ed. Randall K. Burkett. New York: Oxford University Press, 1988.

Brown, Henry. *Narrative of Henry "Box" Brown.* 1849 and 1851. Ed. John Ernest. Chapel Hill: University of North Carolina Press, 2008.

Brown, Lois. *Pauline Hopkins: Black Daughter of the Revolution.* Chapel Hill: University of North Carolina Press, 2008.

Brown, William Wells. *Narrative.* 1847. In *From Fugitive Slave to Free Man: The Autobiographies of William Wells Brown.* Ed. William L. Andrews. Columbia: University of Missouri Press, 2003.

———. *The Escape or a Leap for Freedom.* 1858. Ed. John Ernest. Knoxville: University of Tennessee Press, 2001.

———. *Clotel.* 1853. Ed. M. Guilia Fabi. New York: Penguin, 2004.

Bruce, Dickson D. *Black American Writing from the Nadir.* Baton Rouge: Louisiana State University Press, 1989.

———. *Origins of African American Literature.* Charlottesville: University of Virginia Press, 2001.

Buchanan, Thomas C. *Black Life on the Mississippi: Slaves, Free Blacks, and the Western Steamboat World.* Chapel Hill: University of North Carolina Press, 2004.

Bullock, Penelope L. *The Afro-American Periodical Press, 1838–1909.* Baton Rouge: Louisiana State University Press, 1981.

Cabral, Linda Britton. "Letters from Four Antebellum Black Women Educators to the American Missionary Association, 1863–1870." Ph.D. dissertation. University of Massachusetts at Boston, 2006.

Carby, Hazel. *Reconstructing Womanhood: The Emergence of the Afro-American Woman Novelist.* New York: Oxford University Press, 1987.

Carter, Jennie. *Jennie Carter: A Black Journalist of the Early West.* Ed. Eric Gardner. Jackson: University Press of Mississippi, 2007.

Chan, Chris. "Charles L. Blockson." *African American National Biography.* Ed. Henry Louis Gates Jr. and Evelyn Brooks-Higginbotham. New York: Oxford University Press, 2008. 1: 447–48.

Clamorgan, Cyprian. *The Colored Aristocracy of St. Louis.* 1858. Ed. Julie Winch. Columbia: University of Missouri Press, 1999.

Coan, Josephus. *Daniel Alexander Payne.* Philadelphia: A. M. E. Book Concern, 1935.

Cole, Peter K. *Cole's War with Ignorance and Deception.* San Francisco: J. H. Udell and R. P. Locke, 1857.

Collins, Julia C. *The Curse of Caste*. Ed. William L. Andrews and Mitch Kathun. New York: Oxford University Press, 2006.

Coppin, Fanny Jackson. *Reminiscences of School Life and Hints on Teaching*. 1913. Ed. Shelley P. Haley. New York: G. K. Hall, 1995.

Coultrap-McQuin, Susan. *Doing Literary Business: American Women Writers in the Nineteenth Century*. Chapel Hill: University of North Carolina Press, 1990.

Crafts, Hannah. *The Bondwoman's Narrative*. Ed. Henry Louis Gates Jr. New York: Warner Books, 2002.

Crockett, Davy. *A Narrative of the Life of David Crockett of the State of Tennessee*. Philadelphia: E. L. Carey and A. Hart, 1834.

Crowley, John W. "Slaves to the Bottle: Gough's Autobiography and Douglass's *Narrative*." *The Serpent in the Cup: Temperance in American Literature*. Ed. David S. Reynolds and Debra J. Rosenthal. Amherst: University of Massachusetts Press, 1997. 115–35.

Cunningham, Valerie, and Mark J. Sammons. *Black Portsmouth: Three Centuries of African American Heritage*. Durham: University of New Hampshire Press, 2004.

Daniels, Douglas Henry. *Pioneer Urbanites: A Social and Cultural History of Black San Francisco*. Philadelphia: Temple University Press, 1980.

Daniels, Roger. *Asian America: Chinese and Japanese in the United States since 1850*. Seattle: University of Washington Press, 1988.

Davis, Charles, and Henry Louis Gates, eds. *The Slave's Narrative*. New York: Oxford University Press, 1995.

DeBlasio, Donna M., and Evan Haefeli. "Society of Friends and African Americans." *Encyclopedia of African American History, 1619–1895*. New York: Oxford University Press, 2006.

Delaney, Lucy. *From the Darkness Cometh the Light*. 1891. In *Six Women's Slave Narratives*. Ed. William L. Andrews. New York: Oxford University Press, 1988.

Delany, Martin. *Blake, or the Huts of America*. Ed. Floyd J. Miller. Boston: Beacon, 1970.

DeLombard, Jeannine Marie. *Slavery on Trial: Law, Abolitionism, and Print Culture*. Chapel Hill: University of North Carolina Press, 2007.

Detter, Thomas. *Nellie Brown, or the Jealous Wife with Other Sketches*. 1871. Ed. Frances Smith Foster. Lincoln: University of Nebraska Press, 1996.

Dillon, Merton. *Elijah P. Lovejoy, Abolitionist Editor*. Westport, CT: Greenwood Press, 1980.

Dorr, David F. *A Colored Man Round the World*. 1858. Ed. Malini Johar Schueller. Ann Arbor: University of Michigan Press, 1999.

Douglass, Frederick. *Narrative of the Life of Frederick Douglass*. 1845. Ed. William L. Andrews and William S. McFeely. New York: W. W. Norton, 1996.

Downhour, James G. "Nathaniel Lyon." *Encyclopedia of the American Civil War*. Ed. David S. Heidler and Jeanne T. Heidler. Santa Barbara, CA: ABC-CLIO, 2000. 1233–34.

Dunbar, Erica Armstrong. *A Fragile Freedom: African American Women and Emancipation in the Antebellum City*. New Haven, CT: Yale University Press, 2008.

Durst, Dennis L. "The Reverend John Berry Meachum." *North Star* 7 (Spring 2004). http://northstar.vassar.edu/volume7/durst.html.

Ehrlich, Walter. *They Have No Rights: Dred Scott's Struggle for Freedom*. Westport, CT: Greenwood Press, 1979.

Ernest, John. *Liberation Historiography*. Chapel Hill: University of North Carolina Press, 2004.

———. "Race Walks in the Room." *White Scholars / African American Texts*. Ed. Lisa A. Long. New Brunswick, NJ: Rutgers University Press, 2005. 40–51.

———. "The Reconstruction of Whiteness: William Wells Brown's *The Escape; or, A Leap for Freedom*." *PMLA* 113, no. 5 (October 1998): 1108–21.

Finkelman, Paul. *An Imperfect Union: Slavery, Federalism, and Comity*. Chapel Hill: University of North Carolina Press, 1981.

———. *Slavery and the Courtroom: An Annotated Bibliography*. Washington, DC: Library of Congress, 1985.

Fish, Cheryl. *Black and White Women's Travel Narratives: Antebellum Explorations*. Gainesville: University Press of Florida, 2005.

Fletcher, Robert Samuel. *A History of Oberlin College: From its Foundations through the Civil War*. Oberlin: Oberlin College, 1943.

Flynn, Katherine. "A Case of Mistaken Racial Identity: Finding Emma Dunham (nee Kelley) Hawkins." *National Genealogical Society Quarterly* 94 (2006): 5–22.

———. "Emma Dunham Kelley Hawkins." *Legacy* 24, no. 2 (2007): 278–89.

———. "Jane Johnson Found! But Is She 'Hannah Crafts'? The Search for the Author of *The Bondwoman's Narrative*." *In Search of Hannah Crafts: Critical Essays on* The Bondwoman's Narrative. Ed. Henry Louis Gates Jr. and Hollis Robbins. New York: Basic Civitas, 2004. 371–405.

Foley, William. "Slave Freedom Suits before Dred Scott: The Case of Marie Jean Scypion's Descendents." *Missouri Historical Review* 79 (October 1989): 1–23.

Foner, Philip S., and George E. Walker. *Proceedings of the Black National and State Conventions, 1840–1865*. Volume 2. Philadelphia: Temple University Press, 1980.

Forbes, Ella. *African American Women during the Civil War*. New York: Routledge, 1998.

Foreman, Gabrielle, and Cherene Sherrard-Johnson, eds. *Racial Identity, Indeterminism, and Identification in the Nineteenth Century*. Special issue of *Legacy* 24, no. 2 (2007).

Forten, Charlotte. *The Journals of Charlotte Forten Grimke*. Ed. Brenda Stevenson. New York: Oxford University Press, 1988.

Foster, Frances Smith. "A Narrative of the Interesting Origins and (Somewhat) Surprising Development of African American Print Culture." *American Literary History* 17, no. 4 (Winter 2005): 714–40.

———. "Henry Highland Garnet." *African American National Biography*. Ed. Henry Louis Gates Jr. and Evelyn Brooks-Higginbotham. New York: Oxford University Press, 2008. 3: 452–54.

———. *Witnessing Slavery: The Development of the Antebellum Slave Narratives.* Westport, CT: Greenwood Press, 1979.

———. *Written by Herself: Literary Production by African American Women, 1746–1892.* Bloomington: Indiana University Press, 1993.

———, ed. *Love and Marriage in Early African America.* Durham, NH: University Press of New England, 2008.

Fox-Genovese, Elizabeth. *The Mind of the Master Class: History and Faith in the Southern Slaveholders' Worldview.* New York: Cambridge University Press, 2003.

Gaines, Kevin K. *Uplifting the Race: Black Leadership, Politics, and Culture in the Twentieth Century.* Chapel Hill: University of North Carolina Press, 1996.

Gara, Larry. "William Still." *African American National Biography*. Ed. Henry Louis Gates Jr. and Evelyn Brooks-Higginbotham. New York: Oxford University Press, 2008. 7: 414–15.

Gardner, Eric. "African American Women's Poetry in the *Christian Recorder*, 1855–1865: A Bio-Bibliography with Sample Poems." *African American Review* 40, no. 4 (Winter 2006): 813–31.

———. "Daniel Alexander Payne." *Encyclopedia of African American History*. Ed. Leslie Alexander and Walter Rucker. Santa Barbara, CA: ABC-CLIO, forthcoming.

———. "'Face to Face': Localizing Lucy Delaney's *From the Darkness Cometh the Light*." *Legacy* 24, no. 1 (2007): 50–71.

———. "Frank J. Webb." *African American National Biography*. Ed. Henry Louis Gates Jr. and Evelyn Brooks-Higginbotham. New York: Oxford University Press, 2008. 8: 184–86.

———. "Grace Bustill Douglass." *African American National Biography*. Ed. Henry Louis Gates Jr. and Evelyn Brooks-Higginbotham. New York: Oxford University Press, 2008. 4: 48–50.

———. "James E. M. Gilliard." *African American National Biography*. Ed. Henry Louis Gates Jr. and Evelyn Brooks-Higginbotham. New York: Oxford University Press, 2008. 4: 509.

———. "John Jamison Moore." *African American National Biography*. Ed. Henry Louis Gates Jr. and Evelyn Brooks-Higginbotham. New York: Oxford University Press, 2008. 5: 677–78.

———. "Jonas H. Townsend." *African American National Biography*. Ed. Henry Louis Gates Jr. and Evelyn Brooks-Higginbotham. New York: Oxford University Press, 2008. 7: 625–26.

———. "Mary Webb." *African American National Biography*. Ed. Henry Louis Gates Jr. and Evelyn Brooks-Higginbotham. New York: Oxford University Press, 2008. 8: 187–88.

———. "T. M. D. Ward." *African American National Biography*. Ed. Henry Louis Gates Jr. and Evelyn Brooks-Higginbotham. New York: Oxford University Press, 2008. 8: 107–8.

———. "Thomas Detter." *African American National Biography*. Ed. Henry Louis Gates Jr. and Evelyn Brooks-Higginbotham. New York: Oxford University Press, 2008. 2: 659–60.

———. "'You have no business to whip me': The Freedom Suits of Polly Wash and Lucy Ann Delaney." *African American Review* 41, no. 1 (Spring 2007): 33–50.

Gates, Henry Louis, Jr. *Figures in Black: Words, Signs, and the "Racial" Self*. New York: Oxford University Press, 1987.

———. *The Signifying Monkey: A Theory of Afro-American Literary Criticism*. New York: Oxford University Press, 1988.

Gates, Henry Louis, Jr., Randall K. Burkett, and Nancy Hall Burkett, eds. *Black Biography, 1790–1950: A Cumulative Index*. Alexandria, VA: Chadwyk-Healey, 1991.

Gates, Henry Louis, Jr., and Evelyn Brooks-Higginbotham, eds. *African American National Biography*. New York: Oxford University Press, 2008.

Gates, Henry Louis, Jr., and Nellie McKay, eds. *Norton Anthology of African American Literature*. New York: W. W. Norton, 2004.

Gates, Henry Louis, Jr., and Hollis Robbins, eds. *Black Literature, 1827–1940*. (The Black Periodical Literature Project.) Alexandria, VA: Chadwyck-Healey, 1987–1996.

———, eds. *In Search of Hannah Crafts: Critical Essays on* The Bondwoman's Narrative. New York: Basic Civitas, 2004.

Gernes, Todd. "Poetic Justice: Sarah Forten, Eliza Earl, and the Paradox of Intellectual Property." *New England Quarterly* 71 (June 1998): 229–65.

Gerteis, Louis. *Civil War St. Louis*. Lawrence: University Press of Kansas, 2001.

Getz, Lynne Marie. "Partners in Motion: Gender, Migration, and Reform in Antebellum Ohio and Kansas." *Frontiers* 27, no. 2 (2006): 102–35.

Gibbs, Mifflin Wistar. *Shadow and Light*. 1901. Ed. Tom W. Dillard. Lincoln: University of Nebraska Press, 1995.

Giles, Paul. "Narrative Reversals and Power Exchanges: Frederick Douglass and Print Culture." *American Literature* 73, no. 4 (December 2001): 779–810.

Gilmore, Paul. "'De Genewine Artekil': William Wells Brown, Blackface Minstrelsy, and Abolitionism." *American Literature* 69, no. 4 (December 1997): 743–80.

Glaude, Eddie S., Jr. *Exodus! Religion, Race, and Nation in Early Nineteenth-Century Black America*. Chicago: University of Chicago Press, 2000.

Glazier, Stephen. "John Mifflin Brown." *African American National Biography*. Ed. Henry Louis Gates Jr. and Evelyn Brooks-Higginbotham. New York: Oxford University Press, 2008. 1: 628–29.

Gleason, William. "'I Dwell Now in a Neat Little Cottage': Architecture, Race, and Desire in *The Bondwoman's Narrative*." *In Search of Hannah Crafts: Critical*

Essays on The Bondwoman's Narrative. Ed. Henry Louis Gates Jr. and Hollis Robbins. New York: Basic Civitas, 2004. 145–74.

Graham, Leroy. *Baltimore: The Nineteenth-Century Black Capital.* Washington, DC: University Press of America, 1982.

Gray, Janet. "Passing as Fact: Mollie E. Lambert and Mary Eliza (Perine) Tucker Lambert Meet as Racial Modernity Dawns." *Representations* 64 (Autumn 1998): 41–75.

Greenly, William Jay. *The Three Drunkards.* New Albany, IN: np, 1858.

———. "William Jay Greenly's Antebellum Temperance Drama." Ed. Eric Gardner. *African American Review.* Forthcoming.

Grewal, Inderpal. *Home and Harem: Nation, Gender, Empire, and the Cultures of Travel.* Durham, NC: Duke University Press, 1996.

Griffin, Farah Jasmine, and Cheryl Fish, eds. *Stranger in the Village: Two Centuries of African American Travel Writing.* Boston: Beacon, 1998.

Gross, Ariela J. *Double Character: Slavery and Mastery in the Antebellum Southern Courtroom.* Athens: University of Georgia Press, 2000.

———. "Litigating Whiteness: Trials of Racial Determination in the Nineteenth-Century South." *Yale Law Review* 108, no. 1 (October 1998): 109–88.

———. *What Blood Won't Tell: A History of Race on Trial in America.* Cambridge, MA: Harvard University Press, 2008.

Gunning, Sandra. "Nancy Prince and the Politics of Mobility, Home, and Diasporic (Mis)Identification." *American Quarterly* 53, no. 1 (March 2001): 32–69.

Hall, Francis. *Japan through American Eyes: The Journal of Francis Hall, Kanagawa and Yokohama, 1859–1866.* Ed. F. G. Notehelfer. Boulder, CO: Westview Press, 2001.

Hamilton, Daniel W. "Benjamin Franklin Randolph." *African American National Biography.* Ed. Henry Louis Gates Jr. and Evelyn Brooks-Higginbotham. New York: Oxford University Press, 2008. 6: 505–6.

Hamm, Thomas D. *Earlham College, A History, 1847–1997.* Bloomington: Indiana University Press, 1997.

Handy, James A. *Scraps of African Methodist Episcopal History.* Philadelphia: A. M. E. Book Concern, 1902.

Harper, Frances Ellen Watkins. *Brighter Coming Day: A Frances Ellen Watkins Harper Reader.* Ed. Frances Smith Foster. New York: Feminist Press, 1990.

———. *Iola Leroy.* 1892. Ed. Frances Smith Foster. New York: Oxford University Press, 1988.

———. *Minnie's Sacrifice, Sowing and Reaping, Trial and Triumph.* Ed. Frances Smith Foster. Boston: Beacon, 1994.

Harris, Leslie M. *In the Shadow of Slavery: African Americans in New York City, 1626–1863.* Chicago: University of Chicago Press, 2004.

Hauck, Richard Boyd. *Crockett: A Bio-Bibliography.* Westport, CT: Greenwood Press, 1982.

Heinl, Nancy Gordon. "Ebenezer Don Carlos Bassett." *African American National Biography*. Ed. Henry Louis Gates Jr. and Evelyn Brooks-Higginbotham. New York: Oxford University Press, 2008. Online as part of the Oxford African American Studies Center.

Herman, Janet S. "The McIntosh Affair." *Bulletin of the Missouri Historical Society* 26 (July 1970): 123–43.

Hinks, Peter P. *To Awaken My Afflicted Brethren: David Walker and the Problem of Antebellum Slave Resistance*. University Park: Pennsylvania State University Press, 1997.

"History of Freedom Suits in Missouri." St. Louis Circuit Court Historical Records Project. Online at http://www.stlcourtrecords.wustl.edu/index.php.

Hoare, James E. *Japan's Treaty Ports and Foreign Settlements: The Uninvited Guests, 1858–1899*. Folkestone, Kent: Japan Library, 1994.

Hodges, Graham Russell. "Charles Lewis Reason." *African American National Biography*. Ed. Henry Louis Gates Jr. and Evelyn Brooks-Higginbotham. New York: Oxford University Press, 2008. 6: 530.

———. "Samuel Eli Cornish." *African American National Biography*. Ed. Henry Louis Gates Jr. and Evelyn Brooks-Higginbotham. New York: Oxford University Press, 2008. 2: 430–31.

———. "William T. Hamilton." *Encyclopedia of African American History, 1619–1895*. New York: Oxford University Press, 2006. Online as part of the Oxford African American Studies Center.

Hogue, W. Lawrence. *Discourse and the Other: The Production of the Afro-American Text*. Durham, NC: Duke University Press, 1986.

———. *The African American Male, Writing, and Difference: A Polycentric Approach to African American Literature, Criticism, and History*. Albany: SUNY Press, 2003.

Hoogenboom, Olive. "Richard T. Greener." *African American National Biography*. Ed. Henry Louis Gates Jr. and Evelyn Brooks-Higginbotham. New York: Oxford University Press, 2008. 3: 623–25.

Hopkins, Pauline. *Contending Forces*. 1900. Ed. Richard Yarborough. New York: Oxford University Press, 1988.

Horton, James Oliver. "Black Education at Oberlin: A Controversial Commitment." *Journal of Negro Education* 54, no. 4 (Autumn 1985): 477–99.

Howard, Jennifer. "Literary Geoscapes." *Chronicle of Higher Education* 1 August 2008.

Hubbard, James H. *Orations*. San Francisco: Cuddy and Hughes, 1873.

Hudson, J. Blaine. *Fugitive Slaves and the Underground Railroad in the Kentucky Borderland*. Jefferson, NC: McFarland, 2002.

Hunter, Lloyd A. Review of *Colored Aristocracy*. *Journal of Southern History* 67, no. 2 (May 2001): 452–53.

Hutchinson, Earl Ofari. *Let Your Motto Be Resistance: The Life and Thought of Henry Highland Garnet*. Boston: Beacon, 1972.

Hutchinson, Lowell H. *The Civil War in Kentucky*. Lexington: University of Kentucky Press, 1975.

Jackson, Debra. "Robert Hamilton." *African American National Biography*. Ed. Henry Louis Gates Jr. and Evelyn Brooks-Higginbotham. New York: Oxford University Press, 2008. 4: 28–29.

———. "Thomas Hamilton." *African American National Biography*. Ed. Henry Louis Gates Jr. and Evelyn Brooks-Higginbotham. New York: Oxford University Press, 2008. 4: 29–31.

Jackson, Holly. "Identifying Emma Dunham Kelley: Rethinking Race and Authorship." *PMLA* 122, no. 3 (May 2007): 728–41.

———. "Mistaken Identity." *Boston Globe* 20 February 2005.

Jackson, Luther. *Free Negro Labor and Property Holding in Virginia, 1830–1860*. New York: D. Appleton, 1942.

Jacobs, Harriet. *Incidents in the Life of a Slave Girl*. 1861. Ed. Valerie Smith. New York: Oxford University Press, 1988.

Jaffee, David. "Peddlers of Progress and the Transformation of the Rural North." *Journal of American History* 78, no. 2 (September 1991): 511–35.

Jansen, Marius B. *The Making of Modern Japan*. Cambridge, MA: Harvard University Press, 2000.

Jenstad, Janelle, ed. "Map of Early London." Online at http://mapoflondon.uvic .ca/jenstad.php.

Jockers, Matthew, ed. "Irish American Literature Database." Online at http:// wilsonline.org.

Johnson, Abby, and Ronald Johnson. *Propaganda and Aesthetics: The Literary Politics of African American Magazines in the Twentieth Century*. Amherst: University of Massachusetts Press, 1979.

Johnson, Charles. "The End of the Black American Narrative." *American Scholar* 77, no. 3 (Summer 2008): 32–42.

Johnson, Michael K. *Black Masculinity and the Frontier Myth in American Literature*. Norman: University of Oklahoma Press, 2002.

Johnson, Walter. *Soul by Soul: Life in the Antebellum Slave Market*. Cambridge, MA: Harvard University Press, 1999.

Jolly, Kenneth S. *Black Liberation in the Midwest: The Struggle in St. Louis, 1964–1970*. New York: Routledge, 2006.

Jun, Helen. "Black Orientalism: Nineteenth-Century Narratives of Race and U.S. Citizenship." *American Quarterly* 58, no. 4 (December 2006): 1047–66.

Kaplan, Amy. *The Anarchy of Empire in the Making of U.S. Culture*. Cambridge, MA: Harvard University Press, 2002.

———. "Manifest Domesticity." *American Literature* 70, no. 3 (September 1998): 581–606.

Katz, William Loren. *The Black West*. Rev. ed. New York: Harlem Moon / Broadway, 2005.

Keckley, Elizabeth. *Behind the Scenes*. 1868. Ed. James Olney. New York: Oxford University Press, 1988.

Kelley, Emma Dunham. *Megda*. 1891. Ed. Molly Hite. New York: Oxford University Press, 1988.

Kelley-Hawkins, Emma Dunham. *Four Girls at Cottage City*. 1898. Ed. Deborah E. McDowell. New York: Oxford University Press, 1988.

Kemble, John Haskell. *The Panama Route to the Pacific Coast, 1848–1869*. Glendale, CA: np, 1938.

———. *A Hundred Years of the Pacific Mail*. Newport News, VA: Mariners' Museum, 1950.

Lambert, Mary Tucker. *Loew's Bridge*. 1867. In *Collected Black Women's Poetry*. Volume 1. Ed. Joan Sherman. New York: Oxford University Press, 1988.

———. *Poems*. 1867. In *Collected Black Women's Poetry*. Volume 1. Ed. Joan Sherman. New York: Oxford University Press, 1988.

Lane, Roger. *The Roots of Violence in Black Philadelphia, 1860–1900*. Cambridge, MA: Harvard University Press, 1986.

———. *William Dorsey's Philadelphia and Ours: On the Past and Future of the Black City in America*. New York: Oxford University Press, 1991.

Lape, Noreen Glover. *West of the Border: The Multicultural Literature of the Western American Frontiers*. Athens: Ohio University Press, 2000.

Lapp, Rudolph M. *Afro-Americans in California*. 2nd ed. San Francisco: Boyd and Fraser, 1987.

———. *Blacks in Gold Rush California*. New Haven, CT: Yale University Press, 1977.

LaRoche, Cheryl Janifer, and Ronald D. Palmer. "William Paul Quinn." *African American National Biography*. Ed. Henry Louis Gates Jr. and Evelyn Brooks-Higginbotham. New York: Oxford University Press, 2008. 6: 483–85.

Larson, Ellen N., and Marlene Mitchell. "The Antebellum 'Talented Thousandth': Black College Students at Oberlin before the Civil War." *Journal of Negro Education* 52, no. 5 (September 1983): 142–55.

Leverenz, David. "Frederick Douglass's Self-Refashioning." *Criticism* 29 (1987): 341–70.

Levine, Robert. *Martin Delany, Frederick Douglass, and the Politics of Representative Identity*. Chapel Hill: University of North Carolina Press, 1997.

———. "'Whiskey, Blacking, and All': Temperance and Race in William Wells Brown's *Clotel*." *The Serpent in the Cup: Temperance in American Literature*. Ed. David S. Reynolds and Debra J. Rosenthal. Amherst: University of Massachusetts Press, 1997. 93–114.

———, ed. *Martin R. Delany: A Documentary Reader*. Chapel Hill: University of North Carolina Press, 2003.

Levstik, Frank. "George Boyer Vashon." *African American National Biography*. Ed. Henry Louis Gates Jr. and Evelyn Brooks-Higginbotham. New York: Oxford University Press, 2008. 8: 23–24.

Lott, Eric. *Love and Theft: Blackface Minstrelsy and the American Working Class.* New York: Oxford University Press, 1993.

Lovejoy, Joseph C. *Memoir of the Rev. Elijah P. Lovejoy.* 1838. Freeport, NY: Books for Libraries, 1970.

Luker, Ralph E. "Theophilus Gould Steward." *African American National Biography.* Ed. Henry Louis Gates Jr. and Evelyn Brooks-Higginbotham. New York: Oxford University Press, 2008. 7: 398–99.

May, Ernest R. "Bret Harte and the *Overland Monthly*." *American Literature* 22, no. 3 (November 1950): 260–71.

McAllister, Marvin. *White People Do Not Know How to Behave at Entertainments Designed for Ladies and Gentlemen of Colour: William Brown's African and American Theater.* Chapel Hill: University of North Carolina Press, 2002.

McCandless, Perry. *A History of Missouri: Volume 2, 1820–1860.* Columbia: University of Missouri Press, 2000.

McCarthy, B. Eugene, and Thomas L. Doughton, eds. *From Bondage to Belonging: The Worcester Slave Narratives.* Amherst: University of Massachusetts Press, 2007.

McCaskill, Barbara, and Caroline Gebhard, eds. *Post-Bellum, Pre-Harlem: African American Literature and Culture, 1877–1919.* New York: New York University Press, 2006.

McGinnis, Frederick A. *A History and an Interpretation of Wilberforce University.* Wilberforce: Wilberforce University, 1941.

McHenry, Elizabeth. *Forgotten Readers: Recovering the Lost History of African American Literary Societies.* Durham, NC: Duke University Press, 2002.

———. "Undeniably There: Rethinking Black Presences in the American Past." *American Quarterly* 51, no. 2 (June 1999): 437–46.

McPherson, James M. *The Negro's Civil War: How American Blacks Felt and Acted during the War for the Union.* New York: Vintage, 2003.

Meachum, John Berry. *An Address to All the Colored Citizens of the United States.* Philadelphia: For the Author by King and Baird, 1846.

Miller, Albert G. *Elevating the Race: Theophilus Gould Stewart, Black Theology, and the Making of African American Civil Society, 1865–1924.* Knoxville: University of Tennessee Press, 2003.

Miller, Floyd J. *The Search for Black Nationality: Black Emigration and Colonization, 1787–1863.* Urbana: University of Illinois Press, 1975.

Mitchell, Angelyn, ed. *Within the Circle: An Anthology of African American Literary Criticsm from the Harlem Renaissance to the Present.* Durham, NC: Duke University Press, 1994.

Montesano, Philip. "Philip Alexander Bell." *African American National Biography.* Ed. Henry Louis Gates Jr. and Evelyn Brooks-Higginbotham. New York: Oxford University Press, 2008. 1: 351–52.

Moody, Joycelyn. *Sentimental Confessions: Spiritual Narratives of Nineteenth-Century African American Women.* Athens: University of Georgia Press, 2001.

Moore, Robert, Jr. "A Ray of Hope Extinguished: Slave Suits for Freedom."
  Gateway Heritage 14, no. 3 (1993–1994): 4–15.
Moos, Dan. *Outside America: Race, Ethnicity, and the Role of the American West
  in National Belonging*. Hanover, NH: Dartmouth University Press, 2005.
Morris, Robert C. "Freedmen's Education." In *Black Women in America*. Ed.
  Darlene Clark Hine. Brooklyn: Carlson, 1993. 1: 426–69.
———. *Reading, 'Riting, and Reconstruction: The Education of Freedmen in the
  South, 1861–1870*. Chicago: University of Chicago Press, 1981.
Morse, Mrs. O. E. [Emma]. "Sketch of the Life and Work of Augustus Wattles."
  Collections of the Kansas Historical Society 17 (1928): 290–99.
Moses, Wilson Jeremiah. *Black Messiahs and Uncle Toms: Social and Literary
  Manipulations of a Religious Myth*. University Park: Pennsylvania State
  University Press, 1993.
Mullen, Harryette. "The African-American Strange Family in Virginia
  and Warren County, Ohio." Online at http://www.rootsweb.ancestry.
  com/~ohwarren/Bios/strange.htm.
Mulvey, Christopher. *Transatlantic Manners: Social Patterns in Nineteenth-
  Century Anglo-American Travel Literature*. New York: Cambridge University
  Press, 1990.
Napier, Winston, ed. *African American Literary Theory: A Reader*. New York: New
  York University Press, 2000.
Nash, Gary B. *Forging Freedom: The Formation of Philadelphia's Black Community,
  1720–1840*. Cambridge, MA: Harvard University Press, 1988.
Nell, William Cooper. *Colored Patriots of the Revolution*. 1855. New York: Arno,
  1968.
Nissen, Axel. *Bret Harte: Prince and Pauper*. Jackson: University Press of
  Mississippi, 2000.
Niven, John. *American Presidential Lines and Its Forebears, 1848–1984, from Paddle
  Wheelers to Container Ships*. Newark: University of Delaware Press, 1987.
Nwankwo, Ifeoma Kiddoe. *Black Cosmopolitanism: Racial Consciousness and
  Transnational Identity in the Nineteenth-Century Americas*. Philadelphia:
  University of Pennsylvania Press, 2005.
O'Bryan, Ann. "Mt. Pleasant Library: Reading among African Americans in
  Nineteenth-Century Rush County." [*Indiana*] *Black History News and Notes*
  102 (November 2005): 3–7.
Parker, Elizabeth, and James Abijian. *Walking Tour of the Black Presence in San
  Francisco during the Nineteenth Century*. San Francisco: San Francisco African
  American History and Culture Society, 1974.
Payne, Daniel. *History of the African Methodist Episcopal Church*. Ed. C. S. Smith.
  1891. New York: Arno, 1969.
———. *Recollections of Seventy Years*. 1888. New York: Arno, 1968.
Penn, I. Garland. *The Afro-American Press and Its Editors*. Springfield, MA: Willey
  and Company, 1891.

Peters, Pamela R. *The Underground Railroad in Floyd County, Indiana.* Jefferson, NC: McFarland, 2001.

Peterson, Carla L. *Doers of the Word: African American Speakers and Writers in the North, 1830–1880.* New York: Oxford University Press, 1995.

Picquet, Louisa, and Hiram Mattison. *Louisa Picquet: The Octoroon.* 1861. In *Collected Black Women's Narratives.* Ed. Anthony G. Barthelemy. New York: Oxford University Press, 1988.

Pierson, William. *Black Yankees: The Development of an Afro-American Subculture in Eighteenth-Century New England.* Amherst: University of Massachusetts Press, 1988.

Primm, James Neal. *Lion of the Valley: St. Louis, Missouri.* Boulder, CO: Pruett Publishing, 1990.

Rael, Patrick. *Black Identity and Black Protest in the Antebellum North.* Chapel Hill: University of North Carolina Press, 2002.

———. "Black Theodicy: African Americans and Nationalism in the Antebellum North." *North Star* 3, no. 2 (Spring 2000). http://northstar.vassar.edu/volume3/rael.html.

Redkey, Edwin S., ed. *A Grand Army of Black Men: Letters from African American Soldiers in the Union Army, 1861–1865.* New York: Cambridge University Press, 1992.

Reports of Cases Argued [at the Missouri Supreme Court during 1845]. Jefferson City, MO: James Lusk, 1846.

Rhodes, Jane. *Mary Ann Shadd Cary: The Black Press and Protest in the Nineteenth Century.* Bloomington: Indiana University Press, 1998.

Ripley, C. Peter, ed. *The Black Abolitionist Papers.* Volume IV: The United States, 1847–1858. Chapel Hill: University of North Carolina Press, 1991.

Ristich, Michael J. "J. Henri Burch." *African American National Biography.* Ed. Henry Louis Gates Jr. and Evelyn Brooks-Higginbotham. New York: Oxford University Press, 2008. 2: 53–54.

Robbins, Coy D. *Forgotten Hoosiers: African Heritage in Orange County.* Bowie, MD: Heritage Books, 1994.

———, comp. *Indiana Negro Registers, 1852–1865.* Bowie, MD: Heritage Books, 1994.

Robbins, Hollis. "Blackening *Bleak House*: Hannah Crafts's *The Bondwoman's Narrative.*" *In Search of Hannah Crafts: Critical Essays on* The Bondwoman's Narrative. Ed. Henry Louis Gates Jr. and Hollis Robbins. New York: Basic Civitas, 2004. 71–86.

Romero, Lora. *Home Fronts: Domesticity and Its Critics in the Antebellum United States.* Durham, NC: Duke University Press, 1997.

Rooks, Noliwe. *Ladies' Pages: African American Women's Magazines and the Culture That Made Them.* New Brunswick, NJ: Rutgers University Press, 2004.

Rosenthal, Debra J. "Deracialized Discourse: Temperance and Racial Ambiguity in Harper's 'The Two Offers' and *Sowing and Reaping.*" *The Serpent in the*

Cup: Temperance in American Literature. Ed. David S. Reynolds and Debra J. Rosenthal. Amherst: University of Massachusetts Press, 1997. 153–64.

Rusco, Elmer. *"Good Time Coming?" Black Nevadans in the Nineteenth Century.* Westport, CT: Greenwood Press, 1975.

———. "Thomas Detter: Nevada Black Activist and Advocate for Human Rights." *Nevada Historical Society Quarterly* 47, no. 3 (Fall 2004): 193–213.

"Sanda." [Walter H. Stowers and William H. Anderson.] *Appointed: An American Novel.* Detroit: Detroit Law Printing Company, 1894.

Scharnhorst, Gary. *Bret Harte: Opening the Literary West.* Norman: University of Oklahoma Press, 2000.

Schor, Joel. *Henry Highland Garnet: A Voice of Black Radicalism in the Nineteenth Century.* Westport, CT: Greenwood Press, 1977.

Schweninger, Loren. "Mifflin Wistar Gibbs." *African American National Biography.* Ed. Henry Louis Gates Jr. and Evelyn Brooks-Higginbotham. New York: Oxford University Press, 2008. 3: 483–85.

Scott, Donald. "Octavius Valentine Catto." *African American National Biography.* Ed. Henry Louis Gates Jr. and Evelyn Brooks-Higginbotham. New York: Oxford University Press, 2008. 2: 217–18.

Seematter, Mary E. "Trials and Confessions: Race and Justice in Antebellum St. Louis." *Gateway Heritage* 12 (Fall 1991): 36–47.

Sekora, John. "'Mr. Editor, If You Please': Frederick Douglass, *My Bondage and My Freedom*, and the End of the Abolitionist Imprint." *Callaloo* 17, no. 2 (Spring 1994): 608–26.

Sekora, John, and Darwin T. Turner, eds. *The Art of the Slave Narrative: Original Essays in Criticism and Theory.* Macomb: Western Illinois Press, 1982.

Seraile, William. *Voice of Dissent: Theophilus Gould Steward and Black America.* Brooklyn: Carlson Publishing, 1991.

Shackford, James Atkins. *David Crockett: The Man and the Legend.* Lincoln: University of Nebraska Press, 1994.

Shankman, Arnold M. *Ambivalent Friends: Afro-Americans View the Immigrant.* Westport, CT: Greenwood Press, 1982.

Sherman, Joan R. *African-American Poetry of the Nineteenth Century: An Anthology.* Urbana: University of Illinois Press, 1992.

———. *Invisible Poets: Afro-Americans of the Nineteenth Century.* 2nd ed. Urbana: University of Illinois Press, 1989.

Shockley, Ann Allen, ed. *Afro-American Women Writers, 1746–1933.* Boston: G. K. Hall, 1988.

Shohat, Ella, and Robert Stam. *Unthinking Eurocentrism: Multiculturalism and the Media.* New York: Routledge, 1994.

Simmons, William J. *Men of Mark: Eminent, Progressive, and Rising.* 1887. Rpt. New York: Arno, 1969.

Simpson, Mark. *Trafficking Subjects: The Politics of Mobility in Nineteenth-Century America.* Minneapolis: University of Minnesota Press, 2005.

Smith, C. S. *The Life of Daniel Alexander Payne*. Nashville: African Methodist Episcopal Sunday School Union, 1894.

Southern, Eileen. *Music of Black Americans: A History*. 3rd ed. New York: W. W. Norton, 1997.

Spady, James G. "Robert M. Adger." *African American National Biography*. Ed. Henry Louis Gates Jr. and Evelyn Brooks-Higginbotham. New York: Oxford University Press, 2008. Online as part of the Oxford African American Studies Center.

Stauffer, John. *The Black Hearts of Men: Radical Abolitionism and the Transformation of Race*. Cambridge, MA: Harvard University Press, 2001.

———. "Foreword." *From Bondage to Belonging: The Worcester Slave Narratives*. Ed. B. Eugene McCarthy and Thomas L. Doughton. Amherst: University of Massachusetts Press, 2007. ix–xviii.

———. "The Problem of Freedom in *The Bondwoman's Narrative*." *In Search of Hannah Crafts: Critical Essays on* The Bondwoman's Narrative. Ed. Henry Louis Gates Jr. and Hollis Robbins. New York: Basic Civitas, 2004. 53–68.

———, ed. *The Works of James McCune Smith: Black Intellectual and Abolitionist*. New York: Oxford University Press, 2006.

Stauffer, John, and Timothy Patrick McCarthy, eds. *Prophets of Protest: Reconsidering the History of American Abolitionism*. New York: New Press, 2006.

Stepto, Robert B. *From Behind the Veil: A Study of Afro-American Narrative*. Urbana: University of Illinois Press, 1979.

Sterling, Dorothy. *The Making of an Afro-American: Martin R. Delany*. New York: Doubleday, 1971.

———, ed. *We Are Your Sisters: Black Women in the Nineteenth Century*. New York: W. W. Norton, 1984.

Steward, Theophilus Gould. *A Charleston Love Story*. New York: F. Tennyson Neely, 1899.

———. *Memoirs of Mrs. Rebecca Steward*. Philadelphia: Publication Department of the African Methodist Episcopal Church, 1877.

Steward, Theophilus, and William Steward. *Gouldtown: A Very Remarkable Settlement of Ancient Date*. Philadelphia: J. B. Lippincott, 1913.

Steward, William. "Excerpts from *John Blye*." Ed. Eric Gardner. *African American Review*, forthcoming.

Stewart, Maria W. *Maria W. Stewart: America's First Black Women Political Writer: Essays and Speeches*. Ed. Marilyn Richardson. Bloomington: Indiana University Press, 1987.

———. *Meditations from the Pen of Mrs. Maria W. Stewart*. Washington, DC: np, 1879.

———. *Productions of Mrs. Maria W. Stewart*. Boston: Friends of Freedom and Virtue, 1835.

———. "Two Texts on Children and Christian Education." (Includes "The Proper Training of Children" and "The First Stage of Life.") Ed. Eric Gardner. *PMLA* 123, no. 1 (January 2008): 156–65.

Still, William. *The Underground Rail Road*. Philadelphia: Porter and Coates, 1872.

Stowe, Harriet Beecher. *Key to Uncle Tom's Cabin*. Boston: John P. Jewett, 1853.

Stowe, William. *Going Abroad: European Travel in Nineteenth-Century American Culture*. Princeton, NJ: Princeton University Press, 1994.

Swift, David E. "Charles Bennett Ray." *African American National Biography*. Ed. Henry Louis Gates Jr. and Evelyn Brooks-Higginbotham. New York: Oxford University Press, 2008. 6: 520–21.

Tabscott, Robert W. "Elijah Parish Lovejoy: Portrait of a Radical, the St. Louis Years, 1827–1835." *Gateway Heritage* 8 (Winter 1987–1988): 32–39.

Tanner, Benjamin Tucker. *An Apology for African Methodism*. Baltimore: np, 1867.

Tate, Gayle T. "Prophecy and Transformation: The Contours of Lewis Woodson's Nationalism." *Journal of Black Studies* 29, no. 2 (November 1998): 209–33.

———. "The Black Nationalist–Christian Nexus: The Political Thought of Lewis Woodson." *Western Journal of Black Studies* 19, no. 1 (1995): 9–18.

Taylor, Quintard. *In Search of the Racial Frontier: African Americans and the American West, 1528–1990*. New York: W. W. Norton, 1998.

Taylor, Quintard, and Shirley Ann Wilson Moore, eds. *African American Women Confront the West, 1600–2000*. Norman: University of Oklahoma Press, 2003.

Thompson, Julius E. *Hiram R. Revels, 1827–1901*. New York: Arno, 1982.

———. "Hiram R. Revels, 1827–1901: A Reappraisal." *Journal of Negro History* 79, no. 3 (Summer 1994): 297–303.

Thornbrough, Emma Lou. *The Negro in Indiana before 1900: A Study of a Minority*. 1957. Bloomington: Indiana University Press, 1993.

Thornell, Paul N. D. "The Absent Ones and the Providers: A Biography of the Vashons." *Journal of Negro History* 83, no. 4 (Autumn 1998): 284–301.

Toll, Robert C. *Blacking Up: The Minstrel Show in Nineteenth-Century America*. New York: Oxford University Press, 1974.

Trotter, Joe William. *River Jordan: African American Urban Life in the Ohio Valley*. Lexington: University of Kentucky Press, 1998.

Trotter, Joe William, and Eric Lidell Smith, eds. *African Americans in Pennsylvania*. University Park: Pennsylvania State University Press, 1997.

Tucker, Veta Smith, ed. *Curse of Caste*. Special issue of *African American Review* 40, no. 4 (2006).

Turner, Henry McNeal. *Respect Black: The Writings and Speeches of Henry McNeal Turner*. Ed. Edwin Redkey. New York: Arno, 1971.

Ullman, Victor. *Martin R. Delany: The Beginnings of Black Nationalism*. Boston: Beacon 1971.

Vandervelde, Lea, and Sandhya Subramanian. "Mrs. Dred Scott." *Yale Law Journal* 106, no. 4 (January 1997): 1033–1122.

Vicary, Elizabeth Zoe. "Daniel Alexander Payne." *African American National Biography*. Ed. Henry Louis Gates Jr. and Evelyn Brooks-Higginbotham. New York: Oxford University Press, 2008. 6: 283–84.

Vincent, Stephen A. *Southern Seed, Northern Soil: African American Farm Communities in the Midwest, 1765–1900*. Bloomington: Indiana University Press, 1999.

Vogel, Todd. "The New Face of Black Labor." *The Black Press: New Literary and Historical Essays*. Ed. Todd Vogel. New Brunswick, NJ: Rutgers University Press, 2001. 37–54.

———, ed. *The Black Press: New Literary and Historical Essays*. New Brunswick, NJ: Rutgers University Press, 2001.

Wald, Priscilla. "Hannah crafts." *In Search of Hannah Crafts: Critical Essays on The Bondwoman's Narrative*. Ed. Henry Louis Gates Jr. and Hollis Robbins. New York: Basic Civitas, 2004. 213–30.

Walker, David. *David Walker's Appeal to the Coloured Citizens of the World*. 1829. Ed. Peter P. Hinks. University Park: Pennsylvania State University Press, 2000.

———. *David Walker's Appeal . . . with a Brief Sketch of His Life . . . Also Garnet's Address*. Comp. Henry Highland Garnet. 1848. Salem, MA: Ayer, 1994.

Walker, Juliet, ed. *Encyclopedia of African American Business History*. Westport, CT: Greenwood Press, 1999.

Ward, Andrew. *River Run Red: The Fort Pillow Massacre in the American Civil War*. New York: Viking, 2005.

Watts, Edward, and David Rachels, eds. *The First West: Writing from the American Frontier, 1776–1860*. New York: Oxford University Press, 2002.

Wayman, Alexander W. *Cycopedia of African Methodism*. Baltimore: Methodist Episcopal Book Depository, 1882.

———. *My Recollections of A. M. E. Ministers*. Philadelphia: A. M. E. Book Rooms, 1881.

Webb, Frank J. *The Garies*. 1857. In *Fiction, Essays, and Poetry: Frank J. Webb*. Ed. Werner Sollors. New Milford, CT: Toby Press, 2004.

Weld, Theodore. *American Slavery as It Is: Testimony of a Thousand Witnesses*. 1839. New York: Arno, 1988.

White, Shane. *Stories of Freedom in Black New York*. Cambridge, MA: Harvard University Press, 2002.

Williams, Gilbert Anthony. *The Christian Recorder, African Methodist Church, 1854–1902*. Jefferson, NC: McFarland, 1996.

Williams, James. *Narrative of James Williams*. 1838. Philadelphia: Rhistroic Publishers, 1969.

Willson, Joseph. *Sketches of the Higher Classes of Colored Society in Philadelphia.* Philadelphia: Merrihew and Thompson, 1841. (Reprinted as *The Elite of Our People.* Ed. Julie Winch. University Park: Pennsylvania State University Press, 2000.)

Wilson, Harriet. *Our Nig.* Ed. P. Gabrielle Foreman and Reginald Pitts. New York: Penguin, 2005.

Wilson, Shirley Ann. *To Place Our Deeds: The African American Community in Richmond, California, 1910–1963.* Berkeley and Los Angeles: University of California Press, 2000.

Winch, Julie. "Cyprian Clamorgan." *African American National Biography.* Ed. Henry Louis Gates Jr. and Evelyn Brooks-Higginbotham. New York: Oxford University Press, 2008. 2: 290–91.

———. *Philadelphia's Black Elite: Activism, Accommodation, and the Struggle for Autonomy, 1787–1848.* Philadelphia: Temple University Press, 1988.

———. "Sarah Mapps Douglass." *African American National Biography.* Ed. Henry Louis Gates Jr. and Evelyn Brooks-Higginbotham. New York: Oxford University Press, 2008. 3: 50–51.

Wood, Joseph R. *The Moral of Molliston Madison Clark.* Lewiston, NY: E. Mellen, 1990.

Wright, Arthuree McLaughlin. "Susie Isabel Lankford Shorter." *African American National Biography.* Ed. Henry Louis Gates Jr. and Evelyn Brooks-Higginbotham. New York: Oxford University Press, 2008. 7: 186–87.

Wright, Richard Robert. *Centennial Encyclopedia of the African Methodist Episcopal Church.* Philadelphia: A. M. E. Book Concern, 1916.

Yacovone, Donald. "Jacob C. White, Jr." *African American National Biography.* Ed. Henry Louis Gates Jr. and Evelyn Brooks- Higginbotham. New York: Oxford University Press, 2008. 8: 250–51.

———. "The Transformation of the Black Temperance Movement, 1827–1854: An Interpretation." *Journal of the Early Republic* 8, no. 3 (Autumn 1988): 281–97.

Yellin, Jean Fagan, and Cynthia Bond. *The Pen Is Ours: A Listing of Writings by and about African American Women before 1910.* New York: Oxford University Press, 1991.

Young, James L. *Helen Duval, a French Romance.* San Francisco: Bancroft Company, 1891.

Young, John K. *Black Writers, White Publishers: Marketplace Politics in Twentieth-Century African American Literature.* Jackson: University Press of Mississippi, 2006.

Zboray, Ronald, and Mary Saracino Zboray. *Literary Dollars and Social Sense: A People's History of the Mass Market Book.* New York: Routledge, 2005.

Index